LANGUAGE, DISCOURSE, SOCIETY
General Editors: Stephen Heath, Colin MacCabe and Denise Riley

Published

Stanley Aronowitz
SCIENCE AS POWER

Norman Bryson
VISION AND PAINTING: The Logic of the Gaze

Teresa de Lauretis
ALICE DOESN'T: Feminism, Semiotics and Cinema
FEMINIST STUDIES/CRITICAL STUDIES (*editor*)

Mary Ann Doane
THE DESIRE TO DESIRE: The Woman's Film of the 1940s

Alan Durant
CONDITIONS OF MUSIC

Jane Gallop
FEMINISM AND PSYCHOANALYSIS: The Daughter's Seduction

Peter Gidal
UNDERSTANDING BECKETT: A Study of Monologue and Gesture in the Works of Samuel Beckett

Peter Goodrich
LEGAL DISCOURSE: Studies in Linguistics, Rhetoric and Legal Analysis

Paul Hirst
ON LAW AND IDEOLOGY

Ian Hunter
CULTURE AND GOVERNMENT: The Emergence of Literary Education

Andreas Huyssen
AFTER THE GREAT DIVIDE: Modernism, Mass Culture and Postmodernism

Nigel Leask
THE POLITICS OF IMAGINATION IN COLERIDGE'S CRITICAL THOUGHT

Michael Lynn George
EPOS: WORD, NARRATIVE AND THE *ILIAD*

Colin MacCabe
JAMES JOYCE AND THE REVOLUTION OF THE WORD
THE TALKING CURE: Essays in Psychoanalysis and Language (*editor*)

Louis Marin
PORTRAIT OF THE KING

Christian Metz
PSYCHOANALYSIS AND CINEMA: The Imaginary Signifier

Jeffrey Minson
GENEALOGIES OF MORALS: Nietzsche, Foucault, Donzelot and the Eccentricity of Ethics

Laura Mulvey
VISUAL AND OTHER PLEASURES

Douglas Oliver
POETRY AND NARRATIVE IN PERFORMANCE

Michel Pêcheux
LANGUAGE, SEMANTICS AND IDEOLOGY

Jean-Michel Rabaté
LANGUAGE, SEXUALITY AND IDEOLOGY IN EZRA POUND'S *CANTOS*

Denise Riley
'AM I THAT NAME?': Feminism and the Category of 'Women' in History

Jacqueline Rose
THE CASE OF PETER PAN OR THE IMPOSSIBILITY OF CHILDREN'S FICTION

Brian Rotman
SIGNIFYING NOTHING: The Semiotics of Zero

Raymond Tallis
NOT SAUSSURE: A Critique of Post-Saussurean Literary Theory
David Trotter
CIRCULATION: Defoe, Dickens and the Economies of the Novel
THE MAKING OF THE READER: Language and Subjectivity in Modern American, English and Irish Poetry
Peter Womack
IMPROVEMENT AND ROMANCE: Constructing the Myth of the Highlands

Forthcoming

Lesley Caldwell
ITALIAN WOMEN BETWEEN CHURCH AND STATE
Elizabeth Cowie
TO REPRESENT WOMAN: The Representation of Sexual Difference in the Visual Media
James Donald
THE QUESTION OF EDUCATION: Essays on Schooling and English Culture, 1790–1987
Alan Durant
SOUNDTRACK AND TALKBACK
Piers Gray
MODERNISM AND THE MODERN
Stephen Heath
THREE ESSAYS ON SUBJECTIVITY
Ian Hunter, David Saunders and Dugald Williamson
ON PORNOGRAPHY
Rod Mengham
CONTEMPORARY BRITISH POETICS
Jean-Claude Milner
FOR THE LOVE OF LANGUAGE
Jeffrey Minson
GENESIS OF AUTHORSHIP
PERSONAL POLITICS AND ETHICAL STYLE
Denise Riley
POETS ON POETICS
Michael Ryan
POLITICS AND CULTURE
James A. Snead and Cornel West
SEEING BLACK: A Semiotics of Black Culture in America

Series Standing Order

If you would like to receive future titles in this series as they are published, you can make use of our standing order facility. To place a standing order please contact your bookseller or, in case of difficulty, write to us at the address below with your name and address and the name of the series. Please state with which title you wish to begin your standing order. (If you live outside the United Kingdom we may not have the rights for your area, in which case we will forward your order to the publisher concerned.)

Customer Services Department, Macmillan Distribution Ltd, Houndmills, Basingstoke, Hampshire, RG21 2XS, England.

Culture and Government

The Emergence of Literary Education

Ian Hunter

Lecturer, School of Humanities,
Griffith University, Queensland

palgrave
macmillan

Published by
PALGRAVE MACMILLAN
Houndmills, Basingstoke, Hampshire RG21 6XS and
175 Fifth Avenue, New York, N. Y. 10010
Companies and representatives throughout the world

PALGRAVE MACMILLAN is the global academic imprint of the Palgrave
Macmillan division of St. Martin's Press, LLC and of Palgrave Macmillan Ltd.
Macmillan® is a registered trademark in the United States, United Kingdom
and other countries. Palgrave is a registered trademark in the European
Union and other countries.

ISBN-13: 978–0–333–38825–9
ISBN-10: 0–333–38825–9

This book is printed on paper suitable for recycling and
made from fully managed and sustained forest sources.

A catalogue record for this book is available from the British Library.

Printed and bound in Great Britain by
Antony Rowe Ltd, Chippenham and Eastbourne

To Alison, Dorothy and William Hunter

Contents

Preface

In this book I have set out to reconsider the relation between the idea of culture and the machinery of government. My approach to this question is not through a general theory of culture and society. It concentrates instead on a particular if privileged historical location of this relation, the apparatus of literary education.

In literary education – in the teaching of English and the discipline of literary criticism – generations of cultural historians, critics and theorists have found the exemplary reconciliation of the promise of aesthetic fulfilment and the realities of social existence. They have treated this reconciliation as nothing less than the form of 'man's' cultural completion. Whether it has been conceived of in terms of a gradual synthesis of his divided 'ethical substance', or as a sudden theoretical recovery of his unconscious being, literary culture has been invested with the task of realising 'man's' vocation: to achieve a complete development of human capacities.

Moreover, what appears to be the one attempt to question this conception of literary culture, by recalling it to a broader realm of social relations and activities – I am referring to the tradition of 'cultural materialism' – is, so I will argue, nothing more than a variation on the same theme. It retains the same conception of complete development and is subtended by the same figures of ethical synthesis and theoretical clarification. In fact, it differs only in the form in which it specifies the dialectic of 'man's' ethical substance, opting for the division between his culture and his society rather than that between his intellect and his emotions.

It is the argument of the present work that literary education did not emerge as the (successful *or* failed) reconciliation of the promise of aesthetic culture and the logic of society and that it is not, therefore, the (nearly perfect *or* tragically flawed) vehicle for a complete development of human capacities. Literary education, or 'English', can best be understood as a specialised sector of the apparatus of popular education. This apparatus was not formed on the basis of a compromise between the aesthetic ideal and social necessity. Instead, we describe it as emerging in the autonomous sphere of 'social welfare'; a sphere formed when traditional techniques of individual pastoral surveillance were redeployed in a new machinery of government aimed at the 'moral and physical' well-being of whole populations. It was in this domain that popular education could take shape as an apparatus of moral supervision. And it was as the privileged inheritor of this apparatus – not as the mediator of culture and society – that modern literary education first came into being towards the end of the nineteenth century. So I shall argue.

If this genealogy is correct, then we must give up the idea that English and modern criticism will see to 'man's' cultural completion in either of the two proposed• forms: through an aesthetic reconciliation of his divided ethical substance, or through the theoretical rehabilitation of his unconscious being. Indeed, I will argue that it is necessary to give up the idea that culture forms a totality at all, governed as it is by the figure of a 'complete' development of human capacities. The apparatus of popular education in which English emerged has as its object the formation of a highly specific profile of cultural attributes, in fact the attributes of a citizenry. This profile was produced by an historically unprecedented machinery of social investigation and administration, which began to emerge in England during the late eighteenth century and which by the middle of the nineteenth had largely succeeded in constituting the life of the population as an object of government.

It was in and through this machinery, then, and not through the 'idea of culture', that a uniform development of human attributes became thinkable. The target of this development was not 'man' as the bearer of a divided ethical substance awaiting aesthetic reconciliation, or 'the subject' as the bearer of an unconscious being awaiting theoretical clarification. It was the individual as the member of a population whose health, literacy, criminal tendencies, private sentiments and public conduct had been constituted as objects of a new kind of government attention. Perhaps this list, with its mix of personal and social attributes, gives sufficient preliminary identification of this new form of government: drawing on an administrative apparatus aimed at re-shaping the attributes of whole populations, but operationalised through forms of conscientiousness which permitted individuals to govern themselves. It was on the cultural development of individuals specified in this new manner that literary education eventually went to work. The fact that this development is not a 'complete' one; the fact that it takes place through forms of social organisation organised around techniques of moral supervision (the school); the fact that these techniques are embodied in hierarchical relations between different categories of person (teacher and student) – none of these facts constitute flaws in education generally or in literary education in particular. That they have been taken to is, we shall see, the result of the idea of culture being taken at its own word, instead of in terms of its historical deployment.

No doubt more strands of analysis are drawn on in the writing of a study such as this one than its author can consciously bring to mind. Three such strands can be mentioned, however. First, as the reader will have perhaps already surmised, this study draws on the work of Michel Foucault. From his studies it derives a conception of culture as a patchwork of cultural technologies, together with a mode of describing these technologies – 'genealogy' – which seeks to free them from the sorts of unity imposed by the idea of development towards a goal. Second, a less obvious but if anything more important debt has been incurred to the philosophy of Ludwig Wittgenstein. His work is the source of a particular conception of meaning as a 'dispersed' phenomenon; that is, a phenomenon not determined by a single general form like language or subjectivity, but taking a variety of forms from the motley of cultural technologies in which words are used and from the special activities which are called 'explanations of meaning'. Finally, this study has benefited by some particular initiatives in the field of social theory taken by Paul Hirst and Barry Hindess. Perhaps their work is less evident in the content of the present study than in its general approach to the domain of the 'social'. This is an approach which seeks to avoid the forms of general historical and structural determination; forms whose unity all too often turns out to be a surrogate for the 'complete' development of 'man' long promised by culture.

However, none of the authors mentioned has undertaken a study of the emergence of literary education. The responsibility for bringing their (sometimes conflicting) work to bear on this undertaking rests, therefore, with the present writer.

Brisbane   IAN HUNTER

Acknowledgements

This work is the product of several years of teaching and research in the interdisciplinary milieu of the School of Humanities at Griffith University in Australia. I am indebted to the School's general staff for their contribution to maintaining this environment and to the School Administrator, Pat Noad, in particular. Outside the School, the staff of the library's Inter-Library Loans Service, Kim Hillier and Julie Delman, have been tirelessly efficient in tracking down numerous, sometimes obscure, volumes. Erica Maddock is to be thanked for her careful production of the typescript.

On the academic side, a number of people both inside and outside the School have been no less helpful. Of these I should mention Tony Bennett, Anne Freadman, Mike Gane, Barry Hindess, Colin MacCabe and Ken Ruthven. Terry Eagleton commented generously on an early version of the argument, even though it was in part pitched against his own treatment of the question. To John Frow's conscientiousness and tolerance I owe the benefits of an extended correspondence on the central arguments of the book, even if we did not always agree. Beverley Brown was a searching and generous discussant during her all too short stay in the School. And Noel King has been a bottomless source of references and encouragement.

A special debt has been incurred to Dugald Williamson and Jeffrey Minson, with whom I have worked closely for several years and whose commitment to a common intellectual enterprise has been vital to the development of the present study.

It remains to acknowledge the work of the supervisors of the doctoral research on which this book is based: Stephen Gaukroger for his advice and encouragement, and David Saunders, whose feat was to combine the roles of colleague, supervisor and friend.

I. H.

1

Introduction

I

In 1867 Her Majesty's Inspector Matthew Arnold concluded his 'General Report for the Year' by comparing the public elementary schools of the popular classes with the private schools of the middle classes. He did so 'by placing in juxtaposition a letter written in school by an ordinary scholar in a public elementary school in my district, a girl of eleven years old, with one written by a boy in a private middle-class school, and furnished to one of the Assistant Commissioners of the Schools Inquiry Commission'. The elementary schoolgirl's letter begins in the following way:

> Dear Fanny, – I am afraid I shall not pass in my examination. Miss C– says she thinks I shall. I shall be glad when the Serpentine is frozen over, for we shall have such fun; I wish you did not live so far away, then you could come and share in the game. Father cannot spare Willie, so I have as much as I can do to teach him to cipher nicely. I am now sitting by the school fire, so I assure you I am very warm. Father and mother are very well . . .

While the private schoolboy's epistle betrays a training in a different kind of eloquence:

> My Dear Parents, – The anticipation of our Christmas vacation abounds in peculiar delights. Not only that its 'festivities', its social gatherings, and its lively amusements crown the old year with happiness and mirth, but that I come a guest commended to your hospitable love by the performance of all you bade me remember when I left you in the glad season of sun and flowers.
> And time has sped fleetly since reluctant my departing step crossed the threshold of that home whose indulgences and endearments their temporary loss has taught me to value more and more . . . (Arnold, 1889, pp. 131–2)[1]

1

Just in case we are in any doubt about how to take this comparison, Arnold comments that:

> The stamp of plainness and the freedom from charlatanism given to the instruction of our primary schools, through the public character which in the last thirty years it has received, and through its having been thus rescued, in great measure, from the influences of private speculation, is perhaps the best thing about them. (Arnold, 1889, p. 131)

And if the 'statist' character of his advocacy of popular education tends to unsettle two dominant images of Arnold – as 'prophet of culture' and as bourgeois ideologue – then this disturbance is only compounded by his account of the reason for the superiority of public education.

> It is in this respect that our primary schools compare so favourably with the private adventure schools of the middle class, that class which, Mr. Bright says, is perfectly competent to manage its own schools and education. The work in the one is appraised by impartial educated persons; in the other by the common run of middle-class parents. (Arnold, 1889)

The 'impartial educated persons' are, of course, the inspectorate and the new educational bureaucracy. And the remarkable thing is that Arnold attributes the sincerity and 'freedom from charlatanism' of the popular scholar's letter not to the effects of literature or to the spread of culture, but to the fact that it was produced in a governmental apparatus organised by a certain supervisory function.

In fact, we can discern the main components of modern literary education in Arnold's remarks some half-century before their final synthesis and full actualisation. But they are present in a way that we find difficult to recognise. We can detect, for example, the valorisation of individual self-expression and the condemnation of formulaic composition. Only in Arnold's remarks these are not traced immediately to the expressive powers of literature, but to the deployment of a specific pedagogical system characterised by a special kind of supervision. Moreover, what are we to make of the taken-for-granted centrality of 'culture and criticism' to the emergence of English in the light of these remarks? To be sure, these factors are not absent, but their presence is not that of the driving forces behind the teaching of English. They are present, rather, in the *person* of the inspector whose ethical qualification they secure. They are present, that is, at one remove as the discipline securing the exemplary public standing of the caste of 'impartial educated persons' drawn on to provide the ethical invigilation of a fledgling governmental apparatus.

In short, if we can detect in Arnold's comments the central components of modern English – culture, criticism, and pedagogy – they are not ordered according to that familiar historical logic in which Arnold's role is to mediate culture and criticism at the level of society. According to this logic – which characterises both Marxist and non-Marxist histories of English – the educational system is nothing more than the (true of false) social realisation of the ideal values of culture and criticism. But Arnold's remarks suggest that it is something quite other than this. They suggest that it is a governmental apparatus able to achieve a certain 'humanisation' of the population according to a (supervisory) 'rationality' supported by the apparatus itself. Further, they suggest that on this basis the educational apparatus was able to engage the services of the critic and his culture on its own terms, rather than the other way around. We must therefore seek to describe this rationality according to a different kind of historical logic.

The theme of the present work is the relation between culture and government. More specifically it is concerned with the circumstances in which the reading and criticism of literature lost their function as the aesthetico-ethical practice of a minority caste, and acquired a new deployment and function as an arm of the emergent governmental educational apparatus. It was this complex historical transformation, I shall argue – begun at the end of the eighteenth century but not completed until the first decades of our own – that was responsible for the birth of modern literary education.

Of course, there were literary pedagogies prior to the one that we associate with self-expression, the 'mass' teaching of English literature, and the exemplary role of the teacher-critic; but these were not 'literary education' in the modern sense. In England, the most important prior form of literary pedagogy was of course the teaching of classical grammar and rhetoric in the the network of grammar schools, the handful of Greater Public Schools, the scatter of Dissenting Academies and the two ancient universities. This ensemble of pre-governmental institutions determined what counted as 'education' prior to the beginning of the nineteenth century. But this education was 'literary' only in the pre-modern sense of the word: being concerned with the study of *letters*. Curtius (1948, p. 42) reminds us that '*litteratura* does not at first mean literature in our sense; the *litteratus* is one who knows grammar and poetry (as the *lettre* still is in France), but is not necessarily a writer'. Classical education was not a literary education in our sense. Not only was it directed at a tiny minority of the 'population' (the word is an anachronism in this context), it was also fundamentally concerned with the acquisition of the two ancient languages and the practical mastery of the skills of rhetoric and oratory. Indeed, what is sometimes called 'criticism' in this system was, as Hardison (1962) has shown, itself a branch of oratory: the praise of great authors. In short, the classical education in letters was not what we know as literary education, for what will turn out to be two inseparable reasons: first, because it was not directed at that artefact of modern systems of government, the population; and second, because it was a didactics rather than an aesthetics.

No doubt it seems odd to distinguish modern literary education from its most venerable predecessor by pointing to the emergence of a relation between 'population management' and aesthetics. Modern criticism is after all fiercely anti-didactic and defines itself precisely in terms of the transcendence of social function and political interest. Nonetheless, without anticipating too much of the detail of our argument, we can observe that, despite this intense commitment to the aesthetic, the teaching of English is dependent on the historical emergence of a new kind of educational apparatus: one capable of combining a concern for individual 'self-expression' with new techniques of supervision and discipline operative at the level of the population. And it is precisely this conjunction that we observed informing Arnold's partisan differentiation of popular education from the remnants of the old rhetorical system. The non-rhetorical writing of the popular scholar not only allows a greater access of individuality, its success in this regard is inseparable from its systematic supervision by a corps of 'impartial educated persons'.

It is also this conjunction of aesthetics and government that distinguishes modern literary education from its second-most illustrious predecessor and near relative, Romantic 'aesthetic education'. Unlike classical education, Romantic aesthetic education was directed at the individual's aesthetico-ethical organisation – at producing a synthesis out of the divided 'ethical substance'; and this practice of ethical reconciliation has indeed passed into the modern teaching of English. Unlike the latter, however, the Romantic aesthetics of self-cultivation was for most of the nineteenth century a more or less voluntary 'practice of the self', confined to caste groupings at one remove from the emerging machinery of popular education. Despite some recent claims concerning the ideological function of criticism, Arnold at no point advocated that it be deployed in the popular school (recitation and paraphrase were as far as he went in this regard) or that it be used in the training of teachers. And we shall see that despite Arnold's own axiom that 'culture seeks to do away with classes', criticism for Arnold was in fact that which qualified him for membership of a special purpose-built class: the corps of ethical exemplars deployed to oversee the machinery of popular education. In other words, Romantic criticism and culture possessed no intrinsic generality or democratic drive that operationalised them at the level of the population or realised them in 'society' through the teaching of English in schools. The population, as we shall see, is an artefact of definite systems of administration and investigation; and modern literary education differs from its Romantic predecessor by virtue of its deployment in one such system, the apparatus of popular education.

In brief, modern literary education differs from classical education by virtue of its aesthetic imperative; and it differs from Romantic aesthetic education – to which it is nonetheless related by historical filiation – because this aesthetic imperative is deployed as a discipline in the government of populations. In order to understand the birth of literary education, therefore, we need to be able to describe the circumstances in which the erstwhile caste practice of aesthetic self-culture, or criticism, was redeployed as a discipline in an apparatus aimed at the cultural transformation of whole populations. But we must be able to achieve this objective without subordinating the specific rationality of the pedagogical apparatus – in which the critic first appeared as the locus of a certain kind of ethical supervision – to a general conception of historical development governed by the critic's promise of 'man's' cultural realisation.

The central obstacle confronting this undertaking is the fact that the contemporary history and theory of literary studies is dominated by a particular conception of cultural and historical development. In this conception criticism and culture assume the form of unsurpassable theoretical and historical horizons, because they are deployed as vehicles for the 'complete' realisation of 'man' and the 'total' development of 'society'. And these are the circumstances in which specific dispensations of cultural attributes, such as that achieved by the machinery of popular education, lose historical and political definition; being subsumed within a general logic of 'full' cultural development which is presumed fundamental.

In fact, the conception of complete cultural development as we find it today is the product of two overlapping and inseparable problematics. According to the first, in which criticism duplicates the themes of *cultural history*, the full development of 'man' and 'society' is promised by a fundamental division in the 'ethical substance'. This division assumes many forms – intellect and feeling; freedom and necessity; consciousness and social being – but its central avatar today is that between 'culture and society'. Under this oppositional regimen culture must take the form of a universal dialectic or *reconciliation of ethical division*. Surprisingly enough, criticism in this problematic has never forfeited its original role as the exemplary embodiment of this dialectic and hence of 'man's' cultural completion. In this context the history and theory of English is thus written in terms of the (successful or failed) achievement of this fundamental historico-ethical reconciliation.

In the second problematic, in which criticism duplicates the central concerns of the *human sciences*, 'man's' completion assumes a quite different form. Here it depends on his breaking with the unthought representations presented to him as an empirical or historical being and achieving a *theoretical awareness* of what it is in him that makes them possible. The division in this case is not in the ethical being of 'man' but in the ambivalent topography of 'the subject' formed by the human sciences: a division between empirical consciousness and the linguistic, psychological, or social 'unconscious' on which it is alleged to depend. Nonetheless, this second problematic results in an equally monolithic conception of the history and theory of modern literary education. English in this view is the outcome of the (failed or successful) project to recover from 'the subject's' literary representations the unthought structures that make them possible.

Given that the present work locates its own description of the emergence of English and modern criticism by plotting the historical and theoretical limits of these two models, it is necessary to examine them in a little more detail.

II

Perhaps the most well-known exponent of the *first* model of the development of culture and literary education – the model in which they emerge as the means of reconciling 'man's' divided ethical being – is Raymond Williams. In his seminal *Culture and Society 1780–1950*, Williams provides an exemplary account of the division as a quasi-historical event occuring towards the end of the eighteenth century and synchronised with the ascendancy of 'industrialism'. At this point, says Williams, the organisation of the arts (with their conception of unalienated human fulfilment) began to draw away from the organisation of society (increasingly dominated by a form of production in which 'man's' being is subordinated to the logic of capital accumulation). Williams argues that this division both produced the 'invaluable' idea of culture as the form of human completeness figured forth in 'a total qualitative assessment' of life, while simultaneously inflicting its antinomic form on culture itself. Williams describes this division in culture while commenting on Shelley's *Defence of Poetry*.

> The most obvious criticism of such a position as Shelley's is that, while it is wholly valuable to present a wide and more substantial account of human motive and energy than was contained in the philosophy of industrialism, there are corresponding dangers in specialising this more substantial energy to the act of poetry, or of art in general. It is this specialisation which, later, made much of this criticism ineffectual. The point will become clearer in the later stages of our inquiry, where it will be a question of distinguishing between the idea of culture as art and the idea of culture as a whole way of life. The positive consequence of the idea of art as a superior reality was that it offered an immediate basis for an important criticism of industrialism. The negative consequence was that it tended, as both the situation and the opposition hardened, to isolate art, to specialise the imaginative faculty to this one kind of activity, and thus to weaken the

dynamic function which Shelley proposed for it. (Williams, 1958, pp. 59–60)

Given this exemplary genesis, Williams' history of culture and literary education is wholly contained within the project to end the isolation of art, or to reconcile 'the idea of culture as art and the idea of culture as a whole way of life'. In other words, this history is subsumed by the figure of 'man's' cultural realisation which is the (indefinitely deferred) outcome of such a reconciliation.

Williams' is a relatively ramified form of the model of ethical division and cultural completion, however. We can find a more 'pure' statement of it in Northrop Frye's *The Educated Imagination*. Frye's pretext for the infliction of the ethical split is, appropriately enough, more obviously mythopoeic than Williams', not that this makes any important difference. Frye asks us to imagine ourselves shipwrecked on an uninhabited island and proceeds to derive 'man's' ethical antinomies from his relation to the world.

> The first thing you do is to take a long look at the world around you, a world of sky and sea and earth and stars and trees and hills. You see this world as objective, as something set over against you and not yourself or related to you in any way. And you notice two things about this objective world. In the first place, it doesn't have any conversation. It's full of animals and plants and insects going on with their own business, but there's nothing that responds to you: it has no morals and no intelligence, or at least none that you can grasp . . .
>
> In the second place, you find that looking at the world, as something set over against you, splits your mind in two. You have an intellect that feels curious about it and wants to study it, and you have feelings or emotions that see it as beautiful or austere or terrible. (Frye, 1964, pp. 16–17)

We shall see that this passage could just as easily have been written by Schiller or Fichte, or a number of the other German Romantics. Like them, Frye uses the division of ethical substance as the basis for a 'total history' of culture and society. The sciences and 'didactic' knowledge are the product of 'man's' intellectual side and his moral will. They chain us to the objective world and to the world of limited social purposes and functions. Culture and literature, on the other hand, are products of the feelings or, more accurately, of the reconciliation of 'man's' sensuous identification with things and his intellectual alienation from them. This is why literature, according to Frye, has an essence in the forms of metaphor and myth: types of language which reconcile the *meaning* abstracted from things by the intellect, and the 'embodied imagination' contained in literary *form*. And it is also why literary education holds the key to 'man's' full social being. It is, given the antinomy, the only thing that can save him from the alienating necessities imposed by nature and social organisation (on the one hand) and the abstract violence of his own unrealised intellect and moral will (on the other); and it does so by allowing the former to achieve their full development without imposing on 'man' and the latter to be actualised without the imposition of a 'didactic' order on nature or society. This reconciled state of cultural realisation Schiller (1795, pp. 101–09) associates with the domain of *play*. But then so too does Marcuse (1955, pp. 143–61).

Frye's statement is in fact closer to the Romantic sources of the model. But before we make too much of the difference between his 'cultural idealism' and Williams' 'cultural materialism' we should note their common core. This commonality can be seen, for example, when Williams' (1958, pp. 65–84) exemplifies the 'historical' failure to reconcile 'the idea of culture as art and the idea of culture as a whole way of life'. He does this precisely by pitting Coleridge's confinement to an abstract idea of human fulfilment – disconnected from the 'actual and growing social force' which might have realised it – against Bentham's opposite but complementary imprisonment in the logic of society (the utilitarian calculus), cut-off from the visionary power of moral ideas. As we shall see in more detail below, this dialectic is in fact a variant of Schiller's division between the 'sentimental' (Coleridge) and the 'naive' (Bentham), re-expressed in Frye as the basis of the dynamics of literary education and cultural development. It is worth noting before we pass on to the second model, however, that this first model of cultural completion has spawned two variant and ostensibly opposed forms.

In the first variant, the divided ethical substance is located primarily in 'man' himself – in the gap between his thought and emotions, his moral ideas and his sensuous imagination – and then derivatively in history. In fact, here history functions as the temporal register in which the drama of cultural reconciliation is played out in a more or less mythopoeic manner. This is the case with Frye who, as we have seen, seeks to derive a 'total history' of culture and society from the split in the mentality of a castaway parachuted in from the aesthetic empyrean. But the most well-known example of this variant is, of course, the cultural history employed by F. R. Leavis and the *Scrutiny* circle. Leavis (1952a, 1952b, 1952c) and his collaborators located in sixteenth and seventeenth-century England the image of an 'organic society'. This society was supposedly characterised by its unity of intellect and feeling; by its synthesis of popular and high cultures; and by forms of production in which labour was not an alienation of 'man's' being but an expression of it. Despite the recent and perhaps understandable tendency to poke fun at this conception as a 'peculiarity of the English', it is worth remarking that Leavis' organic society is neither more nor less than a transposition of the image of classical Greek society deployed by the German Romantics, and serves a similar function. It provides, in the form of a retrospective historical projection, the goal of aesthetico-ethical reconciliation used to motivate the practice of criticism in the present.[2]

In the second variant, the divided ethical substance is located primarily in history – in the division between culture and society, civil society and the state or, more recently, between the private and public spheres – and then derivatively in 'man'. This variant, despite its exemplary Hegelian lineage, has – since the celebrated 'materialist inversion' of the dialectic – been increasingly found in Marxist cultural history and criticism. It provides, as we have seen, the schematic genesis for Raymond Williams' history of culture – in the division between culture as art and as 'the way of life as a whole'. In so doing it establishes a form of history in which the completion of 'man's' individual ethical being is made dependent on the socio-aesthetic mediation of the division of labour and the aesthetic totalisation of social relations: the achievement of unalienated labour and true community.[3]

No doubt history in this second variant looks less mythopoeic than in the first. It certainly locates 'man's' cultural realisation in an aesthetic totalisation of society occuring at the end of history rather than in an organic society located at its beginning, thereby substituting utopia for nostalgia. These avatars of cultural criticism and cultural history remain inseparable, however, according to an historical logic which we will investigate in Chapter 3. Leavis can only motivate criticism as a practice of aesthetic reconciliation by appealing to an historical wound in 'man's' ethical being from which culture flows as both sign of injury and promise of cure. But Williams and the contemporary 'cultural studies' movement can only motivate cultural history as a form of social totalisation by deploying criticism as a practice of aesthetic reconciliation. (This is why the literary work remains the privileged image of the true society for this sort of analysis: an image to which the cultural historian has access only through his own reconciliation of form and meaning in the aesthetic reading.) Nor should this surprise us given that both variants are based in the same figure of 'man's' divided ethical substance and differ only over the precedence given to the forms of reconciliation – cultural criticism or cultural history – promising his cultural completion.

In the *second* model of culture and literary education, 'man's' cultural completion assumes a different form. Here it is not characterised by the gradual movements of an historico-ethical dialectic that will eventually reconcile his divided ethical being. It is, rather, marked by a sudden and decisive rupture in 'man's' empirical or historical consciousness and by the theoretical recovery of its unthought conditions of possibility. In its genesis at least, this second model attaches criticism to the human sciences – to linguistics, psychology and sociology; and through this attachment criticism aspires to be something more than an ethics or a means of training sensibilities. It aspires to be a knowledge comparable with the other social sciences. In this model, therefore, the history and theory of literary education are written in terms of a series of (failed or successful) attempts to achieve a rational awareness of 'the subject's' unthought being and to ground culture in a fundamental knowledge of human possibility.

Drawing on the full range of the human sciences, the variants of this model are more numerous than those of its ethical partner. The earliest and perhaps the historically most important version, however, can be found in the early work of I. A. Richards. The figure of theoretical break with experience and rational reconstruction receives an exemplary formulation in the Preface to his *Principles of Literary Criticism*.

> Criticism, as I understand it, is the endeavour to discriminate between experiences and to evaluate them. We cannot do this without some understanding of the nature of experience, or without theories of valuation and communication. Such

principles as apply in criticism must be taken from these more fundamental studies. All other critical principles are arbitrary, and the history of the subject is a record of their obstructive influence. (Richards, 1924, p. 2)

On this basis Richards launched the modern project for a theoretical reconstruction of the field of criticism and culture, drawing his theories of value and communication, at least in part, from behavioural psychology. The history of criticism swept away by this foundational gesture was, according to Richards, characterised by a belief in a 'phantom aesthetic state' or form of experience described in terms of disinterestedness, detachment, impersonality – in fact the attributes of Romantic aesthetic reconciliation. These attributes Richards (1924, p. 15) wished to describe as nothing more than 'a consequence of the incidence of the experience, a condition or an effect of communication'. This move from the immediacy of the aesthetic experience to the theoretical recovery of its unthought conditions, we shall see, typifies the second model: even if the structures of 'unconscious psychological impulses' in which Richards sought to found his theories of value and communication were only the first in a seemingly endless chain of such foundations.

Further along this chain we find Tzvetan Todorov's *Theories of the Symbol*. It is not to psychology that Todorov turns in order to reconstruct criticism as a reflexive knowledge, but to that version of Saussurian linguistics or semiotics characteristic of Russian and Czech formalism. Todorov's book is the subject of a detailed discussion in Chapter 5, so we will not linger over it here. For the moment let us say that, despite its different content, Todorov's 'foundational gesture' takes the same form as Richards'. Criticism becomes 'systematic' and culture acquires the possibility of a rational basis through a breach in 'the subject's' empirical representations that reveals their – this time semiotic – conditions. For Todorov the decisive moment does not occur in the 1920s but in the 1790s, when Romantic criticism overthrew the rhetorical doctrine of imitation. Todorov summarises the central historical argument of his *Theories* in another text written a few years later.

It is with the advent of [German] romanticism that the notion of literature is established in its autonomy, and this is also the beginning of literary theory in the strict sense . . . The concepts of representation and imitation no longer play a dominant role, being replaced at the summit of the hierarchy by the concept of the beautiful, and those related to it: the absence of external finality, the harmonious coherence among the parts of the whole, the untranslatable character of the work of art. All these notions point toward the autonomy of literature and of its works, and lead to an inquiry into their specific properties. It is indeed this inquiry that we find in the romantic texts. (Todorov, 1981, pp. xxv–vi)

These characteristics of the Romantic aesthetic Todorov treats – anachronistically as I will argue – as prefigurations of the 'self-regulating form' which he, following Jakobson (1960), locates as the 'unthought' of literary representation. He thereby produces a history and theory of literary studies in which structuralist poetics is simply the resumption of the fundamental break and theoretical recovery achieved by the Romantics.

Finally, we can complement these psychological and linguistic versions of the second model with a sociological example – Francis Mulhern's *The Moment of 'Scrutiny'*. Mulhern's account of *Scrutiny* is of particular interest for the future course of our argument, because it shows how the model of theoretical clarification of the cultural unconscious deals with some of the actual institutions of literary education. The central point to make regarding his account, however, is that, like Richards and Todorov, Mulhern (1979, pp. 157–76) characterises existing culture and criticism in terms of its unconscious immediacy and its failure to develop a theoretical awareness of its own – this time sociological – possibility. To be sure, Mulhern gives this failure an exemplary sociological explanation, following the lines of analysis thrown out in Perry Anderson's (1969) 'Components of the National Culture'. The failure occurs, argues Mulhern (1979, pp. 3–45), because of an economic and political crisis afflicting the turn-of-the-century imperialist nation states. This crisis apparently outstripped and bankrupted existing sociologies, thereby creating some sort of intellectual and cultural vacuum. This vacuum would have been filled by a Marxist sociology were it not for Leavisite literary criticism which offered an all-too-successful competitor-response to the 'cultural crisis'. Interestingly enough, Mulhern – following Williams this time – accepts the Arnoldian dictum that literature should be a 'criticism of life' and takes issue with *Scrutiny* only for

failing to theorise the material basis of life in social relations: a
failure highlighted by *Scrutiny*'s argument with Marxism over this
very question and its consequent refusal of alliance with the
organised working class (Mulhern, 1979, pp. 63–72, 94–99).

It is not *Scrutiny*'s failure in this regard that is important from our
point of view, however. Much more significant is Mulhern's
invocation of the project for a fundamental clarification of 'the
subject's' unconscious being; because it is only in relation to this
imperative that Mulhern can read-off *Scrutiny*'s 'failure'. This is
what makes Mulhern's sociology of literary education into a variant
of the psychological and linguistic versions of the project proposed
by Richards and Todorov. We have seen that for Richards the
emergence of modern (theoretical) literary education marks the
(limited) success of the project. But we are confronted by the same
model of 'man's' cultural completion in both cases: the figure of the
recovery, through a break in his empirical representations, of the
unthought conditions of 'man's' cultural possibility. What is
important from our perspective is that, whether it is used to mark
success or failure in this regard, the actual apparatus of
governmental pedagogy loses any specific rationality of its own in
this model. As with the ethical model, it is simply the cipher for a
logic of cultural development whose ideal home is in 'criticism and
culture'.[4]

We can suggest, then, that the emergence of the apparatus of
popular education – in which modern literary education was to take
shape – has no logic of its own in either of these models. Certainly
neither of them is able to take into account the unexpectedly
intimate relation between personal expression and public
supervision that we observed informing Arnold's school report. In
fact, the contemporary theory and history of literary education
subjects the sophisticated pedagogical apparatus which made this
function of supervision possible to a double eclipse. On the one
hand, this apparatus is subsumed by a history of culture in which
the educational system is nothing more than a stage on which the
great drama of ethical reconciliation – of intellect and feeling,
meaning and form, or culture and society – is played out. On the
other, it is subordinated to a theory of criticism in which it is
nothing more than a convenient location for the equally dramatic
theoretical rupture in empirical subjectivity that reveals the latter's
unthought social, psychological or linguistic being. If we are to
comprehend the force of the pedagogical imperative in English and

modern criticism – which is as good a formulation of our objective as any – then it is necessary to pay some further attention to the forms of its double exclusion.

III

We are now in a position to put some questions to these two models for the history and theory of English. These questions will be directed at the twin figures of 'man's' divided ethical substance and 'the subject's' unconscious being; that is, at the figures which set the scene for the variant projects of cultural completion and for the variant descriptions of English and modern criticism as the (true or false) vehicles of this completion.

First, let us reconsider the emergence of literary pedagogy as it appears in the first model, the model based on the figure of ethical division and the dialectics of cultural synthesis. It will be recalled that here the deployment of an aesthetic education directed at whole populations is understood in terms of the (complete or partial) reconciliation of culture as art and as 'the way of life as a whole'. Culture in this view is universal in its very idea; and the emergence of a governmental pedagogy is simply a sign of the restoration or anticipation of the 'full' development of human capacities and social relations promised by 'culture and criticism'. The reason for the central role assigned to the prophets of culture – Matthew Arnold in particular – in 'culturalist' histories of literary education should be clear. As both critic and educational bureaucrat Arnold is the prophet of culture armed. Hegel once described Napoleon as the Subject of History on horseback. In our two versions of the history of English, Arnold appears as the Subject of History on the government payroll. His two sides define the space in which the idea of culture as art and as 'the way of life as a whole' achieve their complete and transparent, or partial and distorted, mediation through the emergence of literary education. Hence, in his account of *The Teaching of English in Schools*, Shayer (1972, p. 27) credits Arnold with the paternity of 'creative English teaching' in which 'the whole of society is implicated – every child in a course of humanised studies leading to individual growth and accomplishment within a common bond of civilisation'.

At the same time, we observed that this image of literary education lies at the heart of both variants of the 'culture and society' model. They differ only in their interpretation of 'humanised studies leading to individual growth and accomplishment', according to the options provided by the figures of complete ('culture') and incomplete ('ideology') cultural reconciliation. Let us look a little more closely, then, at literary education as the form in which 'man's' cultural completion is manifested in the popular school. The following remarks on the role of dramatic play in English teaching are taken from John Dixon's *Growth Through English*, the influential digest of a major trans-Atlantic conference on literary pedagogy.

> The taking on of dramatic roles, the dramatic encounter with new situations and with new possibilities of the self, is not something we *teach* children but something they bring to school for us to help them develop . . . To help pupils encounter life as it is, the complexity of relationships in a group and dynamic situation, there is nothing more direct and simple that we can offer them than drama . . . Through the delight of taking a role, of finding new meanings of the body's movements and gestures, young children will come to adapt language as they know it to new roles and levels. And often the language will be the last area in which confidence develops. So 'drama opens up to the inarticulate and illiterate that engagement with experience on which literature rests'. . .
>
> How can a teacher help pupils engaged in so personal a task to weigh up what has been achieved? All of us test the validity of what we have said by sensing how far others that we trust have shared our response. An English teacher tries to be a person to whom pupils turn with that sense of trust. The sensitivity, honesty and tact of his response to what pupils say will confirm their half-formed certainties and doubts in what they have said. A blanket acceptance of 'self expression' is no help to pupils and may well prove a worse hindrance to their growing self-knowledge than a blunt and limited response from the teacher. The more experienced the teacher is in these matters, the more he is able to draw from the pupil the certainties (first) and later the doubts. (Dixon, 1967, p. 38, p. 8)

Here we find most of the features which are taken to typify modern literary education. We find the idea that English provides a unique vehicle for personal expression and individual growth; that it imposes no 'special aptitude' and hence no 'special limitation' on the mind; that this completeness of development is achieved through its closeness to the whole range of 'lived experience'; and that it depends on a special relation to the English teacher whose supervision is not coercive but is, apparently, 'drawn from the pupil' himself. In short, we find all those attributes which – whether they are taken as signs of 'man's' complete or distorted ethical completion – supposedly took shape as English when the 'idea of culture as art' was actualised in 'society'.

What, then, are we to make of the following text? It is taken from David Stow's *The Training System, the Moral Training School and the Normal Seminary*, one of the most important manuals for the design and operation of the nineteenth-century popular school.

> The true character and dispositions are best developed at play with companions similar in years and pursuits. A play-ground, however, may either be a moral training ground, or a mischief-ground. It is the latter too generally when the children are left alone, without any authoritative superintending eye upon them. . .
>
> A play-ground is in fact the principal scene of the real life of children, both in the juvenile and initiatory departments – the arena on which their true character and dispositions are exhibited; and where, free and unconstrained, they can hop and jump about, swing, or play at tig, ball, or marbles. . .
>
> Whilst the pupils sympathise with each other, it is important that the children sympathise with their master. For this purpose, it is necessary that he place himself on such terms with his pupils as that they can, without fear, make him their confidant, unburden their minds, and tell him any little story, or mischievous occurrence. Teachers and parents, desirous of gaining the confidence of their children, must in fact, themselves as it were, become children, by bending to, and occasionally engaging in, their plays and amusements. Without such condescension, a perfect knowledge of real character and dispositions cannot be obtained. (Stow, 1850, pp. 143, 144, 156)

An English teacher may well be 'a person to whom pupils turn with that sense of trust'. But long before the English teacher occupied it, this position of trust and surveillance had been constructed as the position of the ordinary popular school teacher.

Similarly, drama may typify literary education by permitting the 'encounter with new situations and new possibilities of the self'. But long before the emergence of literary pedagogy (and as a condition of this emergence) it was the purpose-built space of the popular school – the playground in particular – that was deployed as 'the principal scene of the real life of children', and as 'the arena on which their true character and dispositions are exhibited'.

In fact, in Stow's remarkable text we find nearly all the features taken to define modern literary education: the problematics of personal expression and individual growth; the idea of complete development; the closeness to experience or 'real life' on which this development depends; and the special relation to the teacher through which the pupil participates in his own supervision – discovering the 'superintending eye' as conscience.

But we find these features in a text which, far from being a hymn to aesthetic education, is a manual for deploying a sophisticated apparatus of pastoral surveillance and moral training. Moreover, we find them in a text that records these innovations in the machinery of popular education developed by Stow at the Glasgow Normal Seminary in the 1820s; that is, at a time when Matthew Arnold was still a babe in arms and Coleridge and Carlyle were still dreaming of education in terms of the formation of a 'National Mind'. In other words, we find the features which were to become characteristic of modern literary education deployed in a supervisory technology in which 'culture and criticism' play no role at all. We must, therefore, prepare ourselves to entertain the possibility that modern literary education was made possible through the deployment of an apparatus that owes little or nothing to literary culture and its promise of 'complete' human development.

At this point we can make two comments by way of prefiguring the argument to come. In the first place, it is impossible to understand the combination of 'personal expression' and moral supervision that characterises popular education by treating it as emerging in the space between the two sides of 'man's' ethical being. It does not matter whether we imagine this space to be defined by the split between the intellect and the emotions, or by that alleged to separate 'culture and society'. And it is equally beside the point whether we decide that the reconciliation achieved by education is a complete one 'in which the whole of society is involved – every child in a course of humanised studies . . .'; or that it is an incomplete one in which the 'failure' of culture to attach its idea of complete development to an 'actual and growing social force' turns it into ideology. We shall see that the apparatus of popular education in which English became possible simply does not emerge in a space defined by a division in 'man's' ethical being and is hence not governed by the variant imperatives of reconciliation. It emerges, rather, in a quite different space defined by quite different historical surfaces. This space we might label – somewhat anachronistically, but for ease of exposition – as the space of *social problems* and *social welfare*. In fact, this was the space in which not drama, but the popular school, opened up 'to the inarticulate and illiterate that engagement with experience on which literature rests', but only because it opened up the inarticulate and illiterate to a new and powerful form of moral supervision.

In the second place, the historical logic according to which this space was formed is not governed by the meeting of the idea of 'man's' cultural fulfilment derived from Romantic aesthetics and the democratic culture 'lived out' in the social relations of the working class – or any other class. Instead, our investigations will show that the space of popular education was delineated by the intersection of two quite different co-ordinates: co-ordinates, moreover, whose meeting was entirely contingent and 'undialectical'. First, we can isolate the co-ordinate formed by the long-standing practice of Christian pastoral care. Directed at the well-being of the individual soul, this practice provided the techniques of personal expression and moral surveillance which pass through Stow to Dixon. Second, we find the co-ordinate formed by the unprecedented technology of social investigation and administration which began to crystallise in England towards the end of the eighteenth century. Directed at the 'moral and physical' condition of entire populations, this technology provided Stow and his cohorts with a means for calculating the need for moral education (the techniques of 'political arithmetic' and 'moral statistics'), and with the administrative machinery in which the attributes of a population or citizenry could be made an object of government (the network of health, penal and 'welfare' institutions aimed at the policing of social space).

Defined by these two co-ordinates, the popular school took shape in a space in which techniques of pastoral surveillance were multiplied and systematised according to a logic whereby the 'moral and physical' well-being of whole populations would be secured through the moral supervision of individuals. This space Foucault has described as that of the *social*, distinguished from 'society' precisely because it is the artefact of piecemeal administrative measures not governed by the dialectics of 'totality'. It was as the result of the organisation of this space that Arnold was able to fix his 'authoritative and superintending eye' on the expressions of 'an ordinary scholar in a public elementary school in my district'.

On the basis of these remarks we can draw three preliminary conclusions which will serve as hypotheses governing the investigations undertaken in Part I of this study.

First, we can begin to call into question the unity and exhaustiveness of the conception of culture that characterises the first model for the history and theory of literary education: that is, the model in which education in general, and literary education in particular, emerge as the (complete or partial) reconciliation of a division in 'man's' ethical substance. The cultural attributes targeted by popular education are not formed according to a logic of 'complete' development derived from the 'idea of culture as art'. Instead, they are built-up from a profile delineated by a specific investigative and administrative machinery aimed at the 'government of populations' and the formation of a citizenry. But this does not mean that such attributes represent only a utilitarian fragment of the complete development of human capacities promised by the totalisation of 'culture and society'. The 'individual' and the 'social' sphere he inhabits are both artefacts of the governmental network which is not subject to a logic of total development. In other words, we can investigate the possibility that popular education (and hence literary education) did not come into being in order to complete 'man', and instead emerged as a local moral technology whose rationality and generality extend only as far as the forms of government defining the sphere of the 'social'. This is the theme of Chapter 2.

Second, the possibility that the cultural attributes targeted by the popular school are, in a certain sense, local and *sui generis*, frees us to set historical limits to the idea of culture itself. This is the objective of Chapter 3. If we are right about the local and 'governmental' character of cultural attributes, what then are we to make of the idea that their formation is governed by an ideal or sum form anticipated in literary culture? We answer this question by tracing the idea of complete development to the local aesthetico-ethical practice of criticism or 'self-culture'. As the telos of a minority ethical practice, this idea – and the figure of ethical division and reconciliation which makes it possible – has no inherent ethical generality or rationality. Aesthetic culture is not the foundation of popular pedagogy, but a distinct minority practice producing a caste of ethical exemplars. These would enter the educational sphere to fulfil a function of moral supervision *defined by it*. The pedagogical apparatus made Matthew Arnold possible, not the other way around.

Third, in the light of the two preceding discussions we can outline a genealogy of modern literary education in which it emerges neither as the vehicle of 'man's' cultural completion, nor as the failed reconciliation of 'culture and society' which gives birth to a moralising ideology. It becomes possible to describe the birth of English as the contingent outcome of the redeployment of the minority aesthetic practice of the ethical exemplar inside a governmental pedagogy organised by the technology of moral supervision. In order to describe this new deployment, however – through which the popular teacher would acquire the exemplary attributes of the critic – we must lower our eyes from the great dialectic reconciling the two sides of 'man's' ethical being: intellect and emotions, culture and society. We must look instead to a series of piecemeal historical changes through which the literary text was able to emerge as the privileged support of the supervisory techniques which David Stow had first invested in the playground. This is the object of Chapter 4, the final chapter of Part I.

IV

Finally, let us conclude this preliminary mapping of the field by putting some questions to the second model of the formation of literary education, the model based on the figure of the theoretical recovery and clarification of 'the subject's' unconscious being. It will be recalled that here the emergence of a rational aesthetic education is treated as the outcome of a decisive rupture in 'pre-theoretical' literary perception: a breakthrough which a theoretical criticism reveals the unthought structures which make such perception possible. The completion of 'man' anticipated in this model is not the outcome of a gradual ethico-historical development. It results from the sudden suspension of what he happens to be and the recovery of a fundamental (linguistic, psychological, social) 'grammar' of all that he might become. It is for this reason, as we have seen, that the actual pedagogical apparatus – itself targeted on a local formation of cultural attributes – loses all specificity in this account: appearing only as the (adequate or inadequate) cipher for the process of theoretical recovery and totalisation occurring on the terrain of 'the subject'.

This figure of theoretical clarification and completion is exemplified well enough in Richards' chapter on 'Sentimentality and Inhibition' in the *Practical Criticism*. Richards begins, as we should expect, by rejecting the idea that the sentiments and emotions are given directly as experience. They are instead, says Richards (1929, p. 260), 'a more or less permanent arrangement in the mind: a group of tendencies towards certain thoughts and emotions organised around a central object . . . A sentiment, in brief, is a persisting organised system of dispositions.' This move from experience to system is of course only the forerunner of an apparently endless series of such moves which will later surface in the work of Todorov and Mulhern, amongst others. On its authority Richards can transform the 'pre-theoretical' meaning of sentimentality as an excessive or crude emotional response. He reconstructs sentimentality as the failure to recover and clarify the unthought system of dispositions or tendencies in the light of the situation which is their target.

> A response is sentimental when, either through the over-persistence of tendencies or through the interaction of sentiments, it is inappropriate to the situation that calls it forth. It becomes inappropriate, as a rule, either by confining itself to one aspect only of the many that the situation can present, or by substituting for it a factitious, illusory situation that may, in extreme cases, have hardly anything in common with it. (Ibid., p. 261)

This failure is what confines 'the subject' to the sphere of 'pre-theoretical' experience and suppresses the totality of possible experiences contained in the underlying structures. And this is what makes Richards' psychological principles into a variant of the linguistic and sociological foundations proposed by Todorov and Mulhern.

The misreadings catalogued by Richards are therefore to be

treated as signs of 'the subject's' failure to clarify the unthought conditions of its recognitions; and Richards conceives his project to be nothing less than the completion of subjectivity through the theoretical recovery of these conditions. What, then, are we to make of the form in which he registers these misreadings? Richards records the following (numbered) student responses and his analysis of them in relation to 'Poem VIII' (Lawrence's *Piano*): the central document for the problems of sentimentality and inhibition.

> With the remark about popular songs . . . we approach the stock-responses difficulty which more than anything else prevented this poem from being read.

> 8.3. *One cannot help disliking* the evocative use of such phrases as 'old Sunday evenings', 'cosy parlour', 'vista of years' etc., which are nothing but so many calls to one's loose emotion to attach itself to them.

A great number could not help themselves:

> 8.31. This poem suggests that some 'Vain inglorious Milton' had unhappily been moved by *that mawkish sentiment with which we so often think of childhood,* to commit to verse thoughts that lie too shallow for words. These thoughts he expresses in phrases culled from *The News of the World* or others [*sic*] his ethereal links with literature.

That the poet might have had a further use for such phrases, beyond that which his readers made of them, they failed to notice in their uneasy haste to withdraw. (Ibid., pp. 108–9)

In their accusations of sentimentality these readers apparently betray their own inhibited emotions. Richards describes the 'further use' that the poet has for the seemingly sentimental phrases in the following terms:

> Whatever its cause, the fact that so many readers are afraid of free expansive emotion, even when the situation warrants it, is important. It leads them, as *Poem VIII* showed, to suspect and avoid situations that may awaken strong and simple feeling. It produces shallowness and trivial complexity in their response. And it leaves those 'sentimental' over-growths that escape the taboo too free a field for their semi-surreptitious existence. The only safe cure for a mawkish attachment to an illusory childhood heaven, for example, is to take the distorted sentiment and work it into close and living relation with some scene concretely and

truthfully realised, which may act as a standard of reality and awaken the dream-infected object of the sentiment into actuality. This is the treatment by expansion, and *Poem VIII* may stand as an example of how it may be done. (Ibid., pp. 269–70)

Now, whatever else is to be said about these misreadings, it is clear that their registration depends upon a certain *relation of supervision and correction* linking the teacher-critic to his students. That this is so can be gathered from the fact that, in a certain sense, the students do not know what they have read until their responses have been corrected by a superior reader. Their relation to the text, as it were, passes through their relation to an individual invested by an exemplary reading. We shall see that this instituted supervisory relation between an individual open to correction and an exemplar who corrects is in fact a condition of existence of misreading and cannot itself be grounded in the latter. In other words, it is not a phenomenon of 'subjectivity' as such.

In fact, at a certain level, Richards himself is aware of this in that the attribution of that specific form of misreading marked by 'sentimentality' typically attaches not to the poem or its author but to the aesthetico-ethical level of the reader. He comments that when we apply the term 'sentimental':

We may mean . . . that the poem was the product of a mind which was too easily stirred to emotion, that it came about through facile feelings, that the *author* was himself sentimental. Or we may mean that *we* should be too easily moved, we should ourselves be sentimental, if we allowed our own emotions a vigorous outing. Sometimes, doubtless, both these assertions are true, but often we are only entitled to make the second. (Ibid., pp. 261–2)

But we can only grasp the full force of this acknowledgement by tracking it to its genesis in the Romantic aesthetic. Here – in a remark which we will cite in part now but in toto later on in our investigations – is Schiller making the same point more than a century earlier.

But it is by no means always proof of formlessness in the work of art itself if it makes its effect solely through its contents; this may just as often be evidence of a lack of form in him who judges it. If he is either too tensed or too relaxed, if he is used to apprehending either exclusively with the intellect or exclusively with the senses, he will, even in the case of the most successfully realised whole, attend only to the parts, and in the presence of the most beauteous form respond only to the matter. (Schiller, 1795, p. 158)

Under these circumstances – straddling aesthetics and the human sciences – the poem is not so much an object of knowledge as a special site (the locus of a special relationship) in which the reader discovers his own incompleteness. We should not feign shock, then, if Friedrich Schlegel draws what is in fact the quite appropriate and accurate conclusion that the ideal reader of criticism or commentary is an individual who only 'half-understands'. True commentary, he remarks

should by no means make everything clear for everybody . . . the reader who only half-understands the work would find such a commentary only half-comprehensible; it would enlighten him in some respects, but perhaps only confuse him the more in others – so that out of this disturbance and doubt, knowledge might emerge, or the reader might at least become aware of his incompleteness. (Schlegel, 1800, p. 66)

We will develop this line of investigation at greater length below, and when we do we will have cause to return to Schlegel's remarkable text. For the present, let us take the preceding remarks as *prima facie* warrants for a proposition to be elaborated in Part II of the present study. We can propose that the act of *theoretical clarification* on which the second model wishes to found literary education is in fact inseparable from the normative imposition of a certain *aesthetico-ethical obligation* (to complete the self) within the context of a specific *relation of supervision and correction*. In other words, we can propose that the 'foundational gesture' of theoretical criticism does not occur on the terrain of 'the subject', and is instead a function of a certain 'practice of the self' deployed as a norm in the pedagogical relationship. At this point we can anticipate the further elaboration of this proposition by making two provisional remarks.

In the first place, it seems likely that modern literary education does not emerge as the result of a fundamental theoretical break which reveals to 'the subject' the unthought conditions of literary representation. Instead, we have given ourselves room to explore the possibility that this 'foundational gesture' is itself a contingent intellectual action imposed as an obligation or norm inside the pedagogical relationship. If this is indeed the case then the 'fundamental clarification' of theoretical criticism is no 'deeper' or more general than the practice of ethical reconciliation that characterises practical criticism. In fact, Richards' own criticism gives us good reason to think that the relation between these two forms is precisely that of an exchange between optional strategies. On the one hand, we have seen that Richards begins his theoretical reconstruction of sentimentality and inhibition by cancelling their experiential character and moving to recover their unthought systemic conditions. But, on the other, this recovery depends on the reader establishing a highly specific relation to his 'self' through the poem.

This relation is one in which his tendency to indulge emotion at the expense of poetic form ('too relaxed') must be played-off against the counter-tendency to suppress emotion in favour of a purely formal or (alternatively) didactic interest ('too tensed'). In other words, we can suggest that what theoretical criticism brings to literary education is not a fundamental knowledge of the latter's conditions of possibility, but two distinct pedagogical imperatives: to clarify 'the subject's' unconscious being and to reconcile the two sides of 'man's' divided ethical substance.

In the second place, we have said enough to suggest that the ground on which two imperatives meet and find their motivation is neither that of 'the subject' (drawn from the human sciences) nor that of 'man' (drawn from the Romantic aesthetic). If we can show that Richards' construction of misreading is representative, then it is not to 'the subject's' unconscious being or to 'man's' divided ethical substance that we must trace the reading of literature. Instead, we shall argue, we must trace it to the special 'educable being' – the 'half-understanding' reader – who is the artefact and outcome of the pedagogical apparatus. We must trace the literary reading, in other words, to the contingent relations of response and correction deployed inside a pedagogy based on techniques of moral supervision. It will be shown that it was these relations and techniques which provided modern criticism with a being characterised by 'pre-theoretical' perceptions and ethical incompleteness.

In short, it seems likely that the being whom modern criticism seeks to 'complete' is not the product of an open-ended 'grammar' of human possibility, or of an ethical division holding out the promise of a 'full' synthesis. Instead, we can suggest that this being is formed according to the specific historical imperatives that arose when criticism (as a practice of the self) was deployed in the apparatus of moral training. These were the circumstances in which the teacher-critic took shape as a public personage combining the attributes of the social scientist (deriving from the gesture of theoretical clarification) and those of the ethical exemplar (deriving from the practice of aesthetico-ethical reconciliation).

In the light of these remarks we can draw three further preliminary conclusions which will serve as the hypotheses governing Part II of this study.

First, we can begin to set limits to the attempt to establish an autonomous history of criticism by appealing to the autonomy of its object, literature or 'literariness'. We have seen that there are two models for such a history. The first finds an unsurpassable historical and theoretical horizon for criticism in the reconciliation of its 'formalist' and 'didactic' tendencies in the aesthetic reading. While the second finds an equally absolute horizon in that moment in which criticism breaks with the 'pre-theoretical' experience of literature and recovers its abstract or unconscious conditions of possibility. It will be shown, however, that the two untranscendable horizons thus proposed – the 'poem itself' and its theoretical unconscious – are in fact themselves the artefacts of two quite local and contingent imperatives deployed as pedagogical norms. We shall argue in Chapter 5 that they are artefacts of the imperative to reconcile an ethical imbalance and thereby construct a self capable of moral action; and the imperative to recover for consciousness that which makes it possible while escaping it. These imperatives, we shall see, are not in themselves literary or aesthetic – being carried out in a variety of other contexts – but are capable of functioning as historical determinants of what is to *count* as 'literary'.

Second, if we are to understand the emergence of modern criticism and its role in literary education we must, therefore, move outside the logic of 'literary' history and describe the lateral intervention of these two quite different pedagogical imperatives. This is the object of Chapter 6. Here it is argued that the Romantic imperative and that of the human sciences were formed as alternative strategic responses to a perceived 'split' in the sphere of 'representation' occasioned by the rise of the positive sciences. The argument here is that the project to reconstruct the lost unity of representation in the register of aesthetics and ethics (Romanticism), and the parallel project to recover it through a certain interrogation of its (newly) unconcious conditions (the human sciences), do not 'extend' or 'improve' criticism by bringing it closer to its object or subject. Instead, they transform what is to *count* as 'criticism' by deploying two quite different activities – a certain ethical practice and a certain intellectual action – in place of the cultivation of taste which characterised eighteenth-century philosophical rhetoric.

Third, given that these two imperatives are not formed on the basis of 'man's' ethical substance or his unconscious being – and are instead local historical responses to the rise of the positive sciences – we cannot look to 'man' or 'the subject' to motivate their meeting at the birth of modern criticism. Neither the project to complete 'man' by reconciling his ethical division in the exemplary practice of the 'close reading', nor the project to achieve this goal by recovering the literary unconscious in a theoretical criticism, can comprehend the circumstances of this meeting. In fact they are the outcome of it. Of the two strategies through which modern criticism attempts to comprehend its birth – the one which would incorporate literary theory into the 'close reading of literature' by treating theory as an abstraction from an unsurpassable aesthetic experience; and the one which would subordinate practical criticism to literary theory by treating the former as the spontaneous expression of a 'pre-theoretical' experience – neither allows us to understand how the two imperatives of modern criticism found their object.

This object, in fact 'the subject' of modern criticism – a being characterised by a pre-theoretical consciousness and a certain ethical incompleteness – is the artefact of a pedagogical apparatus organised around techniques of moral supervision and governed by the special logic of the 'social' sphere. The fallibility and hence the educability of Richards' students, for instance, is the outcome of the relations of surveillance and correction focused on the surface of their literary responses. At the same time – by the time Richards took up his post in Cambridge's fledgling English School – these relations are also informed by the imperatives of ethical reconciliation and theoretical clarification. In short, while the apparatus of popular education provided Romantic criticism and the human sciences with a new kind of person in which their divergent pedagogical imperatives could meet, these imperatives also partially re-shaped the supervisory technology of popular education. At this point of overlap and exchange we find the formation of that ambivalent figure – part ethical exemplar, part social scientist – the teacher-critic. So it is argued in Chapter 7, the final chapter of Part II.

V

The undertaking announced at the beginning of this Introduction – to give an account of the birth of modern literary education – has thus devolved into two distinct but inseparable sub-projects: to describe the emergence of English or literary pedagogy; and to describe the formation of modern criticism. Let us conclude these introductory remarks with a methodological note on the form of description being proposed.

In the case of the emergence of literary pedagogy, it should be clear that the object of our description cannot be a process through which English is supposed to have come into being as the (perfect or flawed) reconciliation of the intellect and the emotions or of culture and society. Neither will our description itself assume the form of a dialectic moving between the exemplary reading of aesthetic texts and an account of their historical contexts: as if this movement guaranteed the completeness of cultural history by reconciling the twin imbalances of 'idealism' and 'historicism'. Instead, here the object of our description will be the contingent historical circumstances in which a minority aesthetico-ethical 'practice of the self' found itself redeployed as a discipline in an apparatus aimed at the moral supervision and cultural formation of populations. This description must therefore take the form of a reconstruction of a governmental technology and an ethical practice: one which remains at the level of the specific and limited domain of 'reason and ethics' formed by their deployment in the sphere of the 'social'.

As far as the formation of modern criticism is concerned, it should be no less clear that our object cannot be the progressive reconciliation of criticism's didactic and formalist tendencies in the goal of the 'close reading'. But neither can it be that moment in which the subject of criticism suspends its 'pre-theoretical' perceptions and achieves a theoretical awareness of their unthought conditions. For these reasons, our own account will not attempt to reconcile didacticism and formalism (which have no special privilege in it); nor will it take the form of an exemplary break with criticism's pre-theoretical past through a recovery of its (linguistic, psychological or social) 'unconscious'. Instead, here the object of our description will be those contingent historical circumstances in which the dual imperatives of the Romantic aesthetic and the human sciences found their object – the object of modern criticism – in the educable individual presented to them by the pedagogical apparatus.

Once again, such a description must take the form of a reconstruction of the historical surfaces on which these twin imperatives emerged and were subject to a profound pedagogical redeployment. Above all, this description must be governed neither by the figure of 'man' and ethical synthesis, nor by the figure of 'the subject' and theoretical clarification. Instead, it must follow the contours of the ensemble of ethical practices, 'intellectual actions', and supervisory techniques which brings these figures into being.

If we adopt Foucault's Nietzschean name for this form of description – 'genealogy' – it is for purely pragmatic reasons. I would just as happily describe this undertaking as a history of literary education, were it not for the fact that 'history' has been so thoroughly colonised by the forms of cultural history and the history of the human sciences. In any case, in referring to Part I of this study as a genealogy of English and Part II as a genealogy of modern criticism, I mean neither more nor less than that they are characterised by the objects and forms of description just catalogued.

Part I

English

2

Government

In her book, *The Preachers of Culture*, Margaret Mathieson outlines four major sources for the genesis and development of English. These are to be located, she argues, in the attacks on the classical curriculum of the grammar schools, culminating in the arguments of the Victorian liberals in favour of 'modern subjects'; in Matthew Arnold's post-Romantic campaign to install literary culture at the centre of popular education; in a tradition of analysis stressing the threats to such a culture posed by the industrialisation of community life and the commercialisation of culture itself; and in the progressive and experimental education of the early twentieth century, with its stress on the creativity of the child-mind and the need for a non-coercive pedagogy. Mathieson sees these factors culminating in a conception of English that elevates it from the rank of 'knowledge subjects' and transforms it into the central vehicle of the child's experience, responsible for the latter's emotional, social and moral development. She also observes that this transformation was accompanied by the elevation of the English teacher into a special personality – combining warmth and morality, sympathy and cultural authority – which, she says, sits oddly with the predominantly working-class origins of English teachers and English itself.

There is much to be learnt from this account and if I dissent from it, it is with a strong sense that it comes closer than any other to the complex of factors which made modern literary pedagogy possible. The central weakness of Mathieson's account, it seems to me, is one that it shares with the standard history of English: the assumption that the developments in popular education from which English emerges are governed by the idea of culture (or the complete development of human capacities) whose privileged expression is the literary tradition. Hence the familiar importance she attributes to Arnold in these developments. I have already indicated some of

33

the problems attendant on this account and sketched-in an alternative lineage for English. Now it is time to develop this sketch in more detail.

We can exemplify the modern face of literary education – which Mathieson characterises in terms of the use of literature in a 'child-centred' pedagogy, overseen by an unobtrusive yet vigilant teacher – by extending the citation introduced earlier from John Dixon's *Growth Through English*. It will be remembered that Dixon advocates the educational centrality of English, and of drama within English, because: 'To help pupils encounter life as it is, there is nothing more direct and simple that we can offer than drama.' He continues:

> So 'drama opens up to the inarticulate and illiterate that engagement with experience on which literature rests'. . . . Drama, like talk, is learning through interaction. The actor may and must find within himself what it is to be angered, hurt, intimidated, ashamed, vindictive . . . but he finds this partly in response to another person. Together they learn to support and confirm each other's discoveries. Because each of us in acting makes public what he knows and can say, others can join in our learning. And the teacher too has the work before him, in progress, open to his sympathetic inspection. Thus he too is positioned to help the work along, to suggest changes of perspective, to focus attention, as the man who observes can. (Dixon, 1967, pp. 38–9)

There is no doubt that we can recognise the face of modern English in these remarks. It is there in the stress on literature as a mode of self-discovery and personal development, open even to the 'inarticulate and illiterate' because of its closeness to experience, and overseen by the non-coercive ministrations of 'the man who observes'. But before we trace in these features the lineaments of the great prophets of culture or the more recent influence of progressive education, and before we decide whether these features reveal the fulfilment or the betrayal of the promise of culture, let us reactivate the comparison with David Stow's 'Training System'. Stow, it will be recalled, wished to make supervised play central to the new organisation of the popular school, urging teachers to 'become children' because: 'Without such condescension, a perfect knowledge of real character and dispositions cannot be obtained.' I will repeat his earlier-quoted remarks, in fuller form, for the reader's convenience:

> The true character and dispositions are best developed at play with companions similar in years and pursuits. A play-ground, however, may either be a moral training ground, or a mischief-ground. It is the latter too generally when the children are left alone, without any authoritative superintending eye upon them. . .
>
> A play-ground is in fact the principal scene of the real life of children . . . – the arena on which their true character and dispositions are exhibited; and where, free and unconstrained, they can hop and jump about, swing, or play at tig, ball, or marbles. In the initiatory school, in particular, the girls and boys of taste may be seen examining the opening flowers planted round the borders, but without presuming to disturb their delicate and downy petals; a few mathematic little men may also be observed arranging the squares and circles which they may have formed in the sandy gravel; and a few of 'cast peculiar' may be seen on the school door steps, sitting in abstract reverie. . .
>
> Amidst this busy scene, the trainer must be present, not to check, but to encourage youthful gaiety. All is free as air, and subject only to a *moral* observation of any particular delinquency, the review of which is reserved for the school gallery. . .
>
> A monitor or janitor won't do as a substitute for the sovereign authority of the master, which all acknowledge and whose condescension, in taking a game or swing with them is felt as a kindness and a privilege, and who, in consequence, is enabled to guide them by a moral, rather than a physical influence. (Stow, 1850, pp. 142–9)

Long before English emerged as the privileged place where 'pupils encounter life as it is', Stow and other popular educationists had successfully launched the popular school with its purpose-built playground as 'the principal scene of the real life of children'. It will be remembered that Stow's text is in fact a manual for the design and organisation of popular schools, recording his experiments at the Glasgow Normal Seminary in the 1820s; that is, at a time when Arnold was still a suckling and progressive education little more than a gleam in Pestalozzi's eye. Yet can't we see in it, albeit in a less sophisticated form, the same stress on self-discovery and 'individual growth', on the techniques of 'learning through play', and on the non-coercive 'moral observation' of the teacher that we have come to identify with English as a distinctively *literary* pedagogy? It is the argument of this chapter that we can. And if this is so then we must revise our view of English as the (true or false) manifestation of literary culture. Instead, we must look at it as largely the outcome of the autonomous development of a special pedagogical technology which, under certain specifiable conditions, found in literature a device which focused and supported the functions of moral supervision.

In my introductory remarks I suggested that this change of focus involved lowering our gaze from the grand movements of the dialectic that is supposed to mediate culture and society. Our new object of attention is a series of less visible transformations in an ensemble of techniques for organising, training, and optimalising large *corps* of the population: techniques which Foucault (1977) calls *disciplines*. It is to this less exalted domain – rather than to the lineage of culture and progressive education – that we must trace Stow's remarks on the supervisory role of play. In fact we can locate Stow's handbook quite precisely by noting that it was first published in 1836, as part of a decisive reform campaign directed at the early 'pre-governmental' pedagogical use of the disciplines: the monitorial schools of the religious school societies.

It is the monitorial school, emerging at the same time as a number of other disciplinary institutions and recommended, as Colquhoun (1806b) makes clear, by its facility in assembling and training large numbers of the population, that forms the prototype of the modern school. Briefly, the disciplines embodied in the monitorial school assumed the following form, as outlined by Joseph Lancaster in his famous *Improvements in Education*.

First, the division of aptitudes to be acquired into elementary skills organised into incremental series. (Reading, for example, was broken down into recognition of the letters, 'sounding out' two-letter syllables, reading three-letter words, etc.) Second, the division of children into an ascending series of 'classes' according to their mastery of the corresponding skills. Third, the sub-division of each class into a hierarchy according to level of attainment in the particular skill. Fourth, the pedagogical method in which the monitor – himself a child – was appointed to oversee the performance of the particular skill which was 'passed along' the class heirarchy rearranging positions as it went. Fifth, the system of visibility in which each child's activities were observed by a monitor who was himself supervised by a higher-level monitor, forming a pyramid of observation at whose apex was the (untrained) 'teacher'. (Foucault (1977, pp. 170-7) describes this pyramid under the heading of 'heirarchical observation'.) Finally, we have the combination of the system of observation with a system of rewards and punishments to intensify the relations of emulation and competition built into the division of skills and classes itself. It was this combination of systematic observation and the internalisation of norms of attainment through emulation that produced the popular schoolroom as a sphere of 'normalising observation'; that is, as a space organised around a type of observation through which children came to *see themselves* according to new social norms which they struggled to attain. It was Lancaster's boast that:

> On this plan, *any boy who can read, can teach;* and the inferior boys may do the work usually done by the teachers, in the common mode: for a boy who can read, can teach, *although he knows nothing about it;* and, in teaching, imperceptibly acquire the knowledge he is destitute of, when he begins to teach, by reading. (Lancaster, 1838, p. 84)

It was precisely this aspect of monitorialism that was attacked by reformers like Stow – less for its inhumanity than for its inefficiency, however. Taught in this preceptual manner, Stow argued, working-class children actually failed to internalise the new social and moral norms. The pedagogical disciplines had to be reorganised around a new 'sympathetic' relation between the children and a specially–trained teacher. The hierarchical observation of the monitorial schoolroom had to be re-invested in the 'moral observation' of the teacher. Let us say for the moment that this intervention consisted in replacing the rigid and anonymous imposition of norms that characterised the monitorial use of the disciplines with the tactics of supervised freedom focused in a new 'personal' relation between teacher and student.[1] It was this transformation, we shall see, that would eventually make it possible for English teachers to advocate 'learning through interaction' while carrying out the functions 'sympathetic inspection' or 'moral observation'.

The first hypothesis to be drawn from our comparison of Dixon and Stow, then, is that, in the first instance at least, we should refer the characteristic features of modern English not to the tradition of literary culture or literary criticism but to certain transformations in the disciplinary technology of nineteenth-century popular education. Unfortunately, this reorientation cannot be achieved simply by turning from the pretensions of literary culture to the facts of educational history. The spell of culture has been cast over the history of education too, which typically assumes the forms of cultural history and is characterised by the same antinomies of human development that we are seeking to forestall in our genealogy of English.

In this instance the cultural dialectic tends to be organised around an opposition between a pedagogy 'imposed' by social utility or political necessity and one developed 'for its own sake', as part of the self-realisation of 'man' or the 'universal class'. Mary Sturt (1967 pp. 1–92), for example, constructs her history of *The Education of the People* around an exemplary transition from a utilitarian and normative pedagogy – symbolised by monitorialism and governed by the maintenance of social order and the relief of poverty – to one expressing the humanitarian goal of 'education for its own sake', characterised by a new 'sympathetic discipline'. While historians like Brian Simon (1960, pp. 126–276), E. P. Thompson (1963, pp. 385–440) and Richard Johnson (1976) for their part emphasise the continuing presence of religious norms and repressive discipline in the 'provided' Sunday school and elementary school systems. They treat this presence as a sign that the process of humanisation and cultural development could not occur through an 'imposed' pedagogy and must instead be looked for in the self-realising educational initiatives of the artisanal and working classes.

It should be clear that these apparently opposed accounts – like the alternative versions of the history of English – both assume that education is a manifestation of culture, pictured as the historical reconciliation of an exemplary opposition between the self-realising and the utilitarian, the self-expressive and the normative. They disagree only over whether this universal movement towards the complete development of human capacities has already occurred or has been blocked by a freezing of the dialectic on the side of 'class cultural control'. However, it seems to be the case that self-realisation and social norms, self-discovery and moral training, are by no means opposed to each other in Stow's modified version of the pedagogical disciplines. Quite the opposite: it was in the supervised freedom of the playground that moral norms would be realised *through* self-expressive techniques; and it was in this space that the forms of self-discovery organised around the individual would *permit* the realisation of new social norms at the level of the population.

In fact, Stow's programme indicates that far from obeying the great dialectic between culture and society or consciousness and social determination – according to which human attributes will either be realised in a moment of reconciliation and transcendence or else repressed by a political imbalance – the transformation of the pedagogical disciplines which would produce English existed on the cusp of two quite different concerns. These were the *religio-philanthropic concern with the moral well-being of individuals,* and the *governmental concern with the 'moral and physical' condition of the population.* The superimposition of these two concerns in the new pedagogy is well illustrated in James Kay-Shuttleworth's testimony to the 1838 sitting of the parliamentary Select Committee on the Education of the Poorer Classes.

Kay-Shuttleworth was soon to be permanent secretary to the Committee of [the Privy] Council on Education, established in the face of fierce religious and political opposition in 1839 as the first government body to have responsibility for overseeing the development of popular education. Evidence given to the Select Committee was concerned with the need for public intervention into the funding, organisation and inspection of schools, and into the training of teachers. Kay-Shuttleworth's testimony concerned the social and moral benefits that would flow from replacing the patchwork of small private and religious schools with large systematically administered institutions, provided that the monitorial discipline of the latter was 'humanised' along Stowian lines. Questioned on the effect of large schools on 'the formation of individual character', Kay-Shuttleworth replied:

I think that the opportunities for moral training among children during their usual associations in periods of recreation, and also while they are trained in the school, are greatly increased when they are in contact with numbers; and that although it may require a larger amount of intelligence and superior vigilance and activity on the part of the master, yet his opportunities, not merely of inculcating moral lessons, but forming good habits, are increased by the accidents which occur when numbers are assembled, and which develop the peculiarities of character, and especially the moral tendencies of different characters, rather than in a small school . . . If the ordinary monitorial system alone were adopted, I cannot conceive that a master ought to be in contact with more than 50 children; but if the ordinary monitorial system be adopted, in conjunction with the gallery employed in infant schools, and which is also employed in the juvenile schools of the Glasgow Normal Seminary, I believe that a very able, intelligent, and active master, may conduct a school containing 200 children, with more success than is ordinarily obtained in schools of not half the number.

But the overlapping of individualising moral supervision and the governmental regulation of the population is focused most sharply in Kay-Shuttleworth's remarks on playgrounds, 'considered an essential part of school discipline for two separate reasons':

first, that it is considered, especially in large towns, that the physical development of children ought not to be impeded by the absence of proper recreation and exercise; but more especially the play-ground is, in the Glasgow Normal Seminary, rendered a source of moral training. The ordinary routine of the school is broken up by occasional recreation, and the languour and irritation which result from fatigue are thus easily got rid of; and during the period when the children are taking recreation they are not abandoned to the mischievous influences of the street or lane in which their parents reside, but they take that recreation under the superintendence of teachers, who endeavour, by careful attention to what occurs without applying any restraint, to exclude the influence of vicious propensities; and, by degrees to establish in the play-ground mutual good offices among the children, and propriety of demeanour. (Parliamentary Papers A, 1838, vol. 6, pp. 532, 547)

Like Stow, Kay-Shuttleworth is concerned to modify monitorialism by installing a pedagogy which will 'develop the peculiarities of character, and especially the moral tendencies of different characters'; and the moral superintendence of the playground remains the emblem of the means by which this shaping of the person might be achieved 'without applying any restraint'. At the same time it is clear that this humanising and individualising pedagogy shares the monitorial imperative to enclose large numbers of children in special purpose-built spaces, where their development might be subjected to a single formative regimen. The concern with general levels of health, sentiment and behaviour devolves from regulatory norms whose object is the population rather than the individual. And the school's role in removing the formation of cultural attributes from the care of family and the companionship of streets places it squarely amongst those other governmental mechanisms – the hospital, the prison, the reformatory – targeted on the nineteenth–century city.

We are confronted by what looks like a paradox, then. The new organisation of the popular school, in which the abolition of coercion and the encouragement of self-expression would permit a profusion of individual characters to show themselves, was at the same time a mechanism for subjecting these characters to new general norms of development. The playground, which provided the space in which children might manifest 'their true character and dispositions . . . free and unconstrained', was also the prophylactic space in which these characters and dispositions could be moulded according to new social norms embodied in the 'moral observation' of the teacher.

No doubt we are ill-prepared to describe such an intimate and reciprocating relationship between the intensification of the personal sphere and the expansion of the sphere of public administration. But this is precisely what we are confronted by in the formation of the popular education system. We can now see more clearly the magnitude of the problem facing the two major versions of the cultural history of nineteenth-century education. Neither a history of the progressive liberation of self-expression from beneath the instrumental norms of government, nor one of its repression by a more subtle re-imposition of such norms, can do justice to the reciprocal relation between the personal and the administered, so evident in Kay-Shuttleworth's testimony.

The individualised self realised through the humanisation of popular pedagogy – despite the fact that it functions as a mirror in which we can still recognise ourselves – seems not to have emerged from a 'culture' or a 'history' any deeper or more general than that involved in the deployment of a new disciplinary technology. This at least is the hypothesis we must form from our observation that the new pedagogical techniques permitting the self-realising manifestation of 'true character and dispositions' also permitted the realisation of new norms for the government of the population. A second hypothesis then: If we are to describe the circumstances in which literature was to provide an embodiment for these techniques – leading to the formation of English – then neither its capacity for realising the self, nor its capacity for collusion in the political repression and displacement of the process of realisation, can form the basis of our description. Instead, we must describe how literature came to be deployed as a privileged device within the apparatus of popular education; one focusing the supervisory strategy that permitted the government of the population to be realised through a tactic of ethical individualisation.

II

Our first task, then, is to describe the initial deployment of these tactics whose consolidated form was to be the popular school. In fact the historical surfaces on which they appeared are personified well enough in the figures of David Stow and James Kay-Shuttleworth. Stow was a religious philanthropist whose conscience, stirred by the moral and physical condition of Glasgow's street children, first led him to form a Sunday school on his own initiative, then a day school in order to further remove these children from their demoralising surroundings.

Kay-Shuttleworth, on the other hand, was the sometime chief public health officer of Manchester, a founder-member of the Manchester Statistical Society, an Assistant Poor Law Commissioner and the author of a much-cited work on *The Moral and Physical Condition of the Working Classes of Manchester in 1832*. His initiatives surfaced in new forms of social observation and administration, aimed at governing the population as a whole, and were realised through an expanding network of medical and social 'police' agencies. The significance of Kay-Shuttleworth's testimony before the Select Committee is that it shows how by 1838 the religio-philanthropic concern with the pastoral care of the individual soul, and the proto-social scientific concern with the 'moral and physical condition' of the population had converged on a common ground: the 'moral training ground' of the popular school. In order to clarify the character of this convergence, however, it is necessary to look briefly at its first incarnation, the turn-of-the-century Sunday school. Here the disciplinary techniques which made the meeting possible were still in the process of assuming their pedagogical form. The means for connecting the care of the individual soul to the government of populations were not yet subject to systematic public administration.

Of course, cultural history has long seen in the Sunday school an emblem of the relation between moral and political guardianship. But in such history – exemplified, for instance, by Edward Thompson's (1963, pp. 385–440) and Brian Simon's (1960, pp. 132–3) accounts of the Sunday school movement – the relation is typically one in which the 'human personality' is repressed or distorted by religious and moral norms serving the economic and political interests of the middle class. In Thompson's Marxian inversion of Weber's thesis on the relation between the protestant ethos and capitalism, the Sunday schools emerge as an important means of inculcating the work discipline required by the factory system, and for displacing the political culture of the subordinate classes. They did this, according to Thompson, by promulgating the doctrine of salvation through 'works', which provided the 'inner compulsion' needed for exploitative factory labour; by translating the demand for political improvement into the eschatological pursuit of divine recompense; and by sublimating this demand into the 'perverted eroticism' of the Methodist conversion process.

Thompson (1963, p. 404) sees the combined process as 'a phenomenon, almost diabolic in its penetration into the very sources of the human personality, directed towards the repression of emotional and spiritual energies'. Or, if not exactly repressed, then these energies were 'displaced from expression in personal and social life, and confiscated for the service of the Church', which in turn served the economic and political interest of the bourgeoisie in securing a work-disciplined labour force.

Simon, who shares the same view of Sunday schools, sees them as the immediate precursors of state popular education, whose function would also be to repress the cultural-political development of the 'human personality' by effecting its displacement onto the terrain of religion and morality. For both writers the undistorted form of this development occurs elsewhere, in the self-educative activities of the artisanal and working classes, like those undertaken by the Chartists and the Corresponding Societies: activities supposedly distinguished by their eschewal of prescriptive religious and moral norms in favour of a rational self-realising pedagogy. Such activities, says Thompson (ibid., pp. 9–10), by mediating the great dialectic between class position and class consciousness, permit the 'making' of a class which 'happens when some men, as a result of common experiences (inherited or shared), feel and articulate the identity of their interests as between themselves, and as against other men whose interests are different from (and usually opposed to) theirs'.

This view of the Sunday schools and hence of the development of popular education has, however, recently been challenged in T. W. Laqueur's *Religion and Respectability: Sunday Schools and Working Class Culture 1780–1850*. Through a meticulously documented analysis of the emergence, popular support, funding, administration, and curriculum of the schools, Laqueur argues that they cannot be seen as distinctively middle-class institutions obeying the logic of 'class cultural control'. He pursues his argument along two intersecting lines.

First, Laqueur does not dispute the claim that Sunday schools subjected working-class children to new norms of cleanliness, punctuality, literacy, conduct and sentiment. In the process such children were, for example, made responsible for their use of time in a way that equipped them for factory labour, *amongst other kinds of work and endeavour*. What he denies is that the organisation embodying these norms was a middle-class imposition, in the sense of arising in response to the needs of factory capitalism and, as Thompson would have it, producing the attributes required by factory labour while repressing or displacing the fundamental 'emotional and spiritual energies' of the 'human personality'.

Although Sunday schools were in part a response to the profound demographic changes accompanying industrialisation, and although the large ones shared forms of disciplinary organisation with the factory system – and, we might add, with prisons, barracks, hospitals and reformatories – Laqueur (1976, pp. 21–62) shows that their rise cannot be correlated either geographically or temporally with the spread of factory production. Moreover, the evangelical and philanthropic currents which surrounded their formation were by no means (middle) class-specific, a fact which Laqueur (ibid., pp. 83–94) demonstrates by analysing the strength of working-class participation in the funding and teaching of the schools. He summarises this line of argument in the following way:

Sunday schools began at a time when the factory system had scarcely gained a foothold and grew to contain millions of children before the factory became the dominant organisation of production. They were as much a rural as an urban phenomenon, as much part of an agrarian as of an industrial economy. Furthermore . . . Sunday school teachers were predominantly working class, funds often came from the working-class community, and indeed the lower orders responded as eagerly to the philanthropic surge of the late eighteenth century as did other strata of society. The great majority of Sunday schools were neither the direct product of industrialism nor of the middle class. (Ibid., p. 216)

But it is Laqueur's second line of argument that bears most centrally on our inquiry into the formation of popular education. If the Sunday school did not arise as an expression of the material and political interests of the middle class, then neither was its action on the individual centrally that of an ideological displacement of political energies into soporific morality or distorted religious gratification. It was not through religious or moral *ideology* that norms took hold of individuals, says Laqueur (ibid., p. 219), but rather through a variety of religious and social *practices*, given new scope and effect by the disciplinary organisation of the school. So, 'The structure of authority, the discipline of time and space, to a lesser extent the organisation of teaching, the rules governing appearance, and the system of rewards and punishments all arose out of the school *qua* school.'

On the one hand, in Laqueur's (ibid., pp. 220–5) description of the meticulous organisation of time and space in the large schools – of their methods for systematically dividing activities and skills into constituent elements performed under the 'moral observation' of the teacher – we can see the indelible marks of those techniques for regulating and intensifying social forces which Foucault has called the 'disciplines'. On the other hand, Laqueur insists that there is no sharp division between these new forms of social regulation and long-standing cultural and religious rites, particularly those of the Christian pastoral or care of the individual soul, which remained central to Sunday school activities. As a result, pedagogical norms and practices could, and typically did, face in two directions simultaneously. The cleansing and grooming required for school attendance, for example, satisfied public norms of health and demeanour embodied in the systematic inspection of the pupils. But at the same time it continued to function as a personal ritual act of observance condensing a wealth of Christian imagery linking care of the body to care of the soul.[2]

It thus becomes clear that, far from retarding the material transformation of social life or displacing it into eschatological fantasies, the moral and religious aspects of the school were inseparable from its emergence as a new form of social organisation directed at precisely such a transformation. In describing these aspects Laqueur is dealing not with a retrogressive ideology but with an ensemble of rites and practices, long responsible for the formation of specific cultural attributes, and now in the process of being incorporated with new and more systematically administered forms of social discipline. This process of incorporation and transposition into a new register is illustrated in the way the skills of reading and writing were deployed in the Sunday school curriculum.

It is true that certain factions of the Sunday school movement – notably the Wesleyan Methodists led by Jabez Bunting and the Tory evangelicals led by Hannah More – opposed the Sunday teaching of writing and arithmetic. This opposition cannot be portrayed, however – in the manner of Simon (1960, pp. 132–3) and Thompson (1963, p. 389) – as an example of religious obscurantism. For one thing, as Laqueur (1976, pp. 124–46) points out, the vast majority of Sunday schools continued to teach writing and arithmetic throughout the controversy; and for another, even the conservative faction was happy for this teaching to occur on week-days and evenings. In other words, the issue is not one of cultural regression but of an attempt to differentiate reading as a long-standing protestant devotional practice[3] from writing and arithmetic as 'secular arts'.

In fact, what the controversy over the teaching of writing ultimately revealed was the impossibility of drawing a line between reading as a religio-ethical practice permitting self-scrutiny and spiritual direction, and writing as a 'secular art' associated with the pedagogical acquisition of social skills and knowledge. Reading and writing, like other Sunday school practices, could face in both directions at once. Once removed from the régime of the protestant household and enclosed in the school, literacy could be connected up to norms other than those regulating the child's devotions and piety. We shall see directly that it was linked through new techniques of social investigation to the child's attributes as a member of the population and as a future citizen of the state – to his health, criminal propensity, sentiments and regularity of habits.

In this new context the sabbatarian distinction between reading as a devotional practice and writing and arithmetic as secular arts became increasingly difficult to maintain. The Christian care of the soul and the governmental administration of the populace converged in the techniques of moral supervision embodied in the Sunday school. And it was precisely this convergence that sparked the opposition of those who wished the schools to remain wholly religious institutions. Opposition was to no avail, however, and even if in the 1840s the Methodist Central Conference did succeed in finally 're-Christianising' its Sunday schools, this was only because the moral pedagogy which had emerged in them was in the process of assuming a new and more powerful form elsewhere, in the publicly administered popular school.

If, then, the organisation of the Sunday school did mark an early articulation of religious supervision and new forms of government, this was not because it emerged as an agency of 'class cultural control', serving the economic and political interests of the middle class. Religious and moral norms entered the schools not as ideology but as popular cultural practices connected to the formation of personal attributes. To be sure, once inside, these practices and norms tended to be absorbed into a more general 'social' concern for the well-being of the scholars. But this was not because the 'human personality' was in the process of emerging from beneath a repressive religious normativity, nor because it was being prevented from doing so by the politically interested re-imposition of such norms. Instead, as we shall see in more detail below, it was a sign that the specifically religious norms and practices related to the care of the individual soul were in the process of being linked to the quite different ones associated with new forms of social investigation and administration, whose object was the moral and physical condition of the population.

Reading, for example, probably did continue to function as a devotional practice closely related to prayer. Here, through the printed word, the child discovered its sinfulness and searched diligently for the signs of grace, the conversion crisis often taking place through the activity of reading itself. But, particularly in big institutions like the Stockport Sunday School, reading took place in

the specially organised time and space of the schoolroom. Here, the
performance of all activities was divided and regulated by norms
embodied in an organised general surveillance which linked
reading to the attributes of punctuality, cleanliness, alacrity and
appropriateness of demeanour and sentiment. The signs of
spiritual condition which reading had supplied to parent or pastor
could thus be transformed into indicators of 'moral and physical'
condition. These were made visible to the teacher in the rank order
of the class, and to the educational reformer as a statistical
percentage of the school population, permitting comparisons with
norms for the population as a whole.

Clearly, the specifically religious features of a practice like
reading become less significant in this process, which saw the
formation of an ethical pedagogy. Nonetheless, it is equally clear
that the ethical function of popular education emerged not as an
ideological supplement to its educative mission, but as an
inescapable component of a pedagogical apparatus directed at
forming the attributes of a population. If the resultant personal
attributes – of punctuality, regularity and the desire for self-
improvement – were found in the factory worker and artisan, they
were also found in the Sunday-school teacher who, from the
beginning of the nineteenth century, was typically a former pupil of
these predominantly working-class institutions. But neither were
these attributes foreign to the militant trade unionists and
Chartists. Their activities not only presupposed literacy, but
literacy as the focus of a self-monitoring and self-improving
regimen which incorporated temperance reform and the reform of
education and domestic life amongst the objects of radical politics.
We shall see that it was no accident, then, that when Lovett and
Collins outlined their utopian project for a humane popular
education – in their *Chartism: A New Organisation of the People* –
they would trace the same convergence between the techniques of
self-development and those of social discipline that had emerged in
the Sunday school and would produce Stow's 'moral training
ground'.[4]

III

We are now better placed to understand the otherwise puzzling
reciprocity between the intensification of individual differences

and the extension of disciplinary norms in the methods of the educational reformers. The first large-scale popular schools did involve the systematic levying of religious and moral norms not, however, in a manner that repressed the collective 'human personality' of the working class, but as adaptations of popular cultural practices and religious techniques associated with the formation of definite personal attributes. Equally, these schools saw the systematisation and transformation of these practices and techniques as they were caught up in new and more general forms of social discipline and organisation. But these changes do not appear to have obeyed a general logic of class domination dictated by the evolution of 'society' as an ensemble of levels governed by its mode of production. It is true that the absorption of pastoral techniques into the new machinery of government produced a pedagogical apparatus whose first target was the children of the working class. But we shall see that this apparatus formed part of a powerful governmental programme operating at a tangent to the main lines of class division and opening onto the new domain of the 'social'.

Laquer's description of the Sunday school suggests that we will not be able to follow this tangent by privileging a line of class domination running from the factory to the school by way of the church: as if this line represented an ultimate horizon for analysis by linking 'society' on the one side to the 'human personality' on the other. Instead, it becomes necessary to describe the co-ordinates which permitted the popular school to emerge in relation to the factory, but also in relation to the family, the reformatory, the Poor Law 'School' and the institutions of public health. It was in the space defined by these co-ordinates that the domain of the 'social' took shape as a sphere of regulated interventions into the life of target populations: the artefact of an ensemble of public campaigns and administrative initiatives. In this domain there appeared a series of new, inter-linked administered spaces where the deployment of social norms was accompanied by a dissemination of individualised 'personalities'. The manner in which these co-ordinates converged in the space of popular education we first noted, personified in the figures of David Stow and James Kay-Shuttleworth, to whom we now return.

In his manual for *The Training System, the Moral Training School and the Normal Seminary*, Stow's account of the origin of his enterprise bears all the marks of religious philanthropy. The

location of his residence forced Stow to pass through Glasgow's
Saltmarket, where

> my eyes and ears were shocked several times a-day by the
> profanity, indecency, filth, and vice, which were exhibited by
> hordes of young and old, and even infants, who were growing up
> pests to society, and ruined in themselves, for whose souls or
> bodies no one seemed to care, and whose wretchedness was
> enough to disgrace a professedly Christian community. (Stow,
> 1850, p. 124)

Even Stow's mature attempts to place such local observation within
a moral topography of Glasgow's class structure remains imbued
with a largely pastoral concern. For example, his enumeration of
'the Sinking class' is based upon including 'the neglectors of
religious ordinances, and the unconcerned about the best interests
of their children or themselves . . . also the dissipated' (ibid., p. 49).
Nevertheless, what Stow considered to be his decisive discovery
concerned new conditions of urban life that had eroded the family's
capacity to supervise children and rendered traditional forms of
pastoral care ineffective. Stow describes the manner in which he

> gradually discovered that one day's *teaching in school* was not
> equal in effect to six days *training on the streets*. . . . I found I had
> been ignorant of the important fact, that teaching is not training,
> and that sympathy and example of companionship are more
> influential than the example and precepts of any master. (Ibid.,
> p. 127)

For all his commitment to the pastoral ideal, Stow was well aware
that factory labour and city living had weakened the old alliance of
parents and priest. Emptied into the streets and lanes of the cities
children formed new and disturbing congregations. It was in these
unholy gatherings that Stow discerned a new force in the
upbringing of children: the unsupervised companionship of the
streets that he called the 'sympathy of numbers', later to be known
as 'peer-group pressure'. Against this force the old system of
parental guidance and pastoral visitation was powerless. The child,
said Stow (ibid., p. 62), 'may not care for the Sunday instructions of
his father or mother, but cares for, and readily copies the language
and bad practices of his street companions. The parents may *teach*,

but companions in reality *train*.' Nonetheless, Stow continued to regard familial sentiments, and Christian morality, as central to the elevation of the 'sunken class'. Popular education thus demanded the transformation of the moral guardianship of parents and priest in a way that took the principle of 'sympathy of numbers' into account. 'To meet *the sympathy of companionship* in what is evil, we ought to oppose it by the only antidote, viz., the sympathy of companionship in what is good' (ibid., p. 65).

It was precisely this, Stow argued, that the Sunday schools and the monitorial schools of Church and Dissent had failed to achieve. As attempts to extend parochial care into the cities, Stow (ibid., p. 21) regarded the former, perhaps unfairly, as 'arranged for instruction or teaching – not for carrying out family training in school, or laying hold of the principle of *the sympathy of numbers* in the real life of the child'. Monitorialism, for its part, while deploying a 'pedagogy of numbers', did so without incorporating the new 'sympathies' of the street children. It enclosed children in a space and formed them according to a pedagogy in which norms were embodied in the apparatus and not in the teacher, whose functions were carried out by other children. As the remote overseer of the machinery of 'hierarchical observation', the teacher could not assume the attributes of parent, spiritual guide and friend, which Stow regarded as necessary for engaging the children's sympathies and bringing the companionship of the street into the moralising space of the school.

Achieving this goal entailed, on the one hand, transforming the humble and untrained school master by systematically equipping him with these new attributes. And if the following quotation – which argues for the right of the teacher to assume the functions of the priest in the guise of the parent – reminds us of Pestalozzi, it is not because Stow had inherited a progressive philosophy of education. It is because his initiatives formed part of a more general 'social' transformation of pastoral techniques.

We highly value the office of the ministry of the gospel. But is there no other mode of preaching or promulgating the word of life? Is the same discourse which is couched in language suited to adults and the cultivated mind, equally applicable to and apprehended by the youthful and the ignorant? Is it understood at all? Are not such discourses to very many the same as if spoken in an unknown tongue? May a father not preach the gospel to his children? May the tender mother not do so to her infant offspring? Does she not do so often in strains so simple that they reach the heart? May the schoolmaster, who represents and takes the place of the parents for a portion of each day, not promulgate the gospel to the young by analysing and picturing out the daily Bible lesson? (Ibid., pp. 14–15)

On the other hand, this change did not hinge on the doctrinal training of the teacher or on the use of catechismal methods. At its centre was the transformation of the organised space of the school, such that it could incorporate the free space of the streets where, through play, the children revealed their 'true selves'.

> In Education, as hitherto conducted in school, we may have had sound instruction, but not physical, intellectual, and moral training. Schools are not so constructed as to enable the child to be superintended in real life at play; the master has not the opportunity of training, except under the *unnatural* restraint of a covered school-room; and it is imagined that, or at least stated, that children are morally trained, without their being placed in circumstances where their moral dispositions and habits may be developed and cultivated; as if it were possible to train a bird to fly in a cage, or a race-horse to run in a stable. (Ibid., pp. 5–6)

It was through such piecemeal changes, then – and not through the supervening advent of a new and humane theory of education – that the old techniques of individual spiritual care and a new awareness of the moral and physical effects of urban space on the populace could meet. They did so in the project to systematically enclose working-class children in a 'morally landscaped' simulacrum of the ungoverned milieu of the streets. In this new purpose-built environment their 'true character and dispositions' would be revealed to the 'sympathetic inspection' of the specially–trained school teacher.

If James Kay-Shuttleworth's endeavours were to issue in this same space, they were governed not by a voluntaristic Christian philanthropy but by a quite different, if convergent, co-ordinate for the social sphere: that of the state's responsibility for the good-order and well-being of its citizens. Kay-Shuttleworth (1862, p. 451) saw popular education as one of those objectives 'too vast, or too complicated, or too important to be intrusted to voluntary associations'. He placed it in the same series as the maintenance of public order and the water supply as legitimate objects of government: objects requiring 'the assertion of the power, and the application of the resources of the majority'. But this expansion of the sphere of public administration is not necessarily a sign of capitalist social relations seeking to consolidate themselves through the apparatus of a middle-class state.

Brian Simon (1960, pp. 163–76) chooses to interpret the new initiatives in this way, however. He treats Kay-Shuttleworth's advocacy of state popular education in the 1830s and 1840s as a sign that the coalition of the middle and working classes which had produced the 1832 Reform Bill had broken up. The political interest of capital shifted toward the need to maintain the working class as a subservient pool of factory labour, and with it the interest of middle-class educationists shifted from 'universal enlightenment' to class domination through moral indoctrination. Kay-Shuttleworth, 'their disciple', completes the transition, according to Simon, by adding religion to popular education, thereby giving the earlier obscurantism of the Sunday school the sanction of the state.

But Kay-Shuttleworth's (1862, p. 453) inclusion of popular education among the objects of government – many of which 'operate almost solely by restraint or coercion, and some interfere constantly with the individual will – even with the rights of property – and subordinate them to the general advantage' – did not obey the logic of the struggle between capital and labour, whose political landmarks are Peterloo and the electoral reform bills. The extension of government into education formed part of a series of parallel interventions into the life of the population which, while they intersected with the great political struggles in a variety of (sometimes surprising) ways, had their conditions of possibility elsewhere.

In the first place, these interventions arose from the deployment of new forms of social investigation and political calculation, typified by the techniques of 'moral statistics'. In a striking analogy at the beginning of his *The Moral and Physical Condition of the Working Classes of Manchester in 1832*, Kay-Shuttleworth compares the 'animal structure', which possesses the special faculty of a unified sensorium to monitor threats to its well-being, with the social structure, which possesses no such faculty.

Society were well preserved, did a similar faculty preside, with an equal sensibility, over its constitution; making every order immediately conscious of the evils affecting any portion of the general mass, and thus rendering their removal equally necessary for the immediate ease, as it is for the ultimate welfare, of the whole social system.

The adjustive powers of the market are not sufficiently sensitive or perceptive to compensate for the lack of such a faculty, and as a result:

> Some governments have attempted to obtain, by specific measures, that knowledge for the acquisition of which there is no natural faculty. The statistical investigations of Prussia, of the Netherlands, of Sweden, and of France, concerning population, labour, and its commercial and agricultural results; the existing resources of the country, its taxation, finance, etc. are minute and accurate. (Kay-Shuttleworth, 1862, pp. 3–4)

Applied to the moral and physical condition of the populace such measures would link the incoherent parts of the 'social body' to a single point of surveillance and regulation, argued Kay-Shuttleworth.

In the following chapter we will investigate the claim that a new conception of the interrelatedness of different spheres of social life can be traced to the idea of culture: an idea modelled on the organic unity of the work of art and subtended by the actual unity of society as a totality governed by its mode of production. At that point in our investigation we shall be well advised to return instead to the new techniques of investigation and administration which themselves connected otherwise distinct social spheres (education and crime; education and health, etc.) on the basis of the delimited political calculations which they made possible. Knowledge of the social sphere was in this sense an artefact 'for the acquisition of which there is no faculty'.

It was not, then, in a consciousness determined by the economic and political interests of the middle class that popular education first appeared as an object of government, but on a surface formed by the systematic deployment of new techniques of social observation and political calculation. And if the interests of the bourgeoisie figured prominently in these new calculations, they were nonetheless 'factorised' with other interests according to a 'political arithmetic' generating its own sphere of political rationality. It was not just with the good order of the working class that Kay-Shuttleworth was concerned, but with their health, literacy, sentiments, domestic life, temperance and criminal propensities, in so far as these had been shown to bear statistically significant relations to each other through an expanding web of social surveys. The interest of the state in popular education, this series suggests, was less the result of the logic of the relations of production and more the product of these 'special measures' of investigation which gave rise to that specific sphere of political interest and rationality which we call 'social welfare'.

In the second place, the formation of this sphere was itself inseparable from the emergence, during the eighteenth century, of new administrative apparatuses constituting new objects of government. As we have already noted, Kay-Shuttleworth was not just a founder-member of the Manchester Statistical Society, he was also at one time Manchester's chief public health officer, an Assistant Poor Law Commissioner and, from 1839, the Secretary of the Committee of Council on Education. As such he was connected directly to most of the key administrative agencies whose generic name in the eighteenth century was 'police', and indirectly to others, including the one we now know as the police. These agencies laid a grid of regulated spaces on the nineteenth-century city, and 'social problems' appearing in any one such space could easily become objects of corrective attention in the others. So, Kay-Shuttleworth explains that the sensitised surface on which the need for public administration of popular education was first registered was itself initially formed in order to monitor threats to public health posed by the outbreak of cholera.

The introduction into this country of a singularly malignant contagious malady, which, though it selects its victims from every order of society, is chiefly propagated amongst those whose health is depressed by disease, mental anxiety, or want of the comforts and conveniences of life, has directed public attention to an investigation of the state of the poor. In Manchester, Boards of Health were established, in each of the fourteen districts of Police, for the purpose of minutely inspecting the state of the houses and streets. These districts were divided into minute sections, to each of which two or more inspectors were appointed from among the most respectable inhabitants of the vicinity, and they were provided with tabular queries, applying to each particular house and street. (Kay-Shuttleworth, 1862, p. 5)

The collection of statistics through which Kay-Shuttleworth mapped the condition of the 'social body' was inseparable from a series of superimposed corrective apparatuses. These permitted new norms for public health, decency, cleanliness and sanitation to fill the grid of surveillance which Patrick Colquhoun had earlier charted in his *Treatise on the Police of the Metropolis*. It was as the agent of these apparatuses, and not as the mouthpiece of middle-class economic and political interests, that the need for government intervention in popular education first appeared to someone like Kay-Shuttleworth. And it did so not simply in the spectre of a politically volatile working class, but as a series of statistical frequencies connecting the condition of streets and housing, poverty, mortality, licentiousness, crime, numbers of taverns and ginshops, church attendance, 'domestic economy' and literacy.[5]

As a result, while Kay-Shuttleworth might well argue in favour of free trade and the abolition of the Corn Laws, he nonetheless denied that the unfettered laws of the capitalist market could secure the well-being of the 'social body'. Depressing wages, for example, by importing cheap Irish labour, was deleterious because:

The low price of the labour of such people depends . . . on the paucity of their wants, and their savage habits. When they assist in the production of wealth, therefore, their barbarous habits and consequent moral depression must form part of the equation. (Ibid., p. 52)

Government must intervene in the education of the people not to protect capitalist relations of production as such, but because such relations will not by themselves produce social good. It is 'Civilisation [that] creates artificial wants, introduces economy, and cultivates the moral and physical capabilities of society' necessary for higher levels of consumption and production; and the civilisation of the working class is dependent on their education (ibid., p. 52). By the same token Kay-Shuttleworth would not support a 'serious reduction of the hours of labour' unless it was accompanied by 'a general system of education'. The attendant lowering of wages would, he argued, be coincident with an increase of the time generally spent by an uneducated people in sloth or dissipation, and hence lead to a deterioration of the moral and physical capacities necessary for consuming the 'comforts and conveniences of life'.[6]

If David Stow's concern with forming moral character began in the tradition of pastoral care for the individual soul, then Kay-Shuttleworth's surfaced inside the new apparatus of social investigation and administration which posed the problem in terms of the moral topographies of whole populations.[7] Stow's understanding of urban life with its powerful 'sympathy of numbers' had driven him to transform the old pastoral techniques by incorporating their powers of moral individualisation in a new machinery for regulating urban space. But Kay-Shuttleworth's plan for state intervention in education was governed by an investigative and administrative mechanism, which operated by dividing the city into similarly norm-saturated spaces. Both reformers agreed that the first attempt to enclose the children of the streets and lanes in moralising environments – the monitorial schools of the two church systems – had failed. In Stow's eyes this was largely because the explicit character of the religious and pedagogical norms required by the method of 'mutual instruction' divorced them from the 'sympathy of companionship' of the streets, the new milieu in which the individual soul or character revealed itself. While for Kay-Shuttleworth such a divorce also removed the schoolchild from the quite different forms of knowledge and regulation which now invested the streets and linked pedagogy to the medical, social and moral government of the population.

The programme to educate 'the whole child – not just the intellectual, but also the moral and physical sides' through a system allowing regulated individual self-expression in play was not, then, the result of a general lifting of utilitarian norms which would lead to an ideal, general development of human faculties. It was, instead, the outcome of those developments which transferred the guardianship of parent and priest onto the teacher as the agent of a new mechanism for policing urban space; that is, which transposed the techniques for the care of the individual soul onto those which regulated the 'moral and physical condition' of the population.

The emblem of these changes – which entailed a new organisation of school space and a new system of teacher training – was the shift from the 'mutual instruction' of monitorialism to the 'simultaneous instruction' of the teacher-controlled classroom. Here, the supervision of the assembled body of children was relayed through the teacher's invigilation of each child. The new methods depended for their efficacy, according to Kay-Shuttleworth:

> on the fact that, by the simultaneous method, the mind of the teacher may be more constantly in contact with that of every child under his care. The moral agencies employed are, under such a method, greatly superior to those in operation where the child receives instruction chiefly, if not wholly, from a boy but little older than himself. (Ibid., p. 253)

But it was the incorporation of the ungoverned environment of the street into the morally improving space of the school, and the reconstruction of the teacher as the sympathetic embodiment of the latter's now unobtrusive norms, which gave the new 'moral agencies' their superiority. More importantly for our argument, it was in this moral simulacrum of 'life' that a literary pedagogy would become possible. Here it would be possible for literature to focus the tactics of supervised freedom. In the process it would assume the role of a repository of ethical experiences, and thereby absorb the key functions of moral training. It is necessary, therefore, to give a brief account of these two decisive changes – in the organisation of pedagogical space and in the social personality of the teacher – before concluding this chapter.

IV

Kay-Shuttleworth's testimony, before the 1838 Select Committee and his subsequent Minutes as Secretary of the Committee of Council on Education, leave us in no doubt that he derived the new structure of pedagogical space from Stow's experiments. In claiming that 'What the suitable school premises for popular education ought to be, remains . . . quite as undefined as the term Education itself. The two ideas are, in fact, inseparable', Stow (1850, p. 7) was asserting the interdependency of the organisation of pedagogical space and goals of popular education. We have already seen that the central requisite of this space was that: 'The physical, intellectual, and moral propensities and habits, must have *free* exercise under a proper superintendence, and the opportunity of development in *real* life, which, to a child is freely at play.' To this end, argued Stow (ibid., p. 7), 'there must be the training school premises, and there must be the trained master'.

As far as school premises are concerned, Stow made two decisive contributions to their modern form.[8] The *first* of these was the gallery or raised, stepped platform. In replacing the molecular sub-divisions of the vast monitorial school-room with a single, more intimate space organised around the superintending eye and voice of the teacher, the gallery was the prototype of the modern classroom. The children must be placed in parallel lines, said Stow (ibid., p. 137) because: 'Semicircles or squares do not secure the eye and attention equally to parallel lines; and should the number of pupils exceed two rows of six each, then each ought to rise a few inches above the other.' He summarises the 'moral agencies' thus made available in the following way:

> The gallery so constructed, enables the trainer with more regularity and precision to conduct the physical exercises, which are requisite according to the age of the pupils, whereby the attention may be arrested and secured. It enables the master and the scholars to fix their eye more easily upon each other while presenting an object, or during the process of picturing out any point of a subject, and also while deducing a lesson. Every word spoken is more easily heard by all; individual, but more particularly *simultaneous* answers are more readily obtained; order is promoted, and instant obedience and fixed attention are more certainly secured . . . Imitation and social sympathy also operate thus more powerfully with children when answering simultaneously or individually . . . And, what is most important of all, breathless attention is secured while the master reviews any case of misconduct of any of the children, or pictures out its consequences. The whole gallery join in this as they do in every one of the exercises, whether secular, religious or moral. (Loc cit.)

Thus placed, the teacher is able to embody the norms of the schoolroom in a personality – part friend, part parent, part director of conscience – in which each child could find himself reflected and judged. At the same time the teacher can develop individual differences and harness the 'sympathy of companionship' between the children by forcing it to pass through his own purifying personality.

You may very soon, by question and answer, exhaust the knowledge of any one child . . . but you cannot so easily exhaust one hundred seated in a gallery, variously constituted as they are, and all being permitted to answer. The master's duty and privilege, is to be, as it were, the filterer, purifying and directing all the answers, and leading them in a proper channel. (Ibid., p. 420)

Stow's *second* contribution was the playground or, as he insisted on calling it, the 'uncovered schoolroom'. In seeking to attach the schoolmaster's 'moral observation' to the free play in which each child revealed its 'true character and dispositions', the playground served as the emblem for the new non-coercive system. It is the playground which mediates most visibly between the norms of the classroom and the ungoverned life of the streets: enclosing the latter within a simulacrum of itself, but one organised in such a manner that the environment itself subjects each child's activities to constant moral superintendence. Stow advises:

Let everything be kept neat and clean, and such important habits will not be lost in after life; the moral taste may be formed, which delights in having the front of every cottage door neat and clean, and its sides decked out with the rose, the clematis, and the woodbine; and similar habits carried out into the crowded lanes of a city, would add greatly to the health, comfort, and happiness of the community. The flowers in the play-ground generate pleasing associations, afford many useful lessons, and assist the trainer occasionally in elucidating Scripture emblems. Flowers or fruit constantly in sight, and within reach, exercise the virtues of honesty and self-denial. The principle, 'Thou God seest me,' coupled with practical forbearance, account for the interesting fact, that in several of the juvenile and initiatory play-grounds, in the poorest districts of Glasgow, and other large towns, children have freely enjoyed themselves from day to day, and yet currants and strawberries have been permitted to ripen, although they have been within the reach of every child. (Ibid., pp. 146–7)

Stow instructs his teachers not to intervene directly in this morally saturated environment, only to observe good and bad conduct which is then taken up in the gallery lesson. Here the children accept the norms governing their conduct as outgrowths of the 'sympathy of companionship' itself, themselves sitting as jurors, 'so that the discovery of the offenders may prove a lesson to all'. This reorganisation of the space of the popular school connected up play and the pedagogical development of the child quite independently of aesthetic theories of the self-realising role of play.

With regard to the training of teachers, Stow's contribution was to be less decisive. Although his method of 'picturing out in words' – that is, the use of familiar figures and illustrations to bring difficult terms before the 'mind's eye' of the child – was endorsed by Kay-Shuttleworth, the latter regarded the system of training used in the Glasgow Normal Seminary as an insufficient preparation for the new position of the teacher. It was Kay-Shuttleworth's achievement – consolidated in his famous Minutes of 1846 – to set in place a quite new apparatus for forming the special status and personality of the popular school teacher. He did so by moving on two different fronts simultaneously.

In the *first* place he moved to transform the social standing and material conditions of popular school teachers by shifting the base of their training and financial support from the two religious societies to the government. The Minutes of 1846 instituted the pupil-teacher training scheme, under which pupils between the ages of 13 and 18 were apprenticed to school masters. Both pupil-teacher and master were the recipients of stipends paid directly to them rather than to the church management boards; and at 18 pupil-teachers could compete for Queen's Scholarships, which would support them during their final two years training in new training colleges. Masters could also qualify for government superannuation pensions. The whole system was to be brought within the superintendence of Her Majesty's Inspectors, who were to examine the scholars at the end of each year of their apprenticeship and award the much-prized certificates on which the new salary level of the trained teacher depended. In this way it was ensured that the Normal Schools would 'be fed with students from the *élite* of the scholars educated in the elementary schools', and the humble and dubious calling of the popular school teacher was set to be transformed into a special agency of government. In his *Explanation of the Minutes of 1846*, Kay-Shuttleworth outlined the implementation of a programme designed to

render the profession of schoolmaster honourable, by raising its character, by giving it the public recognition of impartially awarded certificates or diplomas, and by securing to well-trained or otherwise efficient masters a position of comfort during the period of their arduous labours, and the means of retirement on a pension awarded by the Government. (Kay-Shuttleworth, 1862, p. 481)[9]

But it was Kay-Shuttleworth's *second* set of initiatives – in elaborating the discipline of teacher training – that was to prove decisive in forming the special personage required for the new, morally improving space of the popular school. In this space the teacher needed the sympathy to join the children in their play, while simultaneously remaining the exemplar in whose 'moral observation' each child could find its own conscience. These attributes, Kay-Shuttleworth well realised, could not be formed simply by altering the material conditions of teaching. In his Minutes of 1839 he had moved to establish government sponsorship of a special form of teacher training to replace that offered by the religious societies. (The latter consisted of a bare three months spent passing through the monitorial hierarchy at their central schools in London.) After this initiative foundered, due to religious opposition, Kay-Shuttleworth started his own Normal School or training college at Battersea. This was 'intended to be an institution, in which every object was subservient to the *formation of the character of the schoolmaster*, as an intelligent Christian man entering on the instruction of the poor, with religious devotion to his work'; and Kay-Shuttleworth set out to prove that this goal could be achieved in a non-denominational environment 'without violating the rights of conscience' (ibid., p. 399).

The methods to achieve these ends were in part derived from a visit to De Fellenberg and Vehrli's school for training schoolmasters of the poor at Hofwyl in Switzerland. Here Kay-Shuttleworth had been greatly impressed by the mixed régime of agricultural labour in the beautiful countryside and intellectual labour in the school, a combination which he thought would produce the sympathy required in the popular classroom, while elevating the moral character of teachers in a way that would not raise them above the class they were to serve. In suburban London it was necessary to create a simulacrum of this moralising environment. Kay-Shuttleworth did so by establishing his Normal School as a closed residential community, the model for training colleges until the beginning of this century.[10]

Kay-Shuttleworth's (1868, p. 8) policy was that trainees be 'selected from the classes immediately in contact with the people, and generally from children of the manual-labour class . . . ensuring an identity of interest and harmonious sympathies'; and he perceived that his task was

> to reconcile a simplicity of life not remote from the habits of the humbler classes, with such proficiency in intellectual attainments, such a knowledge of method, and such a skill in the art of teaching, as would enable the pupils selected to become efficient masters of elementary schools. (1862, p. 309)

To this end the Battersea College attempted to duplicate the character-forming environment of Hofwyl, with long hours spent labouring in the school garden as well as practising the art of teaching indoors. But it was the machinery for the moral invigilation of time and space that was decisive in this regard. The day, which began at 5.15 a.m. and ended with prayers at 9.20 p.m., was organised by an exhaustive time-table, each division of which was superintended for 'errors interfering with the formation of habits of punctuality, industry, cleanliness, order, and subordination' (ibid., p. 331). Infringements were individually recorded in a series of special books – the 'time-book', and books for 'household work above stairs', 'below stairs' and 'out-door labour' – from which Kay-Shuttleworth read to the assembled school after morning prayers. However, it was the manner in which moral surveillance was embodied in the relation between the individual scholar and the principal as his director of conscience which shows most clearly how the exemplary attributes of the popular school teacher were to be formed by his own relation to an ethical exemplar. 'There is a necessity for incessant vigilance in the management of a training school,' advised Kay-Shuttleworth, and accordingly:

> The Principal should be *wise as a serpent*, while the gentleness of his discipline, and his affectionate solicitude for the well-being of his pupils, should encourage the most unreserved communications with him . . . He should be most accessible, and unwearied in the patience with which he listens to confessions and inquiries . . . there should be no such severity in his tone of rebuke as to check that confidence which seeks guidance from a superior intelligence. As far as its relation to the Principal only is concerned, every fault should be restrained and corrected by a

conviction of the pain and anxiety which it causes to an anxious friend, rather than by the fear of a too jealous authority. Thus conscience will gradually be roused by the example of a master, respected for his purity, and loved for his gentleness, and inferior sentiments will be replaced by motives derived from the highest source. (Ibid., p. 405)

It was in his own formative passage through the moral régime of the training college that the working-class teacher acquired the attributes of friend, parent and ethical exemplar; that is, the characteristics of the purpose-built personality in whose 'moral observation' the children of the streets and lanes would discover their 'true characters and dispositions'.

V

We are now in a position to see that if the development of popular education came to be focused in the tactics of 'learning through play' and a new and sympathetic relation between the child and a specially-trained teacher, this was not because education had been touched by the humanising hand of the man of letters. The reconstruction of pedagogical space as a morally improving 'learning environment', and the rebuilding of the teacher-student relation into one of correction based on moral emulation, were the product of piecemeal transformations in the pedagogical disciplines. These resulted in an apparatus in which new social norms for the government of the population could surface inside the formation of the individual conscience. And it is in the organisation of this apparatus of moral supervision, and not in the inherent (or ideological) properties of literature or literary criticism, that we can discern the nascent structure of a popular literary education.

On the one hand, English today is characterised by the use of texts as morally charged environments in which students must 'discover for themselves' the growth of their own personalities. On the other, it remains inseparable from the purpose-built, teacher-student relation. Here developmental norms are not imposed directly, but through the 'sympathetic inspection' of 'the man who observes', where they are discovered as conscience. But when popular education emerged it did so precisely as a norm-saturated environment or domain of 'experience', overseen by the unobtrusive but inescapable moral observation of the teacher; and it emerged in this form long before it was thought that literature might have a role to play in the machinery of moral training.

In fact, the history of English is in large part the history of the contraction of the morally managed space of the school into the landscape of the literary text, and the transference of the exemplary attributes of the popular school teacher to the teacher of English. We shall investigate these processes in more detail in Chapter 4. For the moment, let us characterise the broad sequence of the transition by giving two citations which should be placed between those taken from Stow and Dixon, with which we began this chapter.

If in the early decades of the nineteenth century Stow could describe the playground as 'the principal scene of the real life of children . . . – the arena on which their true character and dispositions were exhibited', then by the beginning of the twentieth century it was *art* that was assuming this role. In her book, *Education Through the Imagination*, Margaret McMillan could write in 1904:

> To Art childhood holds out its eager hands. What if these hands are very feeble? What if it has no real conception of beauty as we know it? He goes forward and cannot be held back save by the influence of those around him. He draws as he can or rather writes pictures. He listens to tales of wonder and adventure. He plays and invents plays, if all that is his birthright is not taken away. He not only makes houses, boats, engines, he likes the human model best, puts his toy soldiers in ranks, builds forts for them, is a soldier himself, a prince, a backwoodsman, a pirate, a doctor, a dustman, a preacher. Life is a drama that never ends, but begins over and over again.

While later she describes drama as:

> the great City of Refuge as well as School of almost every type of imaginative and unimaginative! And children appear to understand this far better than older people. Much of their own play is just their own way of getting a stage and being players, and when a teacher accepts this cue, even the dullest children waken up and begin to take an interest as if things had some meaning at last. (McMillan, 1904, pp. 39–40, 98)

Here the tactics of 'normalisation through self expression', made possible within the supervised space of the school, are in the process of migrating to the terrain of art, a move accompanied by the psychologisation of the techniques of moral training. If literature, in the form of drama, appears here as only one of a series of aesthetic devices through which correction could be grafted onto play, and the life of the streets enclosed within the prophylactic space of the school, then by 1921, when the Newbolt Commissioners handed down their report on *The Teaching of English in England*, literature had come to dominate this series. In fact the Newbolt Report devotes a complete chapter to 'The Drama as an Educational Activity', describing its importance in the following terms:

> The pupils who take part in performances of plays must learn to speak well and to move well, to appreciate character and to express emotion becomingly, to be expansive yet restrained, to subordinate the individual to the whole and to play the game, to be resourceful and self-possessed and to overcome and mitigate personal disabilities . . . Incidentally, it has been found that boys or girls usually regarded as stupid, and incapable of learning, have exhibited unsuspected ability in acting and have gained a new interest in themselves and their possibilities. (Newbolt, 1921, p. 316)

In this account the unexpected 'discovery' of personal attributes in the special realm of play is treated as a distinctively literary phenomenon. We are not far away from Dixon's view of drama 'opening up to the inarticulate and illiterate that engagement with experience on which literature rests' and, significantly, the Newbolt Report is amongst the first documents to throw-up the smokescreen of Arnoldian culture as the origin of these developments. But the tell-tale reciprocal relation between self-discovery and the internalisation of norms for appropriate conduct, sentiment and demeanour reveals that what we are witnessing is nothing more than a further mutation in the organisation of the pedagogical disciplines: that organisation which, before Arnold was thought of, had already harnessed the development of self to the government of populations, in a programme for administering the formation of cultural attributes.

We will return to the circumstances surrounding the literary mutation of the pedagogical disciplines below. For the moment, let us draw out two summary points before concluding this chapter.

First, the educational programme for the development of the 'whole child' is not referrable to a universal cultural process in which literature has a privileged role – either as the medium whose self-expressive powers transcend the social norms threatening this development, or as one whose moralising propensity permits the re-imposition of these norms as ideology. Instead, this programme must be referred, in the first instance at least, to those specific circumstances in which the techniques of moral individualisation were placed at the disposal of new forms of social investigation and administration. These were the circumstances permitting the formation of a space in which the development of the self (the 'whole child') became an imperative for the government of populations.

Second, in this space of supervised freedom it would become possible for the literary text to assume the form of a domain of moral experience, at once immediately accessible to the reader yet finally beyond his ethical reach, governed as it was by the recessive norms of 'correction through self discovery'. This unprecedented text, with its surfaces so close to the world of spontaneous play and its depths always withdrawing into an experience never quite grasped, was opened to knowledge only in so far as it opened its reader to knowledge: to the endless ethical inspection of 'the man who observes'. This text, which is no stranger in the world of modern criticism, exists only in the relation between the individual open to correction and the exemplary one who corrects.

No doubt to someone familiar with the usual history of English – in which literary education appears as the brainchild of the nineteenth-century prophets of culture and takes the form of a pedagogical mobilisation of literary criticism – it will seem that we have been on a long and unnecessary detour. I have indicated, however, that it was necessary to take this path in order to show that English is not a manifestation of literary culture: neither of its 'true' form as the vehicle for a complete development of human capacities, nor of its ideological form as the means of repressing this development in the interests of a particular class. It is not to the great dialectic of culture and ideology that we owe the emergence of English, but to the construction of a special *social technology*: the apparatus of popular education.

We have seen that it was the piecemeal modification of the pedagogical disciplines – itself governed by the deployment of the techniques of moral individualisation inside the new machinery for the government of populations – that produced the new forms of social organisation and social agency involved in moral training. Far from being something that literature brought to the educational sphere, the capacity for moral training was something that literature found there already in place, in the form of new techniques for the moral management of experience and a new kind of teacher-student relationship. When, at the turn of the nineteenth century, English began to emerge as a privileged focus for this apparatus, we shall see that it did so neither as the true realisation of 'man's' 'ethical substance', nor as the ideological misrepresentation of his 'social being', but as a distinctive and irreducible *ethical technology*.

I suggested in my introductory remarks that during the nineteenth century the primary reference of 'culture' was to a caste practice of ethical self-development, which was then applied analogically to the culture of races, nations and classes. To a large extent our histories of education and English remain within the shadow of these analogies. Despite claims to the contrary, nowhere in his School Reports does Matthew Arnold advocate that *this* practice of culture – focused for him in the astringent dialectic of his literary criticism – should be democratically disseminated as the basis of popular education. The idea that literary criticism could, or should, be taught in the popular school system never occurred to Arnold, and is in fact a twentieth-century development.

We can now see that this was not the result of an oversight, or worse, the product of an ideological move to arrogate the promise of 'full human development' for a class élite. It is simply a sign that the formation and regulation of cultural attributes undertaken in the popular school was not a manifestation – true or distorted – of the promise of culture. Instead, we have seen that these attributes were artefacts of a new and powerful mechanism of moral training. This mechanism was linked to other parts of the social sphere not through the global functions of culture or ideology, but by the delimited political calculations made available by new techniques of social investigation and administration.

What we must now come to understand is that Arnold's presence in the school system is not a sign of the origins of English in literary criticism, but of the fact that the educational apparatus itself defined a role for the special personality shaped by literary criticism as a caste discipline: the role of Her Majesty's Inspector. In the standard histories, becoming an inspector is portrayed as a convenient means for Arnold to install literary culture in the school system. But in the following chapter I will argue the inverse: that literary culture provided the means for Arnold to become an inspector. In other words, I will argue that it was not as the (true or distorted) realisation of 'man' or 'society' that literary culture would enter the educational apparatus, but as a discipline for forming a special category of person – the person of the ethical invigilator – required by the supervisory strategies of the apparatus itself. We shall further see that if Arnold's critical discipline fitted him for the role of inspector, it was eventually called into play in the training of English teachers for much the same reason: as the means of forming the exemplary attributes of the ethical mentor which were increasingly gravitating to the teacher of English.

It becomes possible to suggest, then, that far from *underpinning* the development of literary education as a special ethical technology, 'culture' has played the role of a local discipline whose wider deployment has been the *result* of that development. However, while indicating the theme of the next chapter, this remark remains premature. Something stands in the way of its further elaboration. This obstacle is the idea of culture itself.

3
Culture

I

We have begun to describe how literary education emerged in the morally managed environment of the popular school. Taking shape as a new means for deploying the disciplinary tactics invested in the 'moral observation' of the teacher, English would in fact become an important agency in forming the cultural attributes of a citizenry. The machinery of popular education therefore provided the first and fundamental 'surface' on which English emerged. The second such surface, we have already indicated, was provided by a specific caste practice of aesthetico-ethical self-cultivation. During the nineteenth century the Romantic culture of the self was a minority avocation, focused in the disciplines of literary criticism and cultural journalism. In this chapter we investigate the circumstances in which this esoteric 'practice of the self' entered the sphere of public education. These were the circumstances in which its exemplary functions entered into an exchange with the supervisory functions of the popular school system: an exchange that was to prove decisive for the formation of English, as we shall see in the next chapter.

The pursuit of this investigation, however, requires that we first impose historical and theoretical limits on the idea of culture or self-realisation that arises from this erstwhile minority practice of the self. To say that in establishing these limits we face formidable obstacles would be a decided understatement. Chief amongst them is the powerful tendency – beginning towards the end of the eighteenth century and subsequently acquiring the authority of Hegel and then of Marx – to universalise the specialist dialectic of ethical cultivation by projecting it as a model for the 'culture' or historical development of 'society as a whole'. Through this philosophico-historical projection – which remains at the centre of contemporary cultural history and the cultural studies movement – what was in fact a specialised ethical practice, initially quite marginal to the new machinery of the social sphere, has been retrospectively transformed into a general principle of 'cultural growth'.

At the same time, the deployment of public education which, in company with the other 'social' apparatuses, brought the formation of cultural attributes within the sphere of systematic administration for the first time, has been marginalised. In its place is projected the image of a general 'cultural process' whereby – either in the dialectic between 'man's' thoughts and feelings, or in the one reconciling his consciousness and his 'social being' – human attributes are formed according to the goal of total development. In this manner, the actual forms of social administration responsible for making the cultural attributes of the population into an object of knowledge and government are reduced to the status of a more or less inadequate (utilitarian) 'machinery' for 'man's' cultural totalisation.

Dropped from the gigantic fingers of the dialectic, or held in them at a safe distance from the 'human personality', the technology of popular education is replaced by culture. Culture assumes the centre of the historical stage: either in the form of an ideal process developing the 'whole man'; or as the totalisation of the 'way of life as a whole' in which society realises itself in 'man'; or, typically, as both. Emblematically, James Kay-Shuttleworth, who was at the very centre of the new machinery in which the systematic administration of cultural attributes became thinkable, is dropped from our histories of 'culture and society' and replaced by the likes of Matthew Arnold, Thomas Carlyle, William Morris or D. H. Lawrence: literary men whose current importance derives, ironically enough, from the fact that this machinery gave them jobs or, through English, deployed their 'lives and works' as exemplary devices in the process of moral training itself.

In short, it is the idea of culture itself – projected from the specialist practice of ethical self-cultivation – that blocks our understanding of the circumstances in which this practice was eventually given a specific role *inside* the social technology of public education, thereby contributing to the formation of English. Today, this obstacle confronts us in two familiar forms.

First, in the form of a theory and history of culture that subordinates the limited and specific cultural programmes of the social sphere to the image of an ideal general development of human faculties and social forces; a development crowned perhaps, with the achievement of historical self-consciousness. Under these conditions it becomes almost impossible to describe the way in which the strategic space of popular education was formed through the layering of other social apparatuses – public health, police, family reform, poverty relief, penality – for which it in turn provided a distinctive focus and support. We have already seen that these programmes were *not* unified by a synthetic *ideal of human development*, culture, that outstripped them all. Instead, they were connected up in limited and specific ways by *administrative calculations*, typified by the use of moral statistics. These calculations functioned as a relay for conceptions of desirable cultural attributes formed within the network of corrective apparatuses itself.

Our conceptions of possible and desirable cultural attributes remain dependent on those historical techniques and institutions. But it is precisely this dependency which the idea of culture presumes to invert. This is what happens when the specific forms in which the administration of cultural attributes first became thinkable are subordinated to a totalising 'cultural process' lodged in the development of the 'whole man' or the 'way of life as a whole'. We shall see that this supposed capacity of the cultural process (and cultural studies) to summate and subordinate the available array of cultural norms and techniques to a 'higher' goal, finally renders it indistinguishable from a transcendental process of 'experience', or historical self-consciousness. The following remarks from Raymond Williams, on the form in which 'meanings and values' relate to cultural technologies, are quite representative in this regard.

> We are most aware of these elements [meaning and values] in the form of particular techniques, in medicine, production, and communications, but it is clear not only that these depend on more purely intellectual disciplines, which had to be wrought out in the creative handling of experience, but also that these disciplines in themselves, together with certain basic ethical assumptions and certain major art forms, have proved similarly capable of being gathered into a general tradition which seems to represent, through many variations and conflicts, a line of common growth. It seems reasonable to speak of this tradition as a general human culture, while adding that it can only become active within particular societies, being shaped, as it does so, by more local and contemporary systems. (Williams, 1961, p. 59)

The *second* form in which we are confronted by the obstacle of 'culture' is in the privileging of a particular discourse or method as the essential vehicle for this 'creative handling of experience', through which 'man's' historical self-formation is supposed to be realised. By the last decades of the eighteenth century the twin exercises of the dramatic meditation (Shaftesbury's 'internal soliloquy') and the medical regimen, which had characterised the minority culture of the self for most of the century, had been decisively transformed by Kantian philosophy. From this transformation emerged two new forms of self culture: a discipline of *aesthetic contemplation* or literary reading, and a discipline of *philosophical history*. The interdependent organisation of the new disciplines is clearly visible in Fichte's lectures *On the Vocation of the Scholar*, delivered at the Jena University in 1794, and in Schiller's letters *On the Aesthetic Education of Man*, published in the following year. No doubt Schiller's (1780) *Essay on the Connection between the Animal and the Spiritual Nature of Man* – in which the dialectic between man's moral and physical sides is still formulated in terms of the medicine of nerve fibres and animal spirits – can be regarded as transitional. But even here the nervous transmission of sensations to the soul is capable of initiating a medical version of man's 'universal history'. Schiller (1780, pp. 267–8) claims: 'Hunger and nakedness first compelled man to hunt, to fish, to rear cattle, to plough and to build . . . The collision of animal instincts drives horde against horde, forges the sword from ore, creates adventurers, heroes and tyrants.'

In the *Aesthetic Letters* it is chiefly through the dialectical exercise of aesthetic contemplation ('play impulse') that the individual reconciles the abstract imperatives of reason ('form impulse') and the embodied imagination of the senses ('sense impulse'). This is achieved in a movement that allows the individual's culture of a self to anticipate the stages through which the state and society must pass in the history of mankind. Neither has the subsequent provision of a 'materialist' version of these stages cancelled the patent given to aesthetic culture as the symbolic vehicle of 'man's' historical making. Consider, for example, Raymond William's comment on the relation between 'thinking about art and thinking about society':

The 'organic society', the 'whole way of life', and similar phrases, are certainly open to charges of obscurity, but they are not in any case likely to be understood except by reference to conceptions of

experience largely drawn from the practice and study of art which
are their basis and substance. (Williams, 1958, p. 145)

In this way, the specialised aesthetic discipline through which
the critic works on the two sides of his 'ethical substance' remains
the model for the dialectical 'cultural process' through which
history will supposedly perfect 'man'. This is the second
impediment we must overcome in our investigation of the
circumstances in which the minority aesthetic culture would obtain
a limited 'social function' through its deployment in the apparatus
of popular education. Otherwise, at every step of the way, we will
be misled by the aura of aesthetic culture; that universalising
embodiment of an essential 'creative handling of experience' on
which – through the dialectic of thought and feeling or culture and
society – the apparatuses of the social sphere are themselves
supposed to depend.

In other words, contrary to one of the central precepts of our
academic upbringing, the chief obstacle to our bringing the idea of
'culture' within the sphere of historical description is *not* that it has
been allowed to function as an a-historical ethical absolute. It is that
it has already been historicised, but in a form which makes the
promised total development of human faculties co-extensive with
'history' as such. Since at least the time of Schiller and Fichte we
have been told that our analysis of culture is insufficiently
dialectical: that it fails to reconcile the abstract consciousness and
the common embodied imagination; or that it has not yet brought
about the synthesis of ethical consciousness with culture as the
'whole way of life'. In the light of the preceding remarks, however,
the suspicion dawns that our investigations of culture have been far
too dialectical, and that the great challenge now confronting anyone
wishing to describe a particular dispensation of cultural attributes
is to establish the historical and theoretical limits of this method.

We have begun to do so by showing that the topography of
popular education in which English first appeared was not formed
through the great movements of the dialectic, with its image of
historical totalisation. Instead, we have seen, this topography was
built up piecemeal, through the layering of specific forms of social
administration and investigation and the systematic deployment of
definite cultural techniques. It was in this manner, and not under
the auspices of aesthetic culture, that popular education acquired a
profile for the cultural attributes of the population; that is, as part of

the corrective network in which these attributes might be formed and maintained. Correlatively, we shall see that for most of the nineteenth century the movements of the dialectic in fact functioned as a sort of aesthetic gymnastic for a tiny minority of 'ethical athletes'. Far from founding the cultural techniques and institutions of the emerging social sphere in an essential 'cultural process', culture and the dialectic remained marginal until the exemplary attributes of the cultivated man were required in the educational apparatus itself.

In other words, in describing the historical formation of English, our task is not to attempt to return culture to 'society' by rooting it in the dialectical development of the 'way of life as a whole', and thereby anticipate the social and democratic realisation of its image of human perfection. Rather, it is to show how culture remained the artefact of a definite and limited ethical practice, quite marginal to the emergent network of institutions and technologies targeted on the well-being of the population. It was in this network, particularly as focused in the moral landscape of the popular school, that the cultural attributes of the population were being delineated; and it was here that literature would acquire a new power and range. Only thus, when we have overcome the overwhelming temptation to transform it into the foundation of the whole network, will we be able to describe how culture acquired limited social functions through a local dissemination of the techniques of ethical self-culture in the apparatus of literary education.

II

Let us continue to pursue this objective by reminding ourselves of the difference between the 'moral machinery' of popular education aimed, as Foucault puts it, at the 'normalisation of the population', and the practice of aesthetic culture, adopted more or less voluntarily by a minority of individuals seeking to shape exemplary lives.

In his manual for the new organisation of the popular school, David Stow defends the cost of purchasing land for playgrounds in the following terms:

There is no doubt a great difficulty in procuring a sufficient extent of ground for the purpose of play-grounds for schools of 80 or 100 pupils; and it is extremely high-priced in the lanes and streets of a crowded city, where moral training is imperiously required; but independently of the moral improvement of the people, the actual cost would be less than is expended upon police, bridewells, prisons, houses of refuge, public prosecutions, and transportation of criminals.

With such machinery in operation, and surrounded for several hours a-day by such a *world* of pupils, it is the province of the shrewd, intelligent and pious superintendent, to watch and direct all their movements; and whilst he daily participates in their juvenile sports, he in consequence *gradually* gains a thorough knowledge of their *true* dispositions, which at the proper time and season, he applauds or condemns on the principles of the system, an example of which is subjoined, and which applause or reproof, be it observed, is not given *at the moment* the circumstances occur *in* the playground, but rather when the children have re-entered the school, and are seated in the gallery. (Stow, 1850, p. 140)

Having thus moved from the moral improvement of the population to the apparatus whose cost it justifies, Stow – in his 'subjoined' example – illustrates the individualising procedures through which this improvement is to be wrought. The example concerns a 'boy who steals his play-fellow's toy' which 'happens in the play-ground, *freely at play*; for it is only when perfectly at liberty that juvenile character is truly exhibited'. According to the procedure, the master who sees all but says nothing to disturb the freedom of play, waits until the children are again seated in the gallery when,

as usual, he commences the process of examination (elliptically and interrogatively, i.e., the children answering questions, and filling in ellipses), in the shape of a story about a boy who stole his neighbour's top or something else. In a moment *the culprit's head head hangs down* – it is unnecessary to mark him out – *he is visible to all* by his downcast and reddened countenance ... In the meantime the trainer reminds the child and all present, that although *he* had not observed him, God assuredly had; or rather, he draws out this statement from the children themselves ... (Ibid., pp. 140–1)

Finally, Stow concludes his demonstration of the apparatus – whose mix of educative, judicial, pastoral and dramaturgical elements remains entirely familiar to us – with the remark that: 'The feelings are thus moulded down to give way to principle; and whilst all see what really is (unfortunately) an every-day exhibition in the world, and what, perhaps, latently exists in themselves, such exhibitions are made in circumstances which naturally call forth, *not imitation*, but *abhorrence.*'

It is possible to draw three points from Stow's demonstration, and these may stand as a summary of our remarks on the formation of popular education in the preceding chapter:

● *First*, the distinctive moral topography of the popular school was delineated by contours linking a governmental calculation of 'social' costs and benefits to a pastoral concern with the individualising moral surveillance of children.

● *Second*, this topography is characterised by the fact that social and moral norms are not deployed in the form of explicit precepts but are, as it were, embedded in the spatial and temporal organisation of the school, and in its instituted relationships, such that the children inhabit a morally managed environment.

● *Third*, at the centre of this moralising landscape stands the omniscient figure of the teacher. The teacher operationalises corrective norms through a mode of surveillance and a 'non-coercive' relation to the child, in which the latter comes to *see himself* according to norms whose very inaccessibility in the teacher establishes the relation of constant emulation.

We have already seen that popular pedagogy was initially almost wholly oral, with little room for literary pursuits save those associated with acquiring the basic skills of literacy.[1] At the same time, in Stow's use of the simple narrative as the means through which the student comes to see himself according to the norms embodied in his teacher's gaze, we can see the embryonic form in which the literary text could assume the shape and acquire the powers of the moralising environment.

Leaving this development to one side for the moment, we can observe that it was in this purpose-built space that new forms of knowledge and government aimed at shaping the attributes of the population were made operative through the forms in which individuals became objects of knowledge and correction. So that when Stow (1850, p. 7) speaks of the need for the popular school to 'cultivate by exercise *the whole man*, in his physical, intellectual, and moral habits – in his thoughts, affections, and outward conduct', he is not in fact attempting to generalise an ideal of individual 'many-sidedness' deriving from aesthetic self culture. This becomes clear once we note that Stow continues by saying that 'this [cultivation] cannot possibly be accomplished within the walls of an ordinary school-room' and, in a remark we have already quoted, goes on to state that 'what education ought to be' and 'what suitable school premises for popular education ought to be' are 'inseparable' questions. In fact, by 'culture' Stow means the operationalising of new norms of cultural attainment in a large-scale programme for governing the population through the moral management of its 'social' environment.

For their part, however, the advocates of aesthetic culture have as their objective something which belongs to a quite distinct sphere of human activity. When Fichte, for example, addressed his students at Jena on their vocation as scholars, he did not begin by introducing them to a statistico-moral analysis of social conditions. Rather, he began by deploying a philosophical specification of the individual ethical substance, dividing it into the side of the free and 'self-identical' moral will, the source of all its own conceptions, and the side of the physical senses, enslaved by sensation to external objects. It was the vocation of the scholar, through the awakening of reason, to establish harmony between the idea of how things ought to be, deriving from 'man's' moral will, and the actual state of the world impressed on him through his senses. This could not be achieved by the will alone, which must therefore be supplemented by 'that skill which is acquired and improved by practice':

The acquisition of this skill, – partly to subdue and eradicate the improper tendencies which have arisen within us prior to the awakening of Reason and the consciousness of our own independence, – partly to modify external things, and alter them in accordance with our ideas, – the acquisition of this skill, I say, is called Culture, . . . Culture differs only in degree, but it is capable of infinite gradations. It is the last and highest *means* to the attainment of the great end of man, when he is considered as of a composite nature, rational and sensuous; – complete harmony with himself. (Fichte, 1794, pp. 154–5)

Schiller, in outlining the form of 'man's aesthetic education, continues the same theme.

> Towards the accomplishment of this twofold task – of giving reality to the necessity within, and subjecting to the law of necessity the reality without – we are impelled by two opposing forces which, since they drive us to the realisation of their object, may be aptly termed drives. The first of these, which I will call the sensuous drive, proceeds from the physical existence of man, or his sensuous nature. Its business is to set him within the limits of time, and to turn him into matter . . . The second of the two drives, which we may call the formal drive, proceeds from the absolute existence of man, or from his rational nature, and is intent on giving him the freedom to bring harmony into the diversity of his manifestations, and to affirm his Person among all his changes of condition. (Schiller, 1795, pp. 79–81)

The role of culture in Schiller's account, while having less of Fichte's Kantian emphasis on making the rational real, and while establishing a more conciliatory relation between man's two impulses, falls, nonetheless, within the same sphere of ethical practice.

> To watch over these, and secure for each of these two drives its proper frontiers, is the task of culture [*Kultur*], which is, therefore, in duty bound to do justice to both drives equally: not simply to maintain the rational against the sensuous, but the sensuous against the rational too. Hence its business is twofold: first to preserve the life of the Sense against the encroachments of Freedom; and second, to secure the Personality against the forces of Sensation. The former it achieves by developing our capacity for feeling, the latter by developing our capacity for reason. (Ibid., pp. 86–7)

Schiller differs from Fichte in investing the mediating action of culture in a third, transcending 'play' impulse which is realised in the work of art and the literary reading. So, in a passage echoed often enough in Coleridge – but also across the whole spectrum of cultural criticism, from Leavis to Lukacs, Morris to Marcuse – Schiller writes:

> The sense-drive wants to be determined, wants to receive its

object; the form-drive wants itself to determine, wants to bring forth its object. The play-drive, therefore, will endeavour so to receive as if it had itself brought forth, and so to bring forth as the intuitive sense aspires to receive. (Ibid., p. 97)

Through play and the sense of beauty, awakened for example in the contemplation of Greek art, 'man' escapes the partial and lop-sided development of his faculties imposed by social utility and anticipates their sum form, embodied, without the abstract violence of reason, in the present.

> Precisely on this account, because [the aesthetic disposition] takes under its protection no single one of man's faculties to the exclusion of others, it favours each and all of them without distinction; and it favours no single one more than another for the simple reason that it is the ground of possibility of them all. Every other way of exercising its functions endows the psyche with some special aptitude – but only at the cost of some special limitation; the aesthetic alone leads to the absence of all limitation. (Ibid., p. 151)

Fichte (1794, pp. 185–7), for his part, invests culture less in aesthetic cultivation than in the scholar's faculty for knowing what 'man's' potential capacities are and for knowing the means through which they are to be developed; that is, in a philsophico-historical discipline which permits him to 'calculate the direction which human progress must take' and to 'declare approximately the particular steps by which it must pass to the attainment of a definite stage of cultivation'. But we should not make too much of the difference between Fichte's philosophical history and Schiller's aesthetic, because both are based on the same image of the harmonious reconciliation or total development of man's divided ethical substance. Fichte's historian can only know the past and anticipate the future forms of man's historical realisation because, through culture, he has reconciled the rational and the sensuous in himself and thereby embodies that great development. And Schiller's critic can only achieve his cultivated reconciliation of conflicting impulses because, through time and historical circumstance, his will is presented with those obstacles whose overcoming represents the unfolding of Reason in history.

Hence arose the long partnership between the disciplines of

aesthetics and philosophical history whose synthetic form –
cultural history – remains at the centre of the contemporary cultural
studies movement. From the outset the totalisation of the self and
that of society have been able to reflect each other through the
medium of the work of art and the sense of beauty. This privileged
reflection remains the basis of our conception of a 'line of common
growth . . . a general human culture'.

> All other forms of perception divide man, because they are
> founded exclusively either upon the sensuous or upon the
> spiritual part of his being; only the aesthetic mode of perception
> makes of him a whole, because both his natures must be in
> harmony if he is to achieve it. All other forms of communication
> divide society, because they relate exclusively either to the
> private receptivity or to the private proficiency of its individual
> members, hence to that which distinguishes man from man; only
> the aesthetic mode of communication unites society, because it
> relates to that which is common to all. (Schiller, 1795, p. 215)

In other words, it seems likely that the continuing project to find a
common foundation for the patchwork of cultural technologies and
institutions in a single cultural or historical 'process' derives from a
specific ethical discipline. According to this discipline, everything
that man might become is dialectically unfolded from (or towards) a
sum form of human capacities supposedly contained in his ethical
substance or 'species-life'. Clearly we are a long way from the
capacities for literacy, cleanliness, self-control, punctuality, good
manners and so on, which popular education derived from the
morally administered environments of the social sphere. Just how
far, we can see by drawing three points of comparison:

● *First*, unlike popular education, 'culture' did not emerge from
  the convergence of pastoral techniques with new forms of social
  investigation and administration in a new machinery for
  governing the population. Instead, it appeared as the term relating
  the two sides of the self in a recently modified but nonetheless
  ancient exercise in *shaping the self*.

● *Second*, the topography of culture was not built up in the
  layering of administered spaces through which public education
  assumed the form of a morally managed environment. Rather, it

was the result of an individual exercise which, by imposing
specific divisions on the 'ethical substance' (into thought and
feeling, consciousness and social being etc.), established culture
as a specific *ethical practice of the self.*

● *Third*, the personal attributes acquired through culture were not
those acquired by a population through the internalisation of
social norms in the supervisory *relation to the exemplar*. They
were those acquired by someone seeking to form himself as an
example to others by subjecting all such norms to a goal of total
development through which the individual constituted his
relation to the self.[2]

We can reaffirm in passing that while aesthetic contemplation
and the reading of literature were at first quite marginal to the oral
environment of the popular school, they provided a central means
for organising the dialectical exercises of the élite culture of the self.
That this ethical practice was to give a decisive inflection to modern
literary education is quite apparent in the following passage from
the *Aesthetic Letters*. Here Schiller – it could just as easily have come
from Lukacs or Leavis – specifies the attributes of the ideal reader
by pitting the didactic tendency against the sentimental.

But it is by no means always a proof of formlessness in the work of
art itself if it makes its effect solely through its contents; this may
just as often be evidence of a lack of form in him who judges it. If
he is either too tensed or too relaxed, if he is used to
apprehending either exclusively with the intellect or exclusively
with the senses, he will, even in the case of the most successfully
realised whole, attend only to the parts, and in the presence of the
most beauteous form respond only to the matter. Receptive only
to the raw material, he has first to destroy the aesthetic
organisation of a work before he can take pleasure in it, and
laboriously scratch away until he has uncovered all those
individual details which the master, with infinite skill, had
caused to disappear in the harmony of the whole. The interest he
takes in it is quite simply either a moral or a material interest; but
what precisely it ought to be, namely aesthetic, that it certainly is
not. (Ibid., pp. 158–9)

III

What is not so apparent is how it was imagined that this practice could be fundamental to a 'general' formation of cultural attributes; given its evident isolation from the new social machinery in which such a formation had emerged as an object of knowledge and government.

On the one hand, this problem was 'solved' by picturing society and the state as collective versions of the subject. The state has an ideal and an actual form, according to Schiller (1975, pp. 11–23), corresponding to man's moral and physical sides. It is the task of the 'statesman-artist' to reconcile the moral imperatives of the former and the utilitarian necessities of the latter through a general cultivation of society as a whole. In Fichte's (1794, pp. 173–4) view, if we apply the 'law' of culture or 'perfect internal harmony' to society, 'then the demand that all the faculties of the individual should be uniformly cultivated includes also the demand that all reasonable beings should be cultivated uniformly with each other'. The 'statesman-artist' cannot achieve this end, however, by a direct legislative empowering of the moral state. This would represent a failure of reconciliation and result in the political tyranny of moral absolutes over the actual diversity of individual dispositions comprising the physical state. Instead, he is to treat society as a work of art, withdrawing from 'premature' political action until moral ends (the 'whole') are freely realised in the impulses of actual individuals (the 'parts'). The cultivated man makes this transformation possible by first reconciling the moral and the sensuous in himself, becoming an example to society at large by embodying the form of its historical development. As Schiller (1975, p. 59) would have it: 'Impart to the world you would influence a Direction towards the good, and the quiet rhythm of time will bring it to fulfilment.'

On the other hand, in case we are immediately tempted to disassociate ourselves from this solution as élitist and a-historical, it is well to remember that the cultivated man can only fulfil this exemplary role as the personification of a much larger dialectic. Schiller (ibid., pp. 73–7) describes this dialectic in his Eleventh Letter as the dialectic between 'person' (the total but unrealised capacities of the self) and 'condition' (the actual but formless materiality of the historical world in which the self is realised). This movement between 'the self and its determinations' is in fact the movement of *history*, through which human capacities are unfolded as partial realisations of their total form.

In other words, it is history which solves the problem of having to account for the actual forms of social organisation in which aesthetic cultivation might conceivably be generalised. And now, are we so sure that our current materialist theories of culture are any less dependent on this conception of history? After all, doesn't Marcuse (1955, pp. 143–61) wish to rehabilitate Schiller's account of play and the aesthetic sphere in order to ground the historical movement towards a society organised around unalienated or self-realising labour? In other words, are our contemporary conceptions of 'culture' any better equipped to give an account of the social formation of cultural attributes, as opposed to one of their historical unfolding from or towards a 'complete' form? Those who think so should perhaps consider that a recent book on *The Idea of the Clerisy in the Nineteenth Century* concludes its argument for democratising the exemplary attributes of the scholar by invoking Schiller's dialectic:

> In conclusion I want to emphasise this sense of a sustained and necessary dialectic between forms of discourse, and (both at a personal and a social level) between on the one hand the highly rationalised and highly formed and on the other, the serial activities of day to day living. (Knights, 1978, p. 232)

We are now in a position to ask the questions to which these remarks have been leading us: What difference did the celebrated 'materialist inversion' of the dialectic make to the conceptualisation of culture? – What is the difference between 'idealist' and 'materialist' cultural theory? At one level, of course, the differences are quite apparent: we have been well schooled in them. Marx substituted man's production of his material existence for Schiller's 'self-creating Intelligence' and Hegel's 'self-positing Spirit'. He was thus able to replace a history of the World-Spirit's approach to self-consciousness with a history of the forms in which 'man' produced his social being. As a result, so we are told, it is no longer the abstract and universal 'man' of philosophy who stands at the centre of history, but the organisation of social classes thrown up by successive modes of production. And it is by drawing on these transformations that a materialist analysis of culture has been able to remove culture from its idealist foundations in the ethical consciousness of the cultivated man and return it to the 'way of life as a whole', from whence it proceeds in the form of class consciousness.

At another level, however, the differences are anything but clear. Despite these transformations, 'cultural materialism' has not given up the deployment of a fundamental ethical substance through whose divisions and reconciliations 'man', or the universal class, is unfolded in history; a history that realises the 'full human potential' contained in the substance itself. The form of this retention is quite apparent in Marx's (1975, pp. 322–400) early analysis of estranged labour and the commodity form. It is here that he posits an ideal or sum form of human capacities – man's 'species-life' – as that which is alienated and deformed under conditions of production in which the labourer produces for the market instead of for his own use or self-realisation. Indeed, the notion of an ideal development of human faculties and that of a total development of society make each other possible in Marx's account of culture and society:

> Just as in its initial stages society is presented with all the material for this *cultural development* [of the 'human senses'] through the movement of *private property* and of its wealth and poverty – both material and intellectual wealth and poverty – so the society that is *fully developed* produces man in all the richness of his being, the *rich* man who is *profoundly and abundantly endowed with all the senses*, as its constant reality. (Marx, 1975, p. 354)

In other words, we can ask whether the shift from the history of the cultivated man to that of the social class is as decisive as it first seems. Despite appearances, the attributes of the working class in this account are *not* the products of definite cultural techniques and forms of social organisation. Instead, they materialise from the dialectic (linking consciousness and social being) which *unfolds them*. Furthermore, the twin injunctions of this *dialectic* – to return consciousness to its determining conditions while bringing the latter within the sphere of consciousness – makes class consciousness look very like the outcome of the exercise through which the cultivated individual establishes the ethical relation to his self.[3]

These suspicions are amply confirmed, it seems to me, if we turn, summarily, to the contemporary materialist analysis of culture. *First*, despite its stated intention of returning culture to the historical process through which man 'makes' his social self, this analysis continues to use the term as the name for a progressive realisation of a sum form of human capacities, leading to self-consciousness. Raymond Williams, for example, in adopting 'the broader historical emphasis of men producing themselves', argues for the recognition of the techniques and practices of such a production 'on the basis of this proposition':

> that no mode of production, and therefore no dominant society or order of society, and therefore no dominant culture, in reality exhausts human practice, human energy, human intention . . . On the contrary, it is a fact about modes of domination that they select from and consequently exclude the full range of human practice. (Williams, 1973, p. 12)

And just in case the implications of this subordination of cultural technologies to culture have escaped us, Williams goes on to identify the cultural practices surrounding 'the formation of a new class' with 'the coming to consciousness of a new class'.

Second, in thus subordinating the social formation of specified cultural attributes to the image of their historical unfolding from or towards a 'full range', contemporary cultural materialism continues to deploy the divided ethical substance, and hence the figure of the 'whole man', as the basis of its historical dialectic. For example, in discussing the Sunday school's 'repression of emotional and spiritual energies', Edward Thompson compares the resultant alienated and distorted emotions of ecstatic Methodism with the differently crippled sensibility of James Kay-Shuttleworth.

> From this aspect, Methodism was the desolate inner landscape of Utilitarianism in an era of transition to the work-discipline of industrial capitalism. As the 'working paroxysms' of the hand-worker are methodised and his unworkful impulses are brought under control, so his emotional and spiritual paroxysms increase. The abject confessional tracts are the other side of the dehumanised prose style of Edwin Chadwick and Dr Kay[-Shuttleworth]. The 'march of intellect' and the repression of heart go together. (Thompson, 1963, p. 402)

Behind the new organisation of pastoral techniques embodied in the Sunday school, and the new administration of cultural attributes provided by popular education – complementary alienations of the total 'human personality' – looms the figure of the 'whole man' as the goal of all historical development. And this goal is approached not through the organised deployment of new cultural technologies but, fundamentally, in the reconciliatory movement between the two sides of 'man's' ethical substance, the 'intellect' and the 'heart'.

Third, at the heart of this dialectic, and organising it as a scholarly exercise, we find the privileged disciplines of cultural history and literary criticism. We can see the form of this exercise in Thompson's Romantic *reading* of historical documents, which works by mediating between the tyranny of intellect and the 'paroxysms' of emotion; this mediation providing the 'experience' through which the scholar understands the dialectic of history by embodying it in himself. And we find it 'theorised' in Williams' (1961, pp. 63–6) concept of the *structure of feeling* which, in reconciling culture as an aesthetic ideal and culture as 'whole way of life', not only specifies the character of class consciousness but also the form of the 'experience' the analyst must share if he is to understand it.

On the one hand, the structure of feeling is, in Williams' (ibid., p. 65) revealing metaphor, that through which 'the changing organization is enacted in the organism: the new generation responds in its own ways to the unique world it is inheriting . . . shaping its creative response into a new structure of feeling'. On the other hand, says Williams (1973, p. 16), in relating aesthetic organisation to social being 'we have no built-in procedure of the kind which is indicated by the fixed character of an object'. Hence, if 'what we are actively seeking is the true practice which has been alienated to an object, and the true conditions of practice – whether as literary conventions or as social relationships – which have been alienated to components or to mere background', then the critic must avoid 'mechanically' reducing aesthetic organisation to social structure or vice versa. Instead, he must free the alienated structure of feeling by reconciling consciousness and social determination in his own reading; that is, he must use the dialectic as a discipline permitting him to understand man's cultural development by realising it in the shaping of his own ethical substance. In this way, Williams (1971, p. 29) believes, 'we can find points of connection that answer . . . to our closest sense of our own living process'.

I am suggesting, then, that the modern cultural studies

movement, with its project to plunge the ideal of aesthetic cultivation into the 'way of life as a whole', and to retrieve it in its socialised form as class consciousness, is in fact a contemporary form of the discipline of ethical self-shaping. On the one hand, it deploys the same image of a class acquiring its attributes through the process of their historical unfolding from (or towards) an ideal or total form, leading ultimately to self-consciousness. On the other, its version of the historical dialectic in which this 'making' occurs, is finally inseparable from the ethical exercise through which the scholar wins the right to embody 'man's' historical realisation by reconciling its poles in himself.[4]

In other words, the contemporary 'materialist' analysis of culture remains as distant as its 'idealist' twin from the social machinery in which cultural attributes have been formed as objects of knowledge and administration. Neither should this surprise us if, as the preceding remarks suggest, the historico-aesthetic analysis of culture has its basis not in competing epistemologies, but in an ethical practice capable of supporting quite contradictory ontological investments of man's ethical substance or 'species-life'. In sketching a genealogy that confines contemporary theories of culture to this specific ethical practice, we set limits to their claims to found the diverse cultural technologies of the social sphere in a single general 'cultural process'. At the same time, we establish the historical and theoretical limits of the dialectical method itself, which – whether issuing in the form of the 'whole man' or the 'common culture' – remains in fact a technique of 'mutual moderation' used in the special practice of ethical self-shaping.

Our first move, then, has been to *withdraw* 'culture' from 'society', and from the relation between them in which each promises the other's totalisation. The object of this tactical withdrawal is to show culture's initially marginal position (as a specialised ethical practice) in relation to the emergent social sphere. Now we are in a position to investigate how, in the series of developments that produced modern literary education, this practice gained a foothold in the morally administered environments of this sphere. We shall see that it did so not as the vehicle for an ideal general process of human realisation underlying them all, but as a repository of techniques for forming a special kind of person that these environments came to require. In short, we can begin to subject culture to the limits of historical description.

IV

No doubt it will be said that this is precisely what Williams himself is doing in his seminal *Culture and Society 1780–1950*, but we must ask leave to doubt this. In the light of the preceding remarks it must be said that 'culture' in that work names nothing other than the dialectical process through which man's universal capacities are unfolded in time. In such a context culture cannot be brought within the sphere of historical description, because it is coextensive with (universal) 'history' and 'society' as such.

It is true that Williams purports to contextualise aesthetic cultivation, describing the transformations undergone during its supposed embodiment in a movement to cultivate 'society as a whole'.

What in the eighteenth century had been an ideal of personality – a personal qualification for participation in polite society – had now, in the face of radical change, to be redefined, as a condition on which society as a whole depended. In these circumstances, cultivation, or culture, became an explicit factor in society, and its recognition controlled the inquiry into institutions. (Williams, 1958, p. 77)

The upshot being, says Williams (ibid., p. 161) in a statement which could well serve as a motto for his work, that 'The arts defined a quality of living which it was the whole purpose of political change to make possible.' But it is simply not the case that 'cultivation or culture' became 'a condition on which society as a whole depended', or a factor whose recognition 'controlled the inquiry into [its] institutions'. Neither could it conceivably have become so. Existing to one side of the new machinery for the moral administration of social space, aesthetico-ethical cultivation was not connected to the instrumentalities of knowledge and power in which the cultural attributes of the population became an object of government. When it eventually was connected to them, it was very much as an adjunct to the sphere of political rationality that *they* defined: aesthetic cultivation playing a role we shall describe as a subsidiary tactic in the new strategies for 'governing the population'. To assert the contrary is to risk confinement to the dialectic between the totalisation of the 'human personality' and that of 'society': confinement, that is, to a contemporary form of ethical self-shaping in which the scholar as universal man mistakes his own cultivation for a more general 'cultural process'.

Let us recall the main outlines of Williams' argument. On the one hand, he claims that despite the idealist and individualist character of its ethics, the 'idea of culture' – that is, of a complete and harmonious development of human capacities – made it possible to conceive of the reshaping of 'society as a whole', and to conceive of the means by which this reshaping might be achieved. Williams (ibid., pp. 85–98) portrays Thomas Carlyle the critic, for example, as providing 'a direct response to the England of his times: to the feel, the quality, of men's general reactions – that structure of contemporary feeling which is only ever apprehended directly'. Carlyle is credited with seeing through the 'external' and 'mechanical' organisation of social life to its 'inward' and 'dynamical' core; with understanding that mutual cultivation of both these sides is required as the means through which 'society struggles to perfection'; with realising that this could not be achieved without leadership or governmental intervention; and with the 'influential' proposal of state popular education as the means of realising this general cultivation: – all this at a time when 'do-nothing' *laissez-faire* liberals and 'paralytic' utilitarians were trusting to the market to achieve civilisation.

Artists and critics like Ruskin and William Morris are, for their part, credited with grasping the quality and organisation of an ideally ordered (self-realising) social existence by deriving them from the nature of the work of art and the life of the artist. This transference, says Williams (ibid., pp. 137–61), made it possible to conceive of the 'organic' interconnections linking all spheres of social life according to the aesthetic ideal of many-sided development, and therefore to propose the uniform cultivation of all individuals in society as a condition of the perfection of each. Again, this breakthrough was supposedly made at a time when the liberal reformists remained committed to an individualistic and economistic conception of social well-being; one well suited to a system of production requiring the degradation of some individuals as a condition of the enrichment of others.

On the other hand, this aesthetic conception of a universal social cultivation could become 'a condition on which society as a whole depended', only because elsewhere it was being objectively realised in a 'growing social force: that of the organized working class'. Needless to say, Williams is less clear about how this was supposed to be taking place. Sometimes it seems that the working class acquired the requisite political interests and attributes simply as the material reflection of the cultivated man. For example, Williams (ibid., pp. 92–3) says of Carlyle's call for more government that 'This, [Carlyle] represents, is the demand of the English working people; and in essence he is again right, . . . the characteristic movements of the English working class, while certainly democratic in the wide sense, have been in the direction of more government . . .' (although this presumably does not apply to that section of the English working class which voted Mrs Thatcher's government into office).

At other times these attributes seem to be spontaneously generated from the 'lived experience' of the working class. This seems to be the case when Williams (ibid., pp. 307–18) locates a materialist correlate for the aesthetic image of the many-sided 'organic society' in the working-class values of 'mutuality' and 'community': in what he calls 'the basic collective idea' arising as 'the property of that part of a group of people, similarly circumstanced, which has become conscious of its own position . . .'.

In other words, 'culture' enters 'society' in Williams' account through a process ('history') in which the 'lived experience' of the working class unfolds the ideal form of human capacities already promised by the figure of the cultivated man: 'The arts defined a quality of living which it was the whole purpose of political change to make possible.' We have already outlined the problems attendant on the general project to make the development of 'culture' and that of 'society' reflect each other through the medium of a total development of human capacities, one leading towards historical self-consciousness. There are two sets of reasons for rejecting Williams' particular version of it.

First, Williams' men of letters were *not* the source of a knowledge of social life and of 'influential' proposals for its governmental regulation at a time when 'do-nothing' liberals were committed to a policy of *laissez-faire* and the law of supply and demand. Neither was their conception of the many-sided unity of the artist's character and works 'influential' in establishing the inter-relatedness of different spheres of social existence in the face of a dogmatically individualist liberalism. Not only did someone like Thomas Carlyle make no use of the new techniques of social statistics – in which the social life of the population was emerging as an object of knowledge – he explicitly repudiated them as 'abstractions', in his essay on *Chartism* for example:

> the condition of the working-man in this country, what it is and has been, whether it is improving or retrograding, – is a question to which from statistics hitherto no solution can be got. Hitherto, after many tables and statements, one is still left mainly to what he can ascertain by his own eyes, looking at the concrete phenomenon for himself. (Carlyle, 1839, p. 158)

In this regard he was, of course, no different from Dickens, whose *Hard Times* made statistical 'Gradgrindery' into a by-word for a certain imbalance in the culture of the self. Disconnected from the available means in which social life became an object of knowledge and regulation, Carlyle's celebrated insight into the 'condition of England question' was in fact nothing more than a fantasmatic projection of the discipline of ethical self-shaping. Under this projection 'England' or 'society' acquired the divided ethical substance ('mechanical' versus 'dynamical') of a collective subjectivity, while 'government' was pictured as the reconciliation of the two sides through which 'society struggles to perfection'.

It is not a question of joining the history of ideas by arguing that the social thought of literary intellectuals 'lacked influence' in government. The point is that the practice through which they shaped their ethical judgements was self-consciously removed – and remains so today – from the new machinery of government in which the regulation of social life became *thinkable*. Thus isolated from the deployment of morally administered social environments in which popular education became conceivable, Carlyle's (ibid., pp. 221–8) educational proposal assumes the utopian form of cultivating 'twenty-four million intellects' ('It is . . . the official person's duty, not ours to mature a plan') into a 'National Mind' able to perfect the world.

Conversely, one only has to observe that Carlyle's *Chartism* essay was written seven years after Kay-Shuttleworth's *The Moral and Physical Condition of the Working Classes in Manchester in 1832*, and in the same year as the establishment of the Committee of Council on Education, to see that 'do-nothing' liberalism was in fact at the centre of a new and powerful apparatus for investigating and regulating social life. It is enough to recall Kay-Shuttleworth's (1862, pp. 451, 453) remarks, quoted in the last chapter, that popular education was one of those governmental initiatives requiring 'the assertion of the power, and the application of the resources of the majority'; initiatives which 'operate almost solely by restraint or coercion, and some interfere constantly with the individual will – even with the rights of property – and, subordinate them to the general advantage'. Furthermore, it was not from a Ruskin's or a Morris's conception of many-sided cultivation that this 'official person' obtained his understanding of the inter-relatedness of different social spheres. This he derived from the overlaying of different corrective apparatuses – police, health, domestic, penal – which produced the profile of attributes that popular education sought to form, and which built up the morally administered environment in which this formation could take place.

It was as the agent of this machinery that Kay-Shuttleworth could subordinate the 'individual will' and the 'rights of property' to a larger conception of the 'general advantage' or social well-being: one to be realised in part through the tutelary transformation of the cultural attributes and forms of consumption of the population. No doubt our characteristic personal attributes and forms of social existence are in large measure due to the historic achievement of this transformation. One can only look forward to the day when the central role ascribed to the 'idea of cultivation or culture' in this achievement – to the idea borne by Coleridge, Arnold, Carlyle, Morris and Lawrence, and the other men of letters who were at best bit-players in it – will be regarded as an historical irony.

Second, neither is there any reason to think that the new profile of cultural attributes was derived from the 'lived experience' of social classes according to the logic of a developing class consciousness. There is no doubt that class differences were at the very centre of new apparatuses of the social sphere, but as the targets of these apparatuses, not as their foundations. We have seen that the topography of class differences – criminal, dangerous, sunken, sinking, labouring, artisanal, respectable – was in fact the product of the multi-valent normative grid that had been laid over urban space. And it was in relation to the thresholds of this grid that popular education could aim to produce a working class with the mental and physical capacities of a citizenry from the 'sunken' condition of the sub-proletariat. That working-class attributes were not unfolded towards a sum 'human' form through a 'popular culture', and were instead largely the artefacts of definite cultural technologies like the popular school, is indicated (we have already noted) by the fact that the Chartists projected their own 'new organisation of the people' using precisely this technology.

Consider the fact, for example, that in Lovett and Collins' famous sketch of the educational wing of this project – at the heart of their critique of rote learning and demand for a pedagogy that would develop 'all the faculties of mind and body' – we find the following:

> While much moral instruction may be conveyed in the school-room, the play-ground will be found the best place for *moral training*; where all [the children's] faculties will be active, and when their dispositions and feelings will be displayed in a different manner than when they are in the school-room, where silence, order and discipline should prevail. But when in the playground, the teacher should incite them to amusement and activity, in order to develop their characters; . . . (Lovett and Collins, 1840, pp. 90–1)

No doubt it is important that in a Chartist school system, had one been built, we would have found the norms of popular democracy – as well as those of punctuality, cleanliness, good manners and the respect for property. But far more important is the fact that we would have found these norms deployed in the same technology of moral supervision around which the governmental pedagogy was organised.

In other words, this technology – which allowed social norms to surface as individual conscience – while responsible for transforming the cultural physiognomies of target classes, arose neither from the 'lived experience' of these classes nor from a mode of production which sought to channel such experience to its own ends. Instead, we have seen that it resulted from the redeployment of techniques of pastoral surveillance in a new and powerful machinery for investigating and regulating social space: a machinery which made the cultural transformation of classes and populations thinkable and possible. The political interests and attributes of the Chartists were just as indebted to this machinery as were those of the liberal reformers. The formation of a proletariat possessing the new 'social' attributes of a citizenry was a common political project although, of course, 'factorised' according to different kinds of political calculation in the two cases.

This is enough to show that Williams' historicisation of 'culture', far from bringing it within the sphere of historical description, in fact allows it to remain coextensive with universal history: time remaining the medium, and dialectic the method, through which 'society' unfolds the 'human personality'. In fact, the new dispensation of cultural attributes was achieved quite independently of 'cultivation or culture' becoming a 'condition on which the whole of society depended', through its supposed embodiment in 'an actual and growing social force: that of the organised working class'. Instead, it was the achievement of new cultural technologies, like the popular school, deployed according to a multi-valent programme for 'governing the population'. Detached from these technologies, literary writing on social questions – Carlyle's essay on *Chartism* or Lawrence's on pornography – remains what it was in Schiller's time: a practice for placing the new machinery of government on one side (the 'mechanical') of the ethical substance and thereby 'transcending' it through the dialectical shaping of an exemplary self.

It seems to me that Williams' attempt to produce a history of 'culture' and 'society' through a reading of the works of the 'prophets of culture'– like Thompson's cultural history of the 'making' of the working class – is essentially a continuation of this practice. The exemplary attributes of the man of letters remain at the centre of our histories of culture because the ethical practice that forms them also forms the capacities and standing of the cultural historian and the literary critic. We can now set limits to these attributes and the history that unfolds them by describing in more detail the ethical practice responsible for them, without seeking to relate this practice to the totalising development of 'society'. Then we will be in a position to understand how the culture of the self found its niche in the new technology of public education: not as a fundamental knowledge of, or vehicle for, man's historical realisation, but as the means of shaping the exemplary ethical personage this technology came to require.

V

The problem as far as 'culture' is concerned is not to reconcile it with the economic and political structure of 'society'. It is to show how at a certain point it functioned as an aesthetico-ethical discipline through which a minority of individuals constituted themselves as subjects of moral action. Foucault has studied this problem under the heading of the 'genealogy of ethics'. Unlike histories of morality the genealogy of ethics is not concerned with the *precepts* of a moral code, but with the *techniques* through which individuals can construct a *relation to the self* as the subject of moral action. In his investigation of classical and early Christian ethics Foucault (1984a and 1984b) studies these techniques of self – what the eighteenth century called 'arts of living' – under four aspects. It is possible to adapt this schema as a summary means of describing that aesthetico-ethical practice which emerged during the eighteenth century, and which was the central determinant of what the nineteenth century called 'cultivation or culture'.

The *first* aspect of this practice concerns *specifying the ethical substance* or delineating that part of the self and its conduct which is relevant to ethical judgement. Foucault points out that such specification is subject to historical variations. While sexuality might be constituted as what one must be most concerned with in some times, in others it is diet, or the intentions lying behind one's actions. In Shaftesbury's *Characteristicks*, it is the thoughts and the feelings or, rather, establishing the appropriate relation between them, that forms the object of ethical concern. The mind or temper is composed of an 'oeconomy of passions' and affections, and the goodness or otherwise of one's actions depends on the balance between the passional forces. 'So that,' says Shaftesbury (1711, II, p. 156) 'according as these Affections stand, a Creature must be good or ill, virtuous or vicious'. By the time of Schiller's *Aesthetic Letters*, Shaftesbury's still partially humoral oeconomy had been successively transformed by a medical-psychological, and then by a Kantian-philosophical, investment of the ethical substance. But it was still in the difficult relation between man's moral and physical sides – or his formal and sensuous impulses – that he might become a 'virtuous or vicious' creature.

The *second* dimension is taken up with what Foucault calls the *mode of subjection*, or the forms in which the individual is led to recognise moral obligation. These may appear in the form of divine laws; imperatives that flow from one's physico-moral constitution; choices in relation to aesthetic ideals; and so on. In the *Characteristicks* the obligation to harmonise the passions and affections appears mainly in the form of a choice to stylise one's public and private life in accordance with an ideal of a beautiful and accomplished existence. For example, one shouldn't indulge the religious affections too far, says Shaftesbury:

For as the End of Religion is to render us more perfect, and accomplish'd in all moral Dutys and Performances; if by the height of devout Extasy and Contemplation we are rather disabled in this respect, and render'd more unapt to the real Dutys and Offices of civil life, it may be said that Religion is then *too strong* in us. (Ibid., p. 160)

According to Schiller (1795, p. 93), however, the mode of subjection is split between a free choice to harmonise the potentially disfiguring impulses of the divided self ('It must be an act of free choice, an activity of the Person which, by its moral intensity, moderates that of the senses . . .') and a universal (Kantian) rule which 'man' must follow in order to be true to his being. 'Such a reciprocal relation between the two drives is, admittedly, but a task enjoined upon us by Reason, a problem which man is only capable of solving completely in the perfect consummation of his existence. It is, in the most precise sense of the word, the Idea of his human nature . . .' (ibid., p. 96.). Indeed, it may be said that the chief function of the idea that culture unfolds human capacities towards an ideal form lodged in history – that is, that there is a human vocation – is to paper-over this split in the recognition of moral obligation.

The *third* co-ordinate for the relation to the self lies in the work done or exercises performed in shaping the ethical substance. These self-shaping activities Foucault calls *ascesis* or *practices of the self*. Once again they vary depending on whether, for example, the work involves discovering one's true self as in sexual confession; demonstrating one's freedom from desire as in exercises of self-denial; showing one's dependence on God as in seventeenth-century puritan spiritual autobiography; and so on. In Shaftesbury's *Soliloquy or advice to an Author* who wishes to constitute himself as a 'moral author', the exercise performed on the mind and passions is one of self-clarification. It begins with the imperative to 'Recognise your-self: which was as much as to say, *Divide* your-self, or Be Two':

And here it is that our Sovereign Remedy and *Gymnastick* Method of Soliloquy takes its Rise: when by a certain powerful Figure of inward Rhetorick, the Mind. *apostrophizes* its own Fancys, raises 'em familiarly without the least Ceremony or Respect. (Shaftesbury, 1711, I, p. 84)

Thus apostrophised, the author's fancies and opinions are open to interrogation in 'self converse', where they can be problematised in the course of forming a balanced judgement. Schiller's exercise of 'cultivation or culture' is more complex, involving as it does a double problematisation ('mutual moderation') of the thoughts and the feelings. This, it was hoped, would allow the cultivated man to combine an aesthetically harmonious development of the faculties with their preparation as the ground of disinterested judgement. For Schiller, we have seen, this was to be achieved by cultivating the sense of beauty or play through the exercise of aesthetic contemplation. Contemplating the statue of a Greek god in the form of a beautiful woman (Juno Ludovisi), for example, would allow one to develop the feelings free of base desires and cultivate the moral sense free of didacticism. Clearly a virtuoso balancing act.

The reading of literature in a manner that refuses to disinter its meaning from an embedded doctrine or intention ('stock notions'), while also refusing to take pleasure in any accidental feelings it gives rise to ('stock feelings'), is a more familiar version of the same exercise. But the cultivation of the 'sense of history' through the discipline of cultural history constitutes, we have observed, a parallel work on the ethical substance. Carlyle's division of society into 'mechanical' and 'dynamical' parts, whose progressive reconciliation is embodied in the critic's own reading of the 'signs of the times', is a case in point. So too is Arnold's opposition of civilisation's 'Hellenising' and 'Hebraic' tendencies and, for that matter, Edward Thompson's double problematisation of religious enthusiasm and the 'abstract' theorising of the radical utilitarians. The decipherment of 'history' is made dependent on the historian reconciling this division in his own ethical substance, for example, on his escaping the 'poverty of theory'.

Finally, the *fourth* aspect comprises the *telos* of the moral subject; that is, it concerns the kind of being to which one aspires through moral action. For some seventeenth-century Puritans, for example, the telos of moral action was the state of earthly sainthood, achieved by purging the desires and temptings of the natural self. In our case, the goal of aesthetico-ethical culture is to achieve a complete or many-sided development of the faculties by reconciling in a developing self the twinned compulsions of reason and the senses, morality and pleasure, consciousness and social determination, and so on. Whether in the guise of the 'whole man' or the 'common culture' – whether in the form of self-realising play or self-realising labour – this goal figures forth the completion of 'man' in that moment when consciousness is returned to the senses or the society 'from which it proceeds', while these senses or this society are brought within the totalising sphere of consciousness. It is through the figuring forth of this telos that the individual constitutes his self and his actions as those of a progressively 'unfolding' moral subject.

From this summary account we can see that the ethical dimension of culture is not founded in a universal moral or historical self-consciousness – whether that of 'man', or the 'universal class'. Instead it must be seen as a product of the specific ethical practice through which a minority of ethical athletes have shaped a relation to the self as the subject of moral action. It is simply not the case that 'cultivation or culture' could restore the sum total of human capacities to their home in 'experience' or 'class consciousness', because the figure of a 'complete development of human capacities' is nothing more than a talisman of the practice of ethical cultivation itself.

In *Culture and Anarchy*, Arnold describes culture as the form in which 'man' pursues the many-sided perfection of his being. But, of course, in his method – in which strict observance of the moral code (Hebraism) and spontaneous perception (Hellenism) are systematically played-off against each other – we find nothing more than a local exercise in the culture of the self. Culture and its dialectic are not therefore the path to the sum form of cultural attributes. Instead, they constitute a technique through which the ethical virtuoso can temporarily withdraw from any given dispensation of cultural attributes in the process of shaping the privileged attributes of a special ethical caste. In other words, the figure of a complete development of human capacities is, as it were, an *emblem* marking out a special category of person whose own attributes are in fact the *highly specialised* ones of the ethical exemplar.

This is *not* to say, however, that men of letters like Arnold and Ruskin *failed* to actualise the human plenitude by, for example, failing to realise it in experience or class consciousness. Neither is it to echo Williams, for example, in saying that:

> both Arnold and Ruskin are, in the end, victims of abstraction in their social criticism: Arnold, because he shirked extending his criticism of ideas to criticism of the social and economic system

from which they proceeded; Ruskin, as becomes apparent in his proposals for reform, because he was committed to an idea of 'inherent design' as a model for society – a commitment which led him into a familiar type of general replanning of society on paper, without close attention to existing forces and institutions. (Williams, 1958, p. 151)

Such a criticism assumes that the prophets of culture *might* have been responsible for realising the sum of human capacities, for example, by founding their critical judgements in a fundamental knowledge of the 'social and economic system from which they proceeded', and thereby attaching them to 'an actual and growing social force'. But all that this assumption shows is that the criticism itself remains within the sphere of ethical self-shaping, as the key use of the term 'abstraction' indicates. On the one hand, Arnold's conception of culture was not a tendentious abstraction from a more fundamental (materialist) knowledge of culture and society. It was, as we shall see in more detail in Part II, the product of a specific and irreducible ethical practice. On the other hand, we have seen that during Arnold's lifetime this practice was simply not connected to the new investigative and administrative machinery in which the cultural attributes of the population had actually been brought within the sphere of knowledge and government.

In other words, Ruskin and Arnold and the other prophets of culture *could not fail* to realise the human plentitude by embodying it in a fundamental knowledge of society, because they *could not try* to do this. When the man of letters did enter the social sphere, he did so not as the true *or* false bearer of a fundamental knowledge but as the embodiment of a special set of personal attributes: those of the *ethical exemplar*. Hence our task cannot be to restore such a knowledge and thereby help to redeem the lost human plenitude by socialising and democratising culture. Rather, it must be to describe the circumstances in which the special attributes of the ethical exemplar were themselves *added to* the profile of cultural attributes, built-up in the morally administered environments of the 'social'. These circumstances can be first discerned as the conditions leading to the formation of the school inspectorate.

VI

Despite the clash of statist and anti-statist forces – itself complex enough to include Tory evangelicals in the former group and radicals like Cobbett in the latter – the contest over popular education during the first half of the nineteenth century was focused in religious rivalry rather than class struggle. By the late 1830s two religious societies – the Dissenting British and Foreign School Society and the Anglican National Society – dominated the field of popular education, except for a remnant of 'dame' and private adventure schools, which were not necessarily educational institutions in the modern sense.

However, as the Manchester Statistical Society's surveys of 1834, 1835 and 1836 revealed, the schools of the two societies catered for only a fraction of the school-age children in the large industrial cities. (For approximately 1 in 14 of the total population, instead of the requisite 1 in 8.) Not only this, but they were conceived of primarily as charities with a strong proselytising function. In a sense they can be regarded as hybrids, having embodied the new disciplinary techniques of hierarchical surveillance and normalising observation in their monitorial systems, but continuing to harness these techniques to a basically catechismal pedagogy aimed at inculcating religious doctrine. By and large the rival religious systems remained to one side of that convergence of pastoral technique and social discipline, which made it possible for a much wider range of social attributes to be incorporated in a 'child-centred' pedagogy.

We have seen that it was this convergence that allowed reformers like Stow and Kay-Shuttleworth to conceive of popular education as a systematic administration of social space, in which the new 'sympathy of numbers' of the big cities would be relayed through the purifying 'moral observation' of the specially-trained teacher. This was the form in which 'public' as opposed to 'voluntary' popular education first became thinkable: as a moral management of the social environment whose scale and character placed it, in Kay-Shuttleworth's (1862, p. 451) words, among the 'objects too vast, or too complicated, or too important to be intrusted to voluntary associations'. These were the circumstances in which – at the hearings of the parliamentary Select Committee on popular education in 1834, 1835 and 1838 – debate over state intervention and the adequacy of voluntary (religious) provision came to be focused in a particular series of questions: questions concerning the narrow and 'mechanical' character of the pedagogy; the role of religious (doctrinal) as opposed to moral training; the untrained character of the teachers and their lack of social and moral standing;

the miscellaneous pedagogy and patchy demographic coverage of the existing provision; and the inability or unwillingness of the religious societies to provide the new apparatus – in particular the playgrounds and galleries – necessary for uniform moral training.

The advocates of state intervention proposed: a national Normal School organised around this new apparatus in which teachers would receive a uniform training; a system of inspection in which continuation of the government grants to the religious societies begun in 1833 would be made contingent on their conforming to the new pedagogy; and a Central Education Department to oversee the development of a single uniform system of popular education. In the event, Church and parliamentary opposition prevented the overseeing body assuming the form of a central ministry and it was created instead by an Order-in-Council in 1839, as a Committee of the Privy Council with Kay-Shuttleworth as its permanent secretary. Moreover, the proposal for a national Normal School which the Committee laid before parliament later in the same year was overwhelmingly defeated by the Church party.

In this regard, however, the beginnings of state intervention in education had its parallel in the development of a national police in England. This was likewise not the outcome of state power acting through the legislative installation of a central ministry. Instead, it was achieved by the creation of regional police commissioners whose investment with a new investigative and administrative apparatus (summarised in Patrick Colquhoun's *A Treatise on the Police of the Metropolis*) meant that existing police agencies would eventually seek their assistance and direction.[5] Kay-Shuttleworth had fully expected the national Normal School initiative to founder. He had already cast his strategy in the creation of an inspectorate which, invested with the new techniques of public education, would form the point at which these techniques were relayed into the voluntary systems.

It is important to note the difference between the Educational Inspectorate and the Factory Inspectorate and the system of Poor Law supervision which preceded it. Unlike the latter two, the schools' inspectorate was not formed to invigilate and enforce a specific set of legally binding provisions and regulations. Except for the withholding of government grants the school inspectors had no formal power over the local clergy and school management boards and, at least initially, had to be *invited* to comment on organisation and pedagogy in the grant-aided schools they visited.

Their functions as defined by the inaugural Minutes of 1839 were: 'to carry on an inspection of schools which have been or may be hereafter aided by grants of public money, and to convey to conductors and teachers of private schools in different parts of the country a knowledge of all improvements in the art of teaching, and likewise to report to this Committee the progress made in education from year to year' (Cited in Ball, 1963, p. 25). The 'improvements in the art of teaching' were precisely those advanced by educationalists like Stow and Wilderspin – particularly the 'simultaneous' method and the use of the gallery and playground – and it was the task of the inspectors to convey these improvements as norms in the process of inspection. This genesis goes some way towards explaining the small numbers and strong *esprit de corps* of the early inspectorate – in 1844 there were only six inspectors for the nearly 800 inspected schools spread across the country – and also the connection between the functions of inspection and the character and ethical standing of the inspector.

Professor Pillans, when questioned by the 1834 Select Committee on the salaries of state school inspectors in France, had replied: 'The situation is an honourable and respected one, rather from the character of the holders than the amount of the yearly salary' (Parliamentary Papers A, 1834–38, 6, p. 65). While Samuel Wood, on being questioned by Lord Morpeth on the possibility of a single system of inspection linking the rival religious networks, had replied: 'I think that if there were a national system, the inspectorship ought to be, in the best sense of the word, national, that is without reference to any peculiarities of opinion.' To which Morpeth responded by indicating the kind of man capable of subordinating sectarian interest to an impartial judgement: 'And you would conceive that a liberal man, although he might approve of the principles of what is now called the national [i.e. Anglican] system, coming into a school taught upon different principles, might be able to form a very impartial idea of the degree of instruction generally acquired?'. 'Certainly', replied Wood (ibid., p. 175).

It was, then, through the deployment of a special public personage that the apparatus of public education was to be put in place, and not through legislative fiat. The inspector had to be a 'liberal man' shaped by a discipline permitting him to withdraw from competing social and religious doctrines, subjecting them to a more balanced and impartial judgement. By displaying this ethical balance in his own person, the inspector would achieve the 'voluntary' adoption of the new measures. These would now appear to the recalcitrant minor clergy and school committees as attributes of a personage whom they wished to emulate. It was not just that the Committee sought men whose training in the 'culture of the self' gave them the public standing of ethical exemplars. Of the 24 men who served as inspectors between 1839 and 1849, all bar two or three were Oxford or Cambridge graduates; a substantial number contributed to literary journals and were authors of books on literary and philosophical themes; three – Morell, Moseley and Cook – had been students of Fichte, Schlegel and Niebuhr (respectively); and most had passed through the two universities when the Anglicisation of Germanic 'culture' – in the works of Coleridge and Wordsworth – was at its high point.[6] It was also that this standing was built into the specification of the position and its function.

In his 'Instructions to Inspectors', Kay-Shuttleworth wrote to them that it was in 'your general bearing and conduct . . . [that] . . . you will . . . best fulfil the purposes of your appointment'. Inspection, he reminded them somewhat disingenuously, was 'not intended as a means of exercising control, but of affording assistance; that it is not to be regarded as operating for the restraint of local efforts, but for their encouragement; and that its chief objects will not be attained without the co-operation of the school committees' (Cited in Ball, 1963, pp. 67–8). That control was exercised, and the objects of national education in large part attained, through the ethical 'bearing and conduct' of the inspectors, seems in fact to be the case.

It is not just that the inspectors possessed the attributes of the ethical exemplar in the eyes of their brothers in literary cultivation. This was clearly so, as we can see in Thackeray's description of John Allen, the first Anglican inspector: 'the man is just a perfect Saint neither more nor less; and not the least dogmatical or presumptuous: but working, striving, yearning, day and night in the most intense efforts to gain Christian perfection . . . no man however can escape from his influence which is perfectly magnetic' (Ball, 1963, p. 71). It is also that the position delineated for them in the moral hierarchy of the emerging education system operationalised the attributes of the exemplar as the form in which public supervision would be *sought* by those lower in the hierarchy.

The following extract from a teacher's obituary for HMI Joseph Fletcher is indicative in this regard:

> I liked Mr. Fletcher, though he did keel-haul me so thoroughly. There was something in his quiet, piercing eye, that while it detected any pretence, beamed with the most generous appreciation for all earnest effort . . . this mind seemed to be so beautifully balanced, that all seemed in perfect harmony . . . He detected weak points with such manifest aims for improvement, that one valued his criticisms almost as highly as his commendations. The latter, too were most remarkably given, not with a positive approval, to engender self-complacency, but always holding out a higher object, ideal, it might be, but still something noble and exalted to be aimed at. If one jumped over the monument, he would incite one to aim at something higher. No one could witness his careful and affectionate teaching without great benefit. No one could be the subject of his day's inspection without becoming wiser and better. (Ball, 1963, p. 230)

At the same time, the inspector was the vehicle for a pedagogy deriving not from the culture of his 'beautifully balanced' mind, but from a far more powerful investigative and administrative agency: one in which his mind was deployed for its exemplary standing, not its comprehension.[7] Regardless of whether Fichte had charged him with calculating 'the direction which human progress must take', each inspector was in fact equipped with a standard 'List of Questions Contained in the Form of Report on a School'. This consisted of 140 questions to be answered for each school visited.

Through this device the inspector was formed not as the Subject of History, but as the agent of a powerful statistico-moral administrative mechanism centred in the office of the Committee. The inspector fed back minutely detailed information on the character of school buildings and grounds; the kind of architecture and apparatus; the qualification and standing of the teacher; and the pedagogical methods in use. ('Obtain a written account, signed by the master, of the routine of employment of each class in the school, for every hour in the day and every day of the week'.) He simultaneously relayed advice on pedagogy (class-teaching not monitorial) and school organisation (use of the gallery and playground; non-coercive discipline) which teachers and committees became less able to refuse the more dependent they became on government funding. Thus constituted, the inspectorate provided the means for the new apparatus of public education to expand *through* the existing voluntary networks, linking them and transforming them into the system of publically administered moral spaces that continues to determine what counts as education.

In other words, it was as an *ethically exemplary personage* that the cultivated man like Matthew Arnold entered the social sphere. He did not do so as the representative of a 'cultural process' or historical dialectic whose movement promised to totalise this sphere as 'society', summating human capacities in historical self-consciousness. On the one hand, Arnold's School Reports, with their attacks on monitorialism and 'rote learning' and their endorsement of individualising non-coercive pedagogy, derive not from the élite literary culture of the self, but from the government apparatus which he and the other inspectors became the exemplary embodiments of. On the other, given that it was this apparatus and not 'culture' that made it possible for the cultural attributes of the population to become objects of knowledge and government, Arnold as critic is not to be blamed for failing to realise the promise of human plenitude at the level of 'society as a whole'. Arnold and the tradition that he represents were simply not that important.

It was in the apparatus of popular education, then, and not in 'man' or 'society', that the élite culture of the self was linked to the machinery for normalising the population. The initial point of contact was the inspectorate. The exemplary standing of the inspectorate allowed the new corrective technologies of the social sphere to penetrate and transform the voluntary school networks. The public control of education was thus achieved not through the exercise of class or state power, but through the form in which a governmental technology personified itself in the ethical authority of the cultivated man. It was in this manner that the minority practice of ethical self-shaping was linked to the strategy for governing the population invested in the morally administered environment of the popular school. Here, the 'relation to the self', through which the member of an ethical élite constituted himself as a moral subject, overlapped the supervisory 'relation to the exemplar' through which the populace internalised new norms of social life. And, most importantly, it was at this point that the literary text bearing the *inaccessible social norms of the classroom* could overlap with the text invested with the *unattainable goal of aesthetic self-realisation*, forming the continuum along which English would emerge.

In fact, once this conduit between a normalising governmental technology and the élite practice of the self was opened, it became impossible to control the flow of ethical authority. The first indication of this was the demand of working-class school teachers that the ranks of the inspectorate be opened to them: that they be given the chance to become their own exemplars. This was, of course, not a demand to democratise culture, but to expand the membership of the ethical élite. It was the first sign that it might be possible for some to pass from being the objects of 'moral observation' to the position of the exemplar who observes. The vehicle of this passage was to be English.

4

English

I

Writing in the November 1887 issue of *The Nineteenth Century*, as part of his battle with the philologists to get literary criticism taught at Oxford, John Churton Collins lamented its absence in the following terms:

> In a country like ours, where the current will always run in a scientific and positive direction, nothing is so much to be regretted as the almost entire absence of any systematic provision for 'musical' culture. [I.e., culture in the sense of the Greek *musike*, or disinterested aesthetic discipline]. At the Universities the want is to some extent supplied by the study of classical literature, but throughout the country our own literature must necessarily be the chief medium for disseminating that culture, if it is to be disseminated at all. Whether English literature is to fulfil this function or not depends obviously on the training of its teachers, and the training of its teachers depends as obviously on the willingness or the unwillingness of the Universities to provide that training. (Collins, 1887, pp. 657–8)

Now, given that Collins very largely succeeded in his campaign,[1] and English Literature (taught at least partly as literary criticism) was introduced at Oxford in 1894 – doesn't this fly in the face of the genealogy of literary education that we have been developing in the preceding chapters? After all, Collins' success surely indicates that the appearance of English Literature in an increasingly national system of education did result from a broader dissemination of culture, and that the teaching of English was indeed the pedagogical manifestation of literary criticism?

D. J. Palmer certainly thinks so. His *The Rise of English Studies* treats the establishment of literary studies at Oxford as a realisation of the vision of the great prophets of culture.

When, some years before, Coleridge had envisaged the role of his National Church, 'at the fountainhead of the humanities, to preserve the stores and to guard the treasures of past civilisation, and thus to bind the present with the past,' he formulated an idea which was to give impetus and shaping spirit to English studies, both as part of a general education, and as an academic discipline on its own merits. (Palmer, 1965, p. 40)

But neither does Chris Baldick disagree. His *Social Mission of English Criticism* improvises on Palmer's somewhat local and commemorative account, incorporating it in a larger history of the relation between culture and society. If it was largely through Arnold's work that culture was denatured – abstracted from the social relations (the 'way of life as a whole') that it should embody, and sublimated by a moralising criticism – this work nonetheless remained unfinished in Arnold's lifetime. Its local completion, says Baldick (1983, p. 60), was left to others, including Collins, who 'were at work bringing about that integration of literary culture into institutional forms which laid the basis of twentieth-century English criticism'. According to Baldick (ibid., pp. 59–106), this consolidation was achieved through a series of ideological deployments of Arnold's moralising and homogenising criticism, in worker education, civil service training and the education of women: the series culminating with the elevation of criticism to the commanding heights of Oxford and Cambridge. These are the circumstances, it is claimed, which in 1921 permitted the Newbolt Report on *The Teaching of English in England* to recommend the installation of English as the hub of a national curriculum, thereby completing Arnold's 'social and cultural crusade' and securing the cultural hegemony of the middle class.

Clearly, in these accounts we are again confronted by the standard history in which English appears as the true or ideologically bastardised offspring of the union of culture and society. But what, then, are we to make of the following remarks by J. A. Green, which appeared in 1913 in *The Journal of Experimental Pedagogy and Training College Record*, edited by Green for the Training College Association? Written some time after culture's victory at Oxford and Cambridge, they call the new specialist training in English into question, rejecting both its philological *and* its critical forms in favour of the tactic of beginning with the actual reading-matter and interests of the working-class child.

The English specialist will hold up his hands in astonishment. Was it for this he received his University training in English? What of his labours in Anglo-Saxon or Early English Texts? What of his critical studies in more modern literature? From the point of view of the school as a whole I am frankly sceptical of its value. I am inclined to think that the influence of the English specialist in the schools has not always been good. A teacher of English stands to his pupils in a different relationship from that of the teachers of Science or History. The latter are concerned primarily with imparting knowledge or teaching how knowledge is to be acquired, but this is not at any rate the chief business of the English teacher, and his special knowledge sometimes clouds his vision . . .

His ultimate object is to save souls, and just as a man may know the Bible thoroughly without having a spark of religion in him, so may an English student have a sound knowledge of the literature of his native land without having any genuine literary feeling. (Green, 1913, p. 207)

Neither should we be misled by the talk of 'saving souls' and 'genuine literary feeling'. Green's pioneering series of articles on 'The Teaching of English' are based around an empirical survey of the reading interests of working children, carried out through the network of Evening Schools. And it is on the basis of this survey that Green argues for his strategy of admitting popular literature (newspapers, 'fun' papers, thrillers, hobby-journals) into the English lesson as a means of grafting learning onto leisure and 'real life'.

Collins might well have resurrected Arnold's dream of refining a national culture. He might well have projected the teaching of criticism in the universities and its dissemination through the school system as the means of achieving this goal. As far as Green is concerned, however, the teaching of English must assume a quite different form if it is to reach the 'inner life of the child', one much closer to psychology. To achieve this end English must allow the child's real life to surface in the classroom, and the teacher's expertise must not prevent the child's actual desires and interests (their 'dwarfed little selves') from emerging for 'sympathetic inspection'. In other words, Green's pioneering project does not derive from the institutionalisation of Arnoldian culture and criticism. It focuses, rather, the techniques of supervised freedom and the teacher-student relationship of the popular school, now, significantly, in the process of opening up to a range of specialist knowledges.

In this context a training in literary history and criticism of the sort devised by Collins and taught by Walter Raleigh and Quiller-Couch is of little use. Of far more importance, says Green, are the emergent disciplines of educational psychology and the tactics of progressive education, at this time grouped together under the heading of 'experimental pedagogy'. Green was anything but eccentric in this regard. We shall see that even in 1921, despite its recommendations for the expansion of specialist English training in the universities, the Newbolt Report had no idea *how* such a training could combine the required personal qualities ('sensitivity') with scholarly expertise ('exact knowledge'). As a result, in keeping with its 'central principle . . . the necessity of keeping literature in close touch with life', the Report (1921, p. 126) finds itself arguing that 'It is by virtue of this principle that a non-specialist teacher endowed with sympathy, humour, wide experience and outlook, is more successful than a highly-trained specialist who lacks these gifts'. It must come as a sobering fact to all those who see in Collins' victory at Oxford the resurgence of Arnold's 'social and moral crusade', and in the Newbolt Report its successful completion, that, despite its appeals to Arnold and its arguments for the training of English teachers at university level, the Report nowhere recommends that this be carried out through a training in literary criticism.

These remarks permit us to draw two preliminary conclusions which will serve as hypotheses governing the direction of this chapter. First, the appearance of English literature at Oxford and Cambridge at the end of the nineteenth century provided neither the intellectual nor the administrative model for the rise of English in the educational system. This event can be regarded as a short-lived pedagogical incarnation of aesthetico-ethical criticism; it signifies a terminal mutation of the nineteenth-century man of letters, rather than a prefiguration of that distinctively twentieth-century personage the teacher-critic. Second, the developments which saw the emergence of modern English were not focused in the culture of the ancient universities, but in the apparatus of popular education, particularly in the machinery of teacher-training and its accompanying special techniques and knowledges. Neither of these remarks should surprise us. They simply summarise and carry forward the arguments of the last two chapters: arguments, on the one hand, that 'culture' provides no general key to the development of 'man' or 'society', and is in principle and practice nothing more than the local accomplishment of criticism as an aesthetico-ethical caste-discipline; and, on the other, that English first emerged as the literary form of the moral disciplines embedded in the prophylactic social space of the popular school.

If literary pedagogy did begin to gravitate to the very centre of the popular curriculum towards the turn of the nineteenth century, then, we have suggested, this was due not to the delayed impact of Arnoldian culture and criticism, but to certain transformations occurring inside the educational apparatus itself. To be sure, nineteenth-century cultural journalism had been responsible for disseminating the image of the critic as an ethical exemplar, and it was as the bearer of this special personality that the critic had entered the school system in the form of Her Majesty's Inspector. But we shall see that it was the manner in which literature inherited the functions of moral training that provided the circumstances in which the persona of the critic would be multiplied in the space of the popular school; that is, the circumstances determining the modern form of English and the special attributes of its teacher.

What Green's articles indicate is that criticism reached the domain of public education by a very circuitous route: a route at whose terminal point – which for the sake of exposition we can locate in I. A. Richards' appointment to the Cambridge English School in 1922 – criticism was by no means the same discipline launched by Collins. It was not, as Palmer and Baldick suggest, a path that criticism followed inexorably in fulfilling the global functions of culture or ideology. On the one hand, we have indicated that modern *literary pedagogy* first emerged as a focus for the tactics of supervised freedom supported by the popular school: the school itself being a locus of the machinery of moral supervision in which the cultural attributes of target populations had been constituted as objects of knowledge and government. This is what made it possible for Green to conceive of English as an ethical technology, capable of revealing the 'inner life' of the child in the normalising milieu of the literature lesson, and for the Newbolt Report to set English apart from the 'knowledge subjects' on the grounds of its 'closeness to life'.

On the other hand, we have also seen that during the nineteenth century *literary cricitism* was primarily a voluntary, minority ethical practice organised around the dialectical antinomies of self-shaping or self-culture. Literature was not yet deployed in a form permitting it to open up whole populations to moral surveillance and correction. Criticism's ethical dichotomies were still the preserve of a small group who used them to shape a specialised ethical self. In this context the title of the Collins' article cited above – 'Can English Literature Be Taught?' – turns out to be less rhetorical than he might have wished; pointing as it does to the difficulties of integrating an autonomous ethical practice into a disciplinary technology organised around surveillance and examination. This begins to suggest why the initial hostilities between philology and cricitism should have been fought over the question of the latter's examinability.

In describing the birth of English, then, it is not to the great and inexorable dialectic of culture and society that we must look. It is rather to those contingent transformations in literary pedagogy that called for the presence of the cultural exemplar in the sphere of government; and to those parallel transformations in criticism that permitted the culture of the self to be redeployed as a device in the government of populations. It is no accident, then, that when these parallel series eventually met in I. A. Richards' experiments in practical criticism, the recondite play of the critical response had itself been transformed into a focus for the tactics of moral supervision. To describe these transformations is the object of the present chapter, even if, as it eventuates, they remained incomplete until the birth of modern criticism, which forms the object of Part II of our study.

II

Let us begin by back-tracking a little. We have seen that the centrality of Arnold in the standard history of English derives from his combining the functions of critic and inspector of popular schools. Arnold's campaign for the teaching of literature in elementary schools is the central image of English emerging as the pedagogical manifestation of literary culture. And whether one regards Arnold's criticism as a betrayal of the promise of culture or as its fruition, 'the key figure here', says Eagleton – and Palmer and Baldick agree – 'is Matthew Arnold'.

What, then, are we to make of the following exchange which took place before the Cross Commission in April 1886, the scene of Arnold's last public testimony on the role of literature teaching in popular education? Arnold was asked: 'Are you aware that at the present time in our elementary schools under the head of "English" a much larger amount of time is given by teachers to working up the children in the grammar side, than in the literary and poetical side?' His response does little to confirm our current view of him as a crusader, ideological or otherwise, for literary studies: 'They can learn their poetry of course very much out of school. I suppose that more time is given, in school, to teaching them grammar.' Pressed on the point of whether he would like to see 'a larger amount of time given to the cultivation of the imagination on the poetry side, and a less amount of time given to the elementary logic on the grammar side?', the old inspector replied:

> No, I should not like to make a distinction unfavourable to grammar. I do not say that more should not be done to develop the imagination of the children, but I would not do it by cutting out the grammar, and there really is no difficulty about it. (Parliamentary Papers B, 1886, 34, p. 210)

Of course, this is not to say that at other times – in his School Reports for 1871 and 1880, for example – Arnold did not advocate an expanded role for poetic recitation (though never for literary criticism). It is simply to indicate that in the context of his testimony, literary subjects did not have an essential privilege. That this is so is demonstrated by the list of subjects which Arnold had endorsed in his School Report of 1876, which the Cross Commissioners quoted for the record.

> But when grammar, geography, English history, and *natur-kunde* are added, as they ought to be, to reading, writing, and arithmetic, as part of the regular school course, little more can be with advantage asked for from the school children with whom [the teachers] may have to deal. (Ibid., p. 209)

Pressed in 1886, Arnold was prepared to add singing and drawing to the list, and we have already quoted his less than enthusiastic endorsement of poetry.

In fact, Arnold's otherwise puzzling relegation of literature to an apparently diverse series of other subjects can only be understood if we revise our account of the history of English and the role of criticism in it. The relation between the prophet of culture and the school inspector in Arnold is anything but direct. Arnold's advocacy of *natur-kunde*, or nature-study, gives the clue we need here. Like the other progressive educationists and parliamentary commissioners who visited the Pestalozzian 'nature-schools' of Switzerland and Prussia, Arnold returned to support the introduction of nature-study with just as much fervour as he advocated poetic recitation. The important point here is that in this regard he was simply following the footsteps of more important educational progressives like David Stow and James Kay-Shuttleworth.[2] As we shall see, there was something about nature-study that permitted its integration with the new and humanised disciplinary techniques emerging in the popular school.

Nature, according to the progressive conception of the child-mind, was a beneficent domain to which working-class children could have direct and empathetic access; without need of bookish preparation or cultured home life, and simply by virtue of their senses and imagination. Like singing and drawing, *natur-kunde* permitted popular school children to freely identify with the object of study, finding in it reflections of their own lives and interests. Hence it functioned as a non-coercive means for bringing the 'real life of the child' into the corrective space of the school. In fact, these subjects were developed for their appropriateness to the new techniques of 'supervised freedom' which, by the mid-nineteenth century, had begun to modify the early monitorial form of popular education. Arnold could include poetic recitation and paraphrase in this series of subjects not because it was the vehicle for a humanising literary culture capable of transforming popular education, but because – like singing, drawing and nature-study – poetry could focus and support the techniques of 'correction through self expression' evolving in the educational apparatus itself.

We can only make sense of Arnold's remarks to the Cross Commission, then, if we treat English as the literary form of a special pedagogy, rather than as the pedagogical form of literary criticism. We must see Arnold's treatment of literature less as the outcome of his own specialist practice of literary criticism, and more as the result of a specific pedagogical strategy. This strategy supported, and was supported by, the entire series of subjects and *it* made Arnold's (limited) advocacy of poetry as an instrument of moral training possible, rather than vice versa. It was in the morally managed space of the popular school, organised around the dual tactics of self-expression and correction, that literature could make the transition from pastime to subject, acquiring in the process the functions of moral training. It was also on the basis of this apparatus that, by the turn of the century, progressive education could take as its object a pedagogy responsive to the 'child's own interests', even while opening those interests to the ever more powerful moral observation of the teacher. It should come as no surprise, then, that the first systematic blueprints for the literature lesson should have emerged in the sphere of progressive and 'experimental' pedagogy (rather than from the pen of a critical journalist like John Churton Collins) and that, initially at least, literature was accorded no special privilege in this sphere.

Margaret McMillan's *Education Through the Imagination* is representative in this regard. Published in 1904 and arguing for a pedagogy that would be simultaneously free and scientific, it is the imagination, art and play rather than literature as such that function as emblems for this project. The double structure of this enlightened pedagogy is nonetheless instructive. On the one hand, freedom and play are necessary if the child's self is to find expression in the school: 'Rules can be learned. But real play is more than the rules, and more than the game. It is the unfolding of one's self in one's own world. No one can teach a child all the movements which are necessary for health. The most important are those which he finds for himself' (McMillan, 1904, p. 26). On the other, it is the job of the school to mould and shape this self in accordance with developmental norms that are supposedly those of life or, more scientifically, the psyche.

> The emotional life is assumed. We know now that the class-room is not a place where all can be done, and experienced. *It is the place where all that has been lived through can be put in order.* But little children of four to seven have not lived long, or lived much. The slum child has hardly lived at all in any real sense . . . [So that] Here, as in a good home, supplementing even the good home, and transforming the bad one, the Nursery School teachers may begin the abolition of Slumdom. (Ibid., pp. 58–9)

Mediating these two movements and, as a result, acquiring a

characteristic complex of functions – vehicle, diagnostic and corrective for the problematic experiences of the child – is the pedagogic deployment of art.[3] 'It is the aim of education not to destroy or repress, but to direct. And to this end in earliest childhood, the preparation for art appears to be the ideal means' (ibid., p. 13). And it is in these circumstances that literature, and centrally drama, can find a place in the classroom, in the same series as singing, drawing, painting and modelling.

> Drama, – Here is the great City of Refuge as well as School of almost every type of imaginative and unimaginative! And children appear to understand this far better than older people. Much of their own play is just their own way of getting a stage and being players. . .
>
> I have seen a class of very dulled and stupefied children, who could understand only a very small range of words, begin to live at once when they allowed to dramatise even a word! . . . A dull almost sub-normal girl of eight allowed to do this became quite normal and even animated-looking within a week. (Ibid., pp. 98–9)

However, if, like Arnold's proposals for recitation and *natur-kunde*, the project for education through art represents a particular use of the moral disciplines invested in the popular school, it also reveals an important transformation of them. The presence of the socio-psychological classification 'sub-normal' in the preceding quotation provides the clue to this transformation. If art was to assume an important pedagogical function, this was not only due to its role as a support for the strategy of moral supervision put in place by Kay-Shuttleworth. By the last decades of the nineteenth century, art was beginning to function as a support for a number of special knowledges which were able to capitalise on the powers of observation and correction produced in the classroom. The following quotation indicates the range of sociological and, more importantly, psychological knowledges which found in child-art a privileged focus for the relations of knowledge and power offered to them by the school.

> Art is the expression of a living force. It is true. It is an inner force that we deny to the poor. And the denial begins in the earliest years. Very soon it tells in the withering of all that, living, seeks

for expression. The drawings of the slum children are saddening, not because they show a lack of hand or eye skill, but because they show us all the weakness and emptiness of the inner life, the dimness of the perception also, of which they are the shadow. (Ibid., p. 57)

The movement of art, and with it literature, to the centre of the curriculum was partly due, then, to its new role as a surface crossed by shadows in which the human sciences could read the signs of 'cultural deprivation'. We will return to the consequences of this scientific investment of the space in moral supervision presently. For the moment, we must conclude our account of the circumstances in which the English lesson emerged as a privileged embodiment of the supervisory machinery.

The conditions permitting literature and the other arts subjects to move to the centre of the popular curriculum are focused in their deployment as supports for the technology of moral supervision and for the special *savoirs* that came to invest this technology. That literature should have gained a place of special privilege amongst these subjects was due not to the visionary or ideological legacy of nineteenth-century criticism, nor to literature's privileged relation to 'experience', but to a number of factors operating quite contingently on these basic conditions. In summary form these factors were:

First, the capacity of literature as an art to be grafted onto language-teaching and literacy as a basic skill, thereby capitalising on the latter's centrality to the elementary school curriculum. Reading and writing had, of course, along with arithmetic, formed the staple of popular education throughout the nineteenth century, taught as the key to all the other capacities required by life in society. As the acquisition of literacy was pushed further back into the elementary grades, higher classes were freed for literature which, taught in the 'self-expressive' manner, could itself claim to be the key to all of language, at the expense of grammar. These are the circumstances in which, by exploiting the newly-won ambiguity of the term 'English', the Newbolt Report (1921, p. 21) could state as 'the two points which we desire to build upon; first, the fundamental necessity of English for the full development of the mind and character of English children, and second, the fundamental truth that the use of English does not come to all by nature, but is a fine art, and must be taught as a fine art.'

Second, unlike music and the visual arts, or at least on a scale quite incommensurate with theirs, literature had itself come to play the role of relay and support for the same moral and social initiatives that had produced the popular school. Serialised in topical journals targetted on the educative bourgeois household, the novels of Dickens, for example, relayed campaigns for educational, industrial and welfare reform through the actions of exemplary characters and narratives. Popular journals like *Comic Cuts* and *Tit Bits* themselves functioned as relays – admittedly often perverse ones – inside the same network. Both popular and serious literature provided the school with points of identification already saturated with the new normativities of the social sphere. As such, they gradually outstripped the other arts subjects in the moral economy of the school, functioning either as a point of identification channeling the degraded inner life of the child into the school, or as a repository of exemplary figures and tactics through which the teacher might mould this life.

Third, no doubt central to the social and pedagogical success of literature in this regard were the functions supported by the erstwhile literary device of *character*. Linking the spheres of literature, pedagogy ('character formation') and the social (cf., the centrality of character types in criminal and medical anthropologies), character became a privileged point of exchange between the school and those other normative environments (family, neighbourhood, reformatory, hospital) that constituted the life of the child. Marjorie Hourd describes the role of character in the drama lesson in this way:

> The teacher's main purpose is to combine the psychological [developmental] and aesthetic [expressive] aims; to mould the child to the character without the loss of any sincerity of expression. Sometimes the child leads the way in this process and only needs to be guided in relation to the other characters, sometimes she needs to be shown what she is capable of. (Hourd, 1949, p. 66)

If, then, in the first decades of this century English was emerging as the privileged vehicle for expressing the life of the child in the moral landscape of the school, this was not due to the filtering down of Arnoldian culture from the universities. It was instead the outcome of a series of changes in the disciplinary organisation of the popular school. As a result of these changes art, and then, increasingly, literature were able to focus the tactics of supervised freedom embodied in the teacher-student couple and to condense the moral topography of the school itself. English was thus able to emerge as an apparently unstructured domain of experience in which the child's moral development was governed by norms which he found in himself.

III

These are the circumstances, then, which in 1921 made it possible for the Newbolt Report to argue for the centrality of English to an education system which it hoped would become truly national on this basis. The Report (1921, p. 19) attributes a quite new importance to the pedagogical use of literature, describing it as 'a possession and a source of delight, a personal intimacy and the gaining of personal experience, an end in itself and, at the same time, an equipment for the understanding of life.' English can take on this new role as the foundation of a national curriculum because:

> In its full sense it connotes not merely acquaintance with a certain number of terms, or the power of spelling these terms correctly and arranging them without gross mistakes. It connotes the discovery of the world by the first and most direct way open to us, and the discovery of ourselves in our native environment. (Ibid., p. 20)

As long as it had teachers who 'keep it close to life – in no case must the real or practical bearing of the experience be neglected or avoided' (ibid., pp. 17–18) – English would overcome the cultural divisions between the classes and produce a national culture. According to the Report it is English Literature's 'closeness to experience' that enables it to function as the vehicle for a universal liberal education. This would be a new form of education, permitting the human faculties to realise their complete form: an education unconstrained by the conventions and norms of its utilitarian and class-based predecessors.

Contemporary discussion of the Newbolt Report divides rather predictably into two categories. There are those like Shayer (1972) who endorse the Newbolt programme more or less on its own terms. Shayer accepts that literature's 'closeness to life' does indeed make English the vehicle for 'man's' cultural realisation, and takes issue only with the extent of the Report's commitment to this goal. On the other hand, 'cultural materialists' like Baldick and Eagleton treat the report as the institutional form of a culture already alienated from the 'way of life as a whole'. This alienation, they claim, is registered in the Report's aesthetic and ethical demeanour, which makes 'closeness to life' into a ideological cover for the cultural hegemony of the middle class and its attendant foreclosure of 'man's' full politico-cultural development.

It should now be clear that both kinds of analysis miss their mark. It was possible to describe the new pre-eminence of English in terms of its 'closeness to life', because English emerged as the privileged embodiment of a social technology which had indeed constituted the life ('moral and physical condition') of the population as an object of knowledge and government. It is quite misleading, however, for Shayer to attribute English's role in channeling the life of the child into the space of the school to the expressive powers of literature. We have seen that English *inherited* the tactics of correction through self-expression, and the functions of moral supervision from an educational apparatus that was not essentially literary. In this context 'life' and the child's discovery of self must be seen as objects constituted by that merger of individualising surveillance and disciplinary organisation which formed the popular school as such.

But it is equally beside the point for Baldick and Eagleton to treat English as an ideology characterised by its capacity to mask the class basis of culture with ethical universals like 'life'. The ethical character of English is not a gloss on the true political organisation of society which it misrepresents. Rather, it is a sign of the fact that English emerged as a support for a machinery of moral training – supervisory techniques, the teacher-student couple, the organisation of pedagogical space and so on. Here social norms are realised not in a specific set of political ideas, but in an ethical technology, susceptible of *varying* political investments, in which the cultural attributes of populations are constructed through the formation of individual selves.

In short the deployment of literary education obeys neither the logic of 'culture' nor that of its twin, 'ideology'. We have seen that the emergence of a pedagogical technology dedicated to the formation of population-attributes was not a manifestation of the complete development of humanity promised by 'culture and criticism'. But neither did it obey a political logic in which the working class would be cheated of the patrimony of history by being paid-off with virtue and nationalist sentiment. Instead, it was the outcome of a series of undirected and piecemeal transformations in forms of ethical discipline and governmental institutions – focused in the incorporation of individualising pastoral supervision into new forms of 'social' investigation and administration. These transformations had positively and directly constituted 'personal life' as an object of 'social' concern. And if English was able to take 'life' as its object, it was because literary pedagogy itself represented a further transformation in this series.

Hence, if we are to describe English as an ethical technology, then we cannot base our investigation on its intrinsic closeness to 'experience' or on its ideological distance from 'the way of life as a whole'. We must concentrate instead on the forms in which English absorbed the tactics and functions of a pedagogy organised around a moral simulation of 'the real life of the child'. It is possible to isolate four dimensions of this process.

First, English emerged as *the privileged vehicle for the techniques of moral training*. Appropriating the key function of language teaching for its own purposes, and exploiting the exchange between aesthetics and social discipline taking place under the heading of 'character analysis', English began to outstrip the other arts subjects, staking its claim to the centre of the popular curriculum as the pre-eminent embodiment of the tactics of moral supervision. It should come as no surprise, therefore, that this claim was made in terms of bringing the 'real life of the child' into the space of the school: that is, in terms of the reciprocal relation between personal expression and social regulation that defined popular education.

On the one hand, the literature lesson, like the playground before it, would permit the child to manifest, with as little constraint as possible, conducts, capacities and sentiments acquired in the streets and the home. It was in this context that the early propagandists for English, like those who banded together to form the English Association in 1906, could argue that English was the only subject capable of expressing the child's 'real experience of life' and was, therefore, the foundation of all other scholastic and vocational capacities. And it is this tactical function of the literature lesson that enables us to make sense of the Newbolt Report's claim that English 'connotes the discovery of the world by the first and most direct way open to us, and the discovery of ourselves in our native environment'. This claim is, of course, familiar and still current. But it should now be clear that it stands in a direct line with Stow's conception of the school as simulacrum of life, in which the 'true characters and dispositions' of the children would be revealed to the moral observation of the teacher.

On the other hand, because the life of the schoolchild was already subject to the corrective attentions of a variety of social apparatuses (but increasingly psychological and welfarist ones) English, as the privileged expression of this life, assumed the role of relay and support for 'governmental' norms. In the process of defending the centrality of elementary schools in national education and the centrality of English in the elementary school, George Sampson – a major contributor to the Newbolt Report – gives the following insight into the regulatory dimension of English:

> Rulers of whatever name or rank may rise and fall; the ultimate power to make or mar the world will always be with the masses. As long as the elementary school is the chief means of humanising the masses, it is the most important school in the country, and no thought or care can be too great for it. (Sampson, 1921, p. 18)

More precisely, emerging as a specialised channel for drawing the life of the child into the norm-saturated environment of the school, the literature lesson would come to function as a surface on which a variety of social and personal deficits could be brought to the attention of a range of special knowledges. John Dixon's *Growth Through English* provides us with the current understanding of this function:

> As we have seen, English is the meeting point of experience, language and society. It implies 'a developmental pattern whose origin and momentum come from outside the school situation, and which is intimately bound up with the individual's whole intellectual, social and spiritual growth' (Whitehead). Such a pattern will be complex and will draw on several disciplines (including psychology and sociology) for a balanced description. (Dixon, 1967, p. 85)

Or, as we found Margaret McMillan saying of the classroom: 'It is the place where all that has been lived through can be put in order.'

Second, English emerged as a *specialised pedagogy based on correction through self-expression.* Taking shape under the combined pressure of the individualising techniques and social normativity that characterised public education, literary pedagogy began to obey a familiar double imperative.

In the first place, it had to approximate as closely as possible the sphere of free play in which unobtrusive norms could work to maximum advantage in revealing the 'true character and dispositions' of children. By 1921, when *The Encyclopaedia and Dictionary of Education* was published, it was English Literature that epitomised 'play, dream-land, freedom, life'. Provided that the teacher is careful not to associate these with 'thoughts of work, of the daily round, of the scholastic prison house', then 'literature will seem to the children something apart from work, something which is not imposed on them, but which belongs to them and springs from them. . .' (Watson, 1921, II, pp. 565–6). In this space the child should be free to respond to literature in terms of 'his own unique experiences' or to express these in writing himself. And it is from here that 'self-expressive' or 'experiential' English would arise.

At the same time, the literature lesson had also to operate as a surface for the decipherment and correction of these individualised responses in the light of general social norms invested in the text and the teacher. As J. A. Green (1913, p. 204) put it in his articles on 'The Teaching of English' in the *Journal of Experimental Pedagogy*, it is only in the space provided by literature for the expression of 'new needs' that 'the boy reveals himself or struggles to do so, and the teacher may find out, whether he has really reached him or no'. Or, as Dixon (1967, p. 8) would have it: 'A blanket acceptance of "self-expression" is no help to pupils and may well prove a worse hindrance to their growing self-knowledge than a blunt and limited response from the teacher.' So that: 'The more experienced the teacher is in these matters, the more he is able to draw from the pupil the certainties (first) and later the doubts.'

The outcome of these two imperatives is a corrective pedagogy based not on the enforcement of fixed norms but on a process of negotiation between personal desires and social norms. Literary education opens the child to a 'moral observation', through which he sees social norms surface in his own desires as 'new needs'.

Dixon emphasises the non-coercive character of the process in a characteristically modern formulation.

> In the heritage model the stress was on culture as a *given*. There was a constant temptation to ignore culture as the pupil knows it, a network of attitudes to experience and personal evaluations that he develops in a living response to his family and neighbourhood. But this personal culture is what he brings to literature; in the light of which he reads linguistic symbols (giving his own precious life-blood!). What is vital is the interplay between his personal world and the world of the writer: the teacher of English must acknowledge both sides of the experience, and know them both intimately if he is to help bring the two into a fruitful relationship. (Ibid., p. 3)

But we must allow J. A. Green to remind us of the source of the rosy light that bathes modern literary pedagogy. Revealed in the free space of the literature lesson, writes Green (1913, pp. 24, 205), 'are dwarfed little selves whose emotional life is bound up with local gossip, the excitement of football, and a humour so crude that their teachers find it difficult to see any fun whatsoever in it'. Certainly, 'What we want is to find for the boy a real motive for writing'. But this is because 'The more he is inspired by that motive, the better his work will be, and the more conscious he will be of its shortcomings'. Through adjustive techniques not unlike those which Donzelot (1979, pp. 169–235) has isolated in modern psychology, literary pedagogy permits social norms to surface as personal desires and personal desires to become the stake in social regulation.

Third, English took shape in, and remains inseparable from, a *special teacher-student relationship*. At the centre of the relay between the personal and the social and defined by its operation, we find the special attributes of the English teacher. These can be understood as literary variants of those which Stow and Kay-Shuttleworth had earlier specified as requisite for the special persona of the popular teacher.

On one side, as the new figure to whom the child would reveal his true self, the English teacher was to inherit and concentrate the attributes of friend and confidant which Stow had deemed necessary to attract and redirect the 'sympathy of numbers'.

> For this purpose, it is necessary that [the teacher] place himself on such terms with his pupils as that they can, without fear, make him their confidant, unburden their minds, and tell him any little story, or mischievous occurence. Teachers and parents, desirous of gaining the confidence of their children, must in fact, themselves, as it were, become children, by bending to, and occasionally engaging in, their plays and amusements. Without such condescension, a perfect knowledge of real character and dispositions cannot be obtained. (Stow, 1850, p. 156)

The transposition of qualities is fairly direct, as we can see in Dixon's (1967, p. 8) remark: 'An English teacher tries to be a person to whom pupils turn with a sense of trust. The sensitivity, honesty and tact of his response to what pupils say will confirm their half-formed certainties and doubts in what they have said.'

On the other side, because it is initially in his *person* that socio-literary norms will be relayed to the child, the English teacher must be equipped with an eye and a voice capable of personifying the whole moralising force of 'great literature' in the classroom. It is for this reason that the Newbolt Report (1921, p. 178) places such great stress on voice training: 'The voice of the teacher is his main instrument, the only model which his pupils will have to follow, and too much attention cannot be paid to it.' At the same time it argues that:

> What we wish to find in the English teacher of the future – and what we look to the Universities to supply – is the combination of a sensitiveness to the aesthetic and emotional appeal of literature with a reverence for exact knowledge and an appreciation of the use of language as an instrument of exact thought. The teacher has to avoid the danger of investing literature with associations that will prevent its being a delight and a refreshment. On the other hand he must avoid the danger of using it to cultivate a shallow impressionism and an insincere fluency . . . (Newbolt Report, 1921, p. 126)

If Kay-Shuttleworth's pedagogue had to combine the attributes of peasant and priest, the 'English teacher of the future' would have to marry the openness of the child to the discrimination of the man of letters, if he was to fulfil the function mapped out for him. The *Educational Encylopaedia* describes the successful English teacher as 'one who understands and appreciates not merely the mind of the poet, but also the mind of the child: he is the thoughtful host who knows that he must use care and discrimination as he pairs his guests for the feast' (Watson, 1921, II, p. 566). Combining sympathy with correction, the nearness of the friend with the remoteness of the moralist, the English teacher is to relay a corrective superintendence by embodying it in his person as sympathetic exemplar.

Marjorie Hourd (1949, p. 129) sums up the relationship in this way: 'A child does not feel free to express himself unless he feels that his expression will be protected. On the other hand, there comes a point when correction and instruction are necessary parts of this very safeguard.' And she characterises the resultant demeanour of the English teacher as one of 'detached warmth': an oxymoron which future ethnographers of our culture will no doubt find remarkable. As we shall see, the formation of this multi-valent personage – which depended on consolidating the tenuous link between the normalising deployment of literature in the school and its exemplary use in the élite culture of the self – was not to be easily achieved.

Finally, English appeared in the guise of *a new formation of the literary text and a new kind of literary reading*. The text of English and the 'response' which delineated it took shape between the spontaneity of 'life' and the normativity of government; between the freedom of an expressive pedagogy and the constraints of a corrective one; and between an individual who spoke in order to manifest a correctable subjectivity and one who listened in order to correct. In other words, the techniques of moral supervision and the special social relationships embodied in the popular school provided the historical surface on which the text of English literature and the mechanism of its reading made their appearance. As a result the reading of literature took on an unprecedented, but now entirely familiar, double aspect.

On the one hand, because it was to provide the child with a simulated domain of experiences in which life in the family and the neighbourhood would find an immediate echo, the literary text had to be immediately accessible to the juvenile mind. The Newbolt Report (1921, p. 87) in fact claims that the qualities of the child's psyche and those of the literary text share a relation of natural reciprocity in this regard: '[Children] have a natural love for beauty of sound, for the picturesque, the concrete, the imaginative, that is to say, for poetry.' As a result even the text of Shakespeare which 'is so remote as to be in an unfamiliar tongue . . . is saved for the schools by his wonderful power of re-telling a story in dramatic form, and his equally wonderful power of characterisation, and, we may add, his incomparable mastery of word-music' (ibid., p. 312).

In a precocious article on 'Literature as a Central Subject', Alice Zimmern (1900, p. 558) had written that 'the great danger in literature teaching is its tendency, in the hands of insufficiently qualified teachers, to degenerate into linguistics'. Relegating all unnecessary linguistic and historical annotation and all intermediary explanation, it was desirable that 'the text alone should be in the hands of the class; all help must come direct from the lips of the teacher'.[4] The 'text alone' and the 'words on the page', which were to provide the exemplary object of the New Criticism, were not, therefore, an error committed by a naive empiricism. Neither were they a ruse perpetrated by a clever obscurantism, bent on preserving the naive immediacy of the text against its demystifying historical context. The literary text lost its linguistic and historical conditions of intelligibility, or at least acquired different and no less fundamental moral conditions, when it was deployed as a device permitting the immediate registration of 'life' on its norm-charged surfaces.

On the other hand, because it acquired this 'immediate' surface inside the very apparatus in which it was invested with corrective norms, the literary text simultaneously acquired a new kind of 'depth', one which every reading would only serve to intensify. Thus the Newbolt Report (1921, p. 204) qualifies its account of Shakespeare's accessibility: 'Besides the sense in which Shakespeare is open to all the world, there is another in which the full knowledge of him is the last reward of prolonged and laborious study.' And in relation to the juvenile reader it remarks that 'Shakespeare is above his head but that is because he is above all our heads'. By these steps we reach the portals of the text which no reading can exhaust – the text of 'infinite meanings' – because each reading opens the reader to the corrective action of exemplary norms.

If modern criticism has come to construe the literary reading as a 'raid on the infinite', always incomplete, always marking a new beginning, this is not because (as it thinks) the literary text contains an inexhaustible supply of meaning due to its openness to an ever-changing domain of experience. Neither is it a sign that the text is a local manifestation of an ideal linguistic calculus capable of infinite actualisations. Rather, it is a sign of the fact that the modern literary text, unlike the text of rhetoric or philology, is not an object of imitation or description, but a more recently elaborated device opening its reader to endless moral invigilation.

It is the ease with which drama reconciles these two dimensions of literary pedagogy that made it the first and paradigmatic 'text' of English. Through performance, drama makes it possible to bypass the linguistic and historical difficulties of the text and forge a seamless link with the pupil's ordinary play and 'talk'. At the same time, it enables the teacher to open the interests and habits thus brought into the school to the norms of conduct and sentiment embodied in exemplary characters and narratives.[5] It is for this reason that the Newbolt Report (ibid., pp. 309–28) devotes a special section to drama, treating it as a means for 'bringing literature to life' even for the linguistically impoverished child, while also observing that:

> The pupils who take part in performances of plays must learn to speak well and move well, to appreciate character and to express emotion becomingly, to be expansive yet restrained, to subordinate the individual to the whole and to play the game, to be resourceful and self-possessed and to overcome or mitigate personal disabilities. (Ibid., p. 316)

In Dixon's (1967, p. 38) claim that 'To help pupils encounter life as it is, the complexity of relationships in a group and dynamic situation, there is nothing more direct and simple that we can offer them than drama', we discovered a more 'psychologised' version of the same strategy.

It should be clear, however, that 'drama experience' is simply the most visible manifestation of the form in which all literary texts are deployed in English. The text immediately open to experience is also the text that no reading can exhaust, because this duality marks the two dimensions of the function of moral training that literature inherits from the supervisory technology of the school. The response which (as a 'valid personal expression') can never be wrong, is simultaneously the response which can never be right; because it marks the point at which the reader is opened to a set of norms relayed through the English teacher's 'sympathetic inspection'.

It is possible to see, then, that the characteristic four-fold structure of English is not the result of the institutional realisation of the expressive powers of literature. Neither does it stem from the deployment of a tendentious criticism whose deceptive immediacy has cast the spell of ethics over the political dynamics of class division. Rather, it is the outcome of those developments in which literature inherited and transformed the functions of an historically specific moral technology. These were the developments that saw English take shape between an individualising moral supervision and the policing of social space; between the expression of the self and its regulation according to social norms; between an individual who spoke in order to be corrected and one who listened to correct; and between a text whose surfaces gave immediate access to the experiences of the self and one in whose depths the fullness of such experience remained forever out of reach, invested as it was by norms known only as desires.

The present study is not a comparative one. However, because in Part II we trace the relations between these developments in English and the emergence of modern criticism – including American New Criticism – it is worth taking a brief note of parallel developments which were occurring across the Atlantic. Consider, for example, an article on 'The Preparation of a Class for a Lesson in Literature' by Sarah McNary, an instructor in the State Normal School of New Jersey. It was published in 1908 in *The Pedagogical Seminary*, a journal overlapping in time with J. A. Green's *Journal of Experimental Pedagogy* and carrying a similar range of articles applying psychology and sociology to educational problems, with a greater emphasis on problem populations: the socially deprived, delinquents, the retarded and the insane. McNary's problem is how to secure an appropriately inward engagement with literature from high school students lacking literary home lives. Her strategy is in fact identical with Green's:

> Lists of words, and a compiler's sketch of an author's life, are not likely to arouse a desire to read a given work; neither device appeals in any way to the life-experience of the pupil, – to his ideas, his emotions, his potential sympathy with the author's mood. Such an appeal must be made skillfully, by personal talk, by suggestive questioning, by carefully elicited reminiscences, above all, by the contagion of the harmony between the teacher and the author. When such an appeal has been made successfully, the soul even of a child may understand the work of an artist, and

the vital essence of a poem may be inwrought into his spiritual fibre. (McNary, 1908, p. 490)

Interestingly enough, she regards this strategy as one that has been developed in infant schools and teacher training seminaries and is now in need of transposition to the high school and university sectors.

It is possible to extrapolate two points from the preceding description, both of which are important for the future course of our discussion. *First,* inside the space mapped out by the four coordinates of English, a new object became possible. This object we now recognise as the *literary response,* and its bearer as the *reader.* If in modern criticism literature has come to be delineated by the contours of the literary response, this is not simply the aftermath of the Romantic re-discovery of affective poetics. 'Responding to literature' is not an eternal hallmark of human nature, but a variable historical artefact of the conditions in which certain kinds of text are deployed. The literary response, for example, played no part in the Renaissance grammar school boy's praise of a great author – the eulogy did not employ the device: 'What does this work mean to me personally?'[6] The literary response as we know it did not become possible until the reading of literature emerged in the space of 'correction through self-expression'; that is, in the sphere of modern public education. It was here that it acquired the curious double aspect, so familiar to us now, of the *personal affirmation* (neither true nor false, judged only for its sincerity) and the *description of literary experience* (judged according to unreachable norms of aesthetico-ethical development).

Second, and of more immediate importance, it was also on the terrain delineated by the four coordinates that a space was marked out for the formerly esoteric practice of criticism or self-culture *inside* the machinery of population management. Once literature was invested by the disciplinary organisation of the school, it became necessary for Kay-Shuttleworth's humble popular school teacher to acquire the attributes of the cultural exemplar. According to the *Educational Encyclopaedia:*

The born teacher of literature . . . is the individual who can enter into the poet's mood and purpose, and interpret them himself or get his students to interpret them in a rich cultivated voice . . . For once he has in his own person exhibited that poetic truth which is 'carried alive into the heart by passion,' once the class has come to realise what glorious fun the rendering of poetry and drama is there will be many ready, nay, eager, to imitate him. (Watson, 1921, II, p. 566)

As the Newbolt Commissioners pointed out, this new dimension of the teacher's persona demanded a new form of training, if English was to successfully assume the functions of moral education.

since the literature lesson is no mechanical matter and is to consist not in the imparting of information but in the introduction of the student to great minds and new forms of experience, it is evidently necessary that the teacher should himself be already in touch with such minds and such experience. In other words, he must himself have received an education of the kind towards which he is to lead his class. . .

Our difficulty would be infinitely lessened if the general population of this country had already for years past been receiving such an education as we now advocate, but in the natural order of things, this could never be; the teacher must exist before the pupil. He is our lever, and we must first apply our whole force to him if we are to raise the mass. (Newbolt Report, 1921, pp. 24–5)

Here we can see how, from inside the apparatus for the moral management of populations, as a condition of its 'aesthetic' reconstruction, the call for the literary cultivation of the popular teacher went out. As the teacher assumed more of the functions of ethical invigilation, and as the English teacher gradually emerged as their privileged embodiment, those attributes first seen in the exemplary literary gentlemen of the inspectorate began to migrate and multiply. These are the circumstances in which the disinterested ethical demeanour of the critic would be married to the non-coercive 'moral observation' of the teacher. In other words, they are the circumstances in which a space was created for the élite culture of the self inside the machinery of population management, thereby opening the possibility for an exchange of functions to take place between the teacher and the critic.

IV

This exchange was by no means easily achieved, however. The reason should be clear. The links between the minority practice of self-cultivation and the machinery for normalising the cultural attributes of target populations were not being forged inside a single domain of human development: 'society' or 'culture' pictured as 'a line of common growth'. The attributes of the working-class children and their teachers were inseparable from a specific cultural technology, in which the life of the family and the neighbourhood was relayed through the supervisory disciplines of the school.

Equally, the capacities and standing of the critic were the product of a quite different minority caste practice from which the man of letters emerged as an exemplar for his own class. This is precisely what is obscured when the emergence of modern literary education is described in terms of developments inside a 'general human culture'; that is, a culture in which differently instituted attributes must appear as incomplete fractions of a single, because 'full', development of human capacities. But it is also what is lost sight of when the different dispensations of attributes are pictured as arising from different positions in the structure of society. Here 'society' itself is invested with the goal of 'complete' development, in relation to which the attributes of specific classes and groups must appear as distorted fragments.

The relationship we are describing, however, was not between fragments of a social or cultural whole. It was between a caste practice and a governmental technology, each of which was not only responsible for a different configuration of the 'person' but was also the terrain of an autonomous ethical or political 'rationality'. Having said this, and in a no doubt utopian attempt to avoid misunderstanding on this point, it is necessary to add the following: these domains were by no means 'absolutely autonomous' of each other, and were quite capable of meeting to form a hybrid politico-ethical programme. After all, it is precisely the *relationship* between these two spheres that is at the centre of our description. I differ from the standard accounts only in affirming that the forging of this relation was not governed by an overarching cultural or historical logic – according to which English moved closer to the 'full' development of human capacities or, on the contrary, further away into the distortions of ideology. Instead, I have argued that the relationship between culture and government was made possible by a series of undirected, piecemeal changes in the technology of public education: changes which demanded the 'mass production' of the cultural exemplar as a condition for the emergence of a specialised ethical technology – English. In short, I have argued that the conditions permitting literary education to emerge on the cusp of the government of populations and the culture of the self were not 'social' or 'cultural' but, for want of a better word, technical: as long as it is kept in mind that these were techniques of the soul as well as the body, and were indeed targetted on different social and moral classes.

That this is so is indicated, as I had begun to say, by the nature of the difficulties which stood in the way of the Newbolt programme. Its proposal, to concentrate on the literary formation of the teacher as the 'lever' capable of 'raising the mass' of the population, was confronted by two inter-related sets of problems.

The *first* set arose in relation to the need to systematise the new form of teacher training. In keeping with its foundational claim that English was not just another 'knowledge subject', but the key to the acquisition of experience and the formation of character, the Report signalled the new centrality of English via the slogan: 'Every teacher in English is a teacher of English'. And in these terms it recommended that English, taught along the new lines, form a central element in the curricula of the training colleges and universities. The Report (1921, p. 247) envisages that 'The academic English staff will thus in a special sense be the "teachers of the teachers" of the great English-speaking democracies'. At the same time, the attributes of the English teacher were in fact those of a special personality formed within the apparatus of popular education: the teacher must have the capacity to delight in literature, to 'believe' in it, to mediate between the mind of the poet and that of the child – all in accordance with the disciplinary tactic of 'keeping literature in close touch with life'. For this reason the Report cannot formulate a general academic programme for the systematic formation of these attributes. It thus remains caught in the cleft stick of advocating a systematic specialist training in English as the key to generalising the functions of moral pedagogy, while denying that any specialist knowledge can in fact form the personality of the 'born' English teacher.

Apart from asking for a training that would combine 'sensitivity' and 'exact knowledge', we have seen that the best the Report can manage in this regard is a double negation.

The teacher has to avoid the danger of investing literature with associations that will prevent its being a delight and a refreshment. On the other hand, he must avoid the danger of using it to cultivate a shallow impressionism and an insincere fluency, in which case it simply feeds the 'lie in the soul' from which it is the aim of the best education to deliver us. (Ibid., p. 126)

With hindsight we can see that this dilemma arose with the need to adapt the tactics of moral supervision, which English acquired in the normalising environment of the popular school, to pedagogies of a quite different (academic) type.

The *second* set of problems is focused by the difficult relation between literary criticism and historical philology. The 'aesthetic' reconstruction of the pedagogical disciplines might well have necessitated that the persona of the teacher be supplemented by the exemplary attributes of the critic. Equally, the Report might well lean to the idea of placing criticism at the centre of a university training in English in order to achieve this end. But we have seen that nineteenth-century criticism was neither a pedagogical discipline nor a positive knowledge, like philology. It was a minority ethical practice of the self disseminated largely through cultural journalism; and it was in this form that it entered the English schools of Oxford and Cambridge in the 1890s.

As a species of voluntary self-cultivation organised around the antinomies of the ethical substance – thought and feeling, consciousness and history, etc. – criticism could not compete with philology as a *knowledge* of language and literature, and was understandably denounced by the philologists as dilettantish. At the same time, it was not yet connected to the techniques of supervised freedom which secured popular literary pedagogy's 'closeness to life'. Hence it was also denounced by specialists in the new English, like J. A. Green, because this meant it could be 'crammed' like any other 'knowledge subject'. As a result, although it favours instituting a systematic university training in criticism as the linchpin of a teacher training system – as the means of joining the disciplinary formation of a special personality to systematic training in an 'exact knowledge' – the Report does not have at its disposal a criticism possessing this synthetic power.

In fact both sets of problems are focused in the Newbolt Report's complex response to the question of examinations. In discussing this question the Report (ibid., pp. 295–309) is well aware that if

English was to assume its place at the centre of a national curriculum, then it had to be incorporated into the emerging network of public scholarship and university entrance examinations. This network provided the key to linking the class-differentiated elementary, grammar and university sectors into a single, if still differentiated, educational system. The Report is equally clear-sighted, however, about the difficulties of achieving such an incorporation.

While tests and examinations were a feature of the popular school, they were employed as techniques of moral supervision. Their object was not what the student knew, but knowledge of the student. In this regard, the following remarks cited on the education of workers had a general application.

> It matters little to the worker whether a poem is a lyric or an epic, whether it is in trochees or iambics. He wants to know what it means, how it interprets life, the source and secret of its inspiration. It is obvious that before the teacher can go far he must know each student, and build his syllabus upon that foundation. (Ibid., p. 273)

The object here was not primarily the acquisition of skill and knowledge, but the formation of conscience in the special relation of identification and correction set up between teacher and student and now mediated by the literary text. Hence as far as literary education is concerned:

> The test of its success is not that students should be able to talk fluently, or even intelligently, about literary history, but that they should have been penetrated by the power of some great writer, should have made something of him at least a part of themselves, and should have acquired insensibly an inner standard of excellence. (Ibid., p. 274)

J. E. Barton's testimony to the commission concluded with the statement that:

> To examine on [literature as an art] was very difficult. It was certainly not to be done by finding out what a boy did not know. If a wide choice of questions was given, and the questions were simple, it was perhaps possible to find out what a boy liked and

felt. But many boys of 16, though they were beginning to feel something, had as yet no power of expression. (Ibid., p. 307)

While the English Association went so far as to say that:

Purely external examinations in English Literature, in which there is no direct contact between the examiner and the teacher cannot be approved . . . Since the style of question set determines the method of teaching, examining bodies usurp functions which properly belong to the school. (Ibid., p. 303)

The demand that the student respond in terms of his own thoughts and feelings, rather than via something learned, was not testimony to the privileged access that literature has to the soul. It arose only after literature had assimilated the techniques of moral supervision through which the 'true character and dispositions' of the student were revealed to the normalising observation of the teacher. It was in this apparatus that literature *acquired* a privileged access to the soul: a soul itself insensibly acquired in the instituted space between self-expression and social normativity. The problem confronting the Newbolt Commissioners was that despite the necessity for English to be incorporated in a system of national external examinations, the conditions in which English had emerged made the functions of teaching and examination inseparable. And if, in a very significant phrase, the Report baptised the object of the English examination as the 'first-hand knowledge of literature', this was only because such a 'knowledge' made it possible for the teacher to 'find out what a boy liked and felt'.

But if what was required was a literary discipline that was open to external examination as a knowledge, yet continued to function as a means of forming the moral attributes of students and their teachers, then no such discipline was available. As an examinable knowledge English literature already formed a branch of Anglo-Saxon and Old English studies, treated via philology in terms of sound shifts, historical morphology and the relations between dialects. Clearly this would not do for a subject connoting 'the discovery of the world by the first and most direct way open to us, and the discovery of ourselves in our native environment'. But neither would an approach to English through history or sociology, as these knowledges must themselves remain handmaidens to the moment of the 'literary response'. Deriving ultimately from the unconditional relation between the mind and the 'text itself', great literature is 'a timeless thing, which can never become old-fashioned or out of date, or depend for its importance upon historical considerations' (ibid., p. 205).

Furthermore, despite the pressure to make the literary cultivation of the teacher the key to its entire project, the Newbolt Report could not solve these problems by making nineteenth-century criticism itself into an examinable subject. Following John Churton Collins down this path – which entailed asking questions like: 'The epithet which best characterises Shakespeare is "myriad-minded". Discuss that statement' – meant that English would fail in both directions. Such questions did allow English to appear as an examinable knowledge, but in this case what was learned were critical judgements which, shorn of their ascetic function, looked pale and precious in comparison with the monumental achievements of Indo-European philology.[7] At the same time, because such questions *could* be learned or 'crammed', examining in criticism meant that English forfeited the 'personal' response which was the key to the disciplinary function of the new literary pedagogy. According to the Report (ibid., p. 308): 'It would be fatal to encourage formulas for the purpose of expressing feeling and admiration.' (Even though this is precisely what was encouraged by grammar schools prior to the emergence of a morally managed social sphere.)

In fact, this impasse cannot be resolved within the terms of the Report. Despite the fact that it assembles most of the elements responsible for the emergence of literary pedagogy as the central ethical technology of an inter-linked national curriculum, the Report lacks the *means* of forming English as an examinable knowledge without forfeit of its disciplinary function. The impasse is well characterised in P. J. Hartog's *Examinations and Their Relation to Culture and Efficiency*.

> It may be held, and I should agree, that culture is as individual a thing as conscience; that culture may be killed, that it cannot be caught, by examinations. Yet teachers who realise all this, who think examinations in their subject mischievous rather than helpful, implore the authorities to include it in every possible examination syllabus. Why? Because, under the present *regime*, a

subject that is not examined in is likely to disappear speedily from our teaching curricula. (Hartog, 1918, p. 9)

And apart from some less than prophetic remarks on the need for a 'literary philology', the Report could do little more than advocate that unstable amalgam of philology and criticism – the 'language and literature' department – which characterised a university training in English until the appearance of I. A. Richards. As far as the problem of examinations was concerned the Report (1921, p. 309) recommended nothing more than 'that oral examination in English should be resorted to more frequently as affording the best means of lessening the angle between the view of the examiner and that of the teacher'. But this was tantamount to shelving the whole problem, as it tacitly recognised in the Report's (ibid., p. 309) closing remark on the topic: 'The part of the examiner is to bring as many as possible to the starting point, to accompany them to his furthest limit, and then to bid them pass on, with the ideal teacher, beyond his range.'[8]

A sideways glance at the American context reveals a similarly unstable amalgam of elements. Here the emergence of university language and literature departments witnessed a parallel battle between the philologists and the men of letters, although one decisively inflected by the emergence of the graduate school system. Indeed, John Churton Collins' broadsides found a ready American audience. We have already noted that the new pedagogical use of literature, stressing its immediacy and 'closeness to life', was being advocated in American teacher training colleges by the turn of the century. Small wonder, then, that the machinery for integrating these elements first tested by Richards should have found an American correlate in the emergence of the New Criticism.[9] This is to anticipate our argument, however.

In the first decades of this century 'English' did not name a single subject, but a loose ensemble consisting of a literary pedagogy supporting the tactics of supervised freedom embodied in the popular school; the minority caste practice of self-culture carried out through the ethical dialectics of criticism; and, on the margins, the knowledge of language and literature made available by historical philology. It should now be clear that the gradual emergence of English at the centre of a national curriculum was not the result of the delayed institutionalisation of Arnoldian culture and criticism. Neither did it occur at the behest of a culture promising the 'full' development of human capacities or an ideology threatening to withhold this development in the interests of a particular class. Rather, the imperative to deploy the persona of the cultivated man within the sphere of governmental pedagogy was the outcome of those contingent changes which made moral supervision dependent on the teacher acquiring the exemplary attributes of the critic. What was thrown up by the campaign for the systematisation of teacher training – and what was focused by the impasse over the examinability of English – was the need for a new technical organisation for the components of the 'English complex'. This would have to be an organisation capable of linking a pedagogy in which literature opened the population to moral supervision; a caste practice in which literature provided the antinomies for shaping the exemplary moral self; and a science in which literature was the object of a positive, examinable knowledge.

V

In fact, if we are to understand the conditions in which the esoteric discipline of the critic came to play a role in the government of populations – forming the 'lever' which would 'raise the mass' – then we cannot base our description on the great dialectic between culture and society. Instead, we must return to the less glorious relations between an emerging literary pedagogy, on the one hand and, on the other, an equally embryonic educational psychology and progressive pedagogy: these last two sharing the single title of 'experimental pedagogy' until the 1920s. It was in the field formed by this group of relations – seeming with hindsight to be characterised by an overlapping of boundaries and a blurring of functions – that, as we have noted, the first blueprints for the literature lesson appeared. We shall now see that it was also in this field that the exemplary cultivation of the critic could enter into an exchange with the supervisory functions of the popular school teacher. This exchange in turn made it possible for English to assume the form of an examinable knowledge without forfeiting its powers of 'character formation', as we shall see in more detail in Part II of our study.

Of course, the broad development of educational psychology and progressive education fall outside our central focus. We are concerned with them only at the point of their emergence in the space of the popular schoolroom where, alongside English, they were able to draw on the unprecedented powers of observation and correction made available. As early as 1835 we find the Scots barrister and educationist James Simpson attempting to provide psychological principles for the apparatus of popular education. Drawing on a prevalent philosophical psychology which divided the human faculties into three classes – the animal propensities, the moral sentiments and the intellectual powers – Simpson's *The Philosophy of Education* aimed to provide a rational basis for the mixture of monitorialism and Stowian 'moral observation' which he advocated. And testifying before the 1835 sitting of the Select Committee on the Education of the Poorer Classes, he argued that:

> Education, above all, is essentially the improvement of the faculties named, to the end of regulating the animal propensities, increasing the activity of the moral sentiments, and enlarging the power of the intellectual faculties. (Parliamentary Papers A, 1834–38, 6, p. 443)

True to his enlightenment origins, Simpson wanted teachers and students to be trained in this theory of mind so that education might proceed on principled rational grounds. The Committee remained sceptical, however, with one member remarking:

> Does not all that resolve itself into this; that the master observes his scholars, and prohibits that which is conventionally considered bad, and inculcates that which is conventionally considered good; and how is that necessarily connected with the theory of mind which you have developed, and why should the same power of direction not be effective if this theory of the mind were not understood? (Ibid., p. 444)

In fact, psychology did not enter the educational domain as a foundational knowledge. Rather, the reverse is the case: educational psychology was itself a child of the new pedagogical apparatus. It drew on existing theories of mind and new quantificational techniques only to codify a dispensation of attributes and capacities unthinkable outside the norm-charged space of the classroom. At the centre of the educational psychology which was taking shape at the end of the nineteenth century we do not find the old faculties of will, intellect and emotion, or the privileged relation between mind and body. Instead, we find a quite new array of objects: attention span, speed of response, verbal and arithmetical competence, vivacity of mental imagery, memory retention and intelligence. This new psychology was not a psychology of 'man' but of individual differences, varying according to norms embodied in the classroom and distributed into categories like intelligent, average and 'feeble-minded'. By subjecting cultural practices and their bearers to a single formative regimen operative in the moral observation of the teacher, the school made normative social aptitudes visible as general human attributes.

In short, the school made it possible for the acquisition of capacities to emerge in a field of frequencies distributed around *governmental norms*, which statistical techniques could transform into *human averages*: a move from the 'norm' to the 'normal'.[10] And it was in this form that educational psychology 'discovered' pedagogical capacities as individual psychological states or functions.

Nikolas Rose provides corroboration for this account in his article on 'The Psychological Complex'. Here Rose argues that in moving from experimenting on the faculties to testing 'tasks of behaviour', psychology acquired new objects and functions in the sphere of social administration. In basing its tests on behavioural norms embodied in the apparatuses of population management (prisons, asylums, reformatories, hospitals, schools) psychology began to form its objects (psychological functions in general, 'intelligence' in particular) according to specific governmental strategies: strategies which it in turn 'psychologised'. Rose summarises the two-fold consequence of this transition in the following way:

Firstly, measurement has become a question of differentiating between individuals through sequential comparisons, ranking them upon a linear series according to some characteristic regarded as having a continuous distribution whose pattern follows the normal curve. Intelligence thus becomes a unitary characteristic which can be treated according to the statistics of large populations, in which individual scores receive their pertinence from the perspective of the population itself and their relation to its norms. And secondly, intelligence has become the measure of the outward and visible effects (behaviours) of an internal and biological cause (sensory abilities). (Rose, 1979, p. 54)

Emerging as a parallel modification of the pedagogical disciplines, English, by the turn of the nineteenth century, had begun to borrow from the field of psychology and in fact underwent a parallel mutation in form and function. Sometimes this borrowing was quite direct, as in the case of E. Allison Peers. Peers used his English classes to perform a series of tests designed to discover the role of mental imagery in the understanding of literature. The tabulated results of these tests were published in *The Journal of Experimental Pedagogy and Training College Record* in 1913–14, and if the results are of no particular significance, Peers' method certainly is.

Peers presented a range of classes with a selection of poetry extracts, some chosen for their imagaic character and some for their 'underlying ideas'. He then asked each class to record the images experienced while reading these extracts and any ideas they conveyed. What is of interest to us is the manner in which this method converts pedagogical practices and norms into techniques for 'discovering' the presence of psychological capacities and distributing them as individual deviations from normal psychological functions. In fact, Peers' criterion for the 'understanding' of poetic images and ideas is the normative and pedogogical one of being able to 'picture out' the images and paraphase the ideas when asked to do so by the teacher. At the same time, by translating *normative marks* (arrived at on the basis of these 'tasks of behaviour') into *statistical expressions of the normal*, he is able to convert these local and normative techniques of understanding poetry into the behavioural signs of interpretive processes hidden deep within each child by nature.

Of course, it is not Peers' particular methods that characterise the future form of literary education. When we next meet the psychological testing of literary abilities, in I. A. Richards' famous experiments in practical criticism, the diagnostic functions of the test will be subordinated to those of the literary seminar. Moreover, in Richards' discussion of 'The Normality of the Artist' in his *Principles of Literary Criticism*, it is the 'exemplar' sense of 'normal' that is to the forefront, rather than its role as a standard defining pathological deviations. Nonetheless, it is important that the literary response should have acquired a diagnostic function and a normalising role, of whatever sort. And we simply cannot understand this mutation unless we understand the exchanges that occurred inside the space of the school between emergent literary and psychological pedagogies.

These exchanges did make it possible for literary pedagogy – which until this time had functioned as a species of moral supervision – to be reconstituted as a knowledge: one taking as its object the hidden states and processes underlying the student's literary response. Moreover, if this modified the teacher-student relation – allowing the former a more 'forensic' relation to the latter and hence permitting some separation of teaching and testing – it did so without jeopardising its normalising function, which remained embedded in the structure of the test.

However, if literary pedagogy was thus 'psychologised', the forms of psychological development in their turn received a distinctively aesthetic patterning. The same exchange made it possible for the discipline of aesthetic self-culture to take its place in the normalising apparatus of the school. Educational psychology had, as it were, allowed the classroom tactics of moral supervision to surface 'inside' the student, where they appeared in the form of individualised psychological states and processes. And it was in this individualised and psychological form that the tactics of popular education could enter into an exchange with the esoteric dialectics of self-cultivation. For the first time, if he stayed in school long enough, the popular scholar could be presented with the difficult task of reconciling his thoughts and his feelings, and moderating his moral impulses in the light of his sensuous ones. If this made it possible for the student to become responsible for shaping his own self in the advanced stages of his literary education, it did so by incorporating self-cultivation itself into the supervisory relation between teacher and student. Here modern criticism could acquire its normalising function.

Hence, it came about that English took shape in a space defined by two intersecting functions: a pedagogical function in which the literary response provided access to norms of psycho-moral development now embedded deep in the child; and a critical function for which the literary response provided a means of shaping a self in whom others would find themselves shaped – the self of the teacher-critic. It was in this space that English could emerge as an examinable knowledge without losing its disciplinary power, while its teacher could acquire the attributes of the critical exemplar without forfeiting those of the moral superintendent. In short, it was in this space that culture's grand promise of a complete development of human faculties found its niche in the governmental administration of cultural attributes. If we are to delineate the contours of this space it is necessary to examine in a little more detail the overlapping of literary and psychological pedagogies in which they were formed.

VI

In the first place, with regard to the 'psychologisation' of literary pedagogy, we have noted that as early as 1904 Margaret McMillan was using child art and literature to decipher the deprived 'inner lives' of slum children and the 'stunted imaginations' of 'sub-normals'. But as McMillan herself was quick to point out – in a remark whose frankness is revealing in relation to later apologists for English – these techniques were not to remain confined to popular and therapeutic education.

> Much is said in this book about the poorest class of children, but of course we are not thinking of any one class alone. The feeble-minded have helped the gifted, because it has been easier in some ways to study their slower development than to follow the flight of the quicker mind. The poor also have a great service to render, though a very sorrowful one. (McMillan, 1904, pp. 14–15)

That these techniques for the detection and management of socio-psychological failure have continued to function as a coordinate for the development of English is evident in Dorothy Heathcote's (1968) use of them in reformatories, and David Holbrook's (1961 and 1964) use of them in Secondary Modern and Comprehensive schools. But it is their less overtly therapeutic use inside the literature lesson that typifies modern English. In this regard Marjorie Hourd's *The Education of the Poetic Spirit* is representative of the main line of development, whose later incarnations include Frank Whitehead's *The Disappearing Dais*, John Dixon's *Growth Through English* and Denys Thompson's collection *Directions in the Teaching of English*.

Drawing her model of psycho-social maturation from the child-psychology of Susan Isaacs (1930),[11] Hourd uses the dramatisation of epics and romances as a means of monitoring and regulating the development of pre-adolescent students. The capacity of this tactic to transform social norms into those of the child's own unfolding psycho-social sensibility is evident in the following:

> The *Iliad* has always seemed to me to be the perfect material for dramatisation in this transitional stage between later childhood and early adolescence. As can be seen in these examples the emotional reactions of the chief characters have a primitive sublimity well within the child's grasp. It is true that very different levels of understanding have been reached in these confessions, but Elizabeth has penetrated deeply into the sources of conflict in Achilles. She has her finger right on the pulse of the Oedipus Complex, and the homosexual stress in his character . . . Unconsciously the child is expressing herself; she is consciously enjoying a good tale. . .
>
> The children are establishing themselves socially in relation to others, and Achilles, Hector, Priam and the rest line up with their fellow beings as part of the environment. So whereas Shakespeare and the mature dramatist reflect their times and search through their characters for the universal human feelings, the child reflects her home and school background whilst unconsciously seeking her own prototype. (Hourd, 1949, pp. 40–1, 55)

Or, as Whitehead would have it:

> The growth of [the young child's] language-powers is insepar-ably bound up with his developing consciousness of the world around him, with his relationships to the people in his family circle about whom he cares most deeply, with his control of his inner fantasies and the feelings they give rise to, and with his growing socialisation – his possession, that is to say, of the values of the civilisation in which he is growing up. (Whitehead, 1969, p. 19)

If English has been able to find in the literary response a means of deciphering in the student 'the values of the civilisation in which he is growing up', this is because at a certain point in its formation it assimilated the psychological 'introjection' of socio-pedagogical norms.

But, in the second place, this assimilation was also a transformation. If Hourd (1949, p. 16) could claim to have shown 'how mental health is maintained through the teacher's skill in leaving the way open between feeling and expression and indeed how children seek for themselves this therapy which lies in acting, speaking and writing', she was equally emphatic that the role of the English teacher was not that of the psycho-therapist. This role was a distinctively aesthetic and ethical one. If psychology provided a means of reading the patterns of development hidden in the child, these patterns nonetheless took shape in relation to the organisation of literature and its appreciation.

> We have seen that drama has a double psychological function. It acts as a release of phantasy and also a means of grasping reality. Both aspects are equally important and finally inter-dependent. Just as in play-writing it is necessary to take hold of the values intrinsic to the source, so in play-acting it is most important to remember that two ends must be served, the child's development on the one hand, and the interpretation of the play on the other. (Ibid., p. 63)

In other words, if literary pedagogy learnt from psychology how to locate the norms of moral training in the internal dynamics of 'child development', these norms remained those embedded in literary pedagogy itself. And it was in relation to the 'tasks of behaviour' set by this pedagogy – recitation, dramatisation, 'creative writing', interpretation – that developmental norms were established.

Emerging in the space defined by these contrapuntal strategies, it is no wonder that English took shape as a hybrid technology combining therapeutic and ethical functions. Neither should we be surprised that in the kind of 'maturity' which English took as its goal, a form of psycho-moral moulding of the sensibility should have been carried out according to the norms of aesthetic organisation.

Hourd herself characterises English in terms of its two aims, psychological and aesthetic; and their combination in her model programme permits the literary syllabus to double as a model of 'personality development'. Up until adolescence, Hourd (ibid.,

p. 66) remarks: 'The teacher's main purpose is to combine the psychological and aesthetic aims; to mould the child to the character without the loss of any sincerity of expression.' At this crucial threshold, however, the aims begin to receive different emphases; and this leads to the ultimate ascendency of the aesthetic aim, depending on age and, significantly, the type of school.

> I would say that between nine and twelve these two aims could be kept in fairly good balance, but that between the ages of twelve and fifteen the psychological purpose should be weighted more heavily, whilst in later adolescence, that is in the fifth and sixth forms of the grammar school, the aesthetic aim would take precedence. (Ibid., pp. 63-4)

In short, as the anthropologists remind us, adolescence is not a purely biological threshold. It occurs within the normative pattern of a particular administration of life, and is often connected to systems for differentiating the special social personalities such a 'form of life' requires.

Such is the case here. The supercession of the psychological aim by the aesthetic, which is achieved through the introduction of poetry writing and appreciation, is linked to the segregation inside a governmental pedagogy of a stratum from which the next generation of teachers will be drawn. The important thing for us to observe is that with the ascendency of the aesthetic aim, the disciplinary techniques 'interiorised' by psychology are reshaped by the categories and practices of aesthetic self culture, which thereby finally enter the social sphere.

This reshaping is achieved in two stages. First, in the creative writing exercise of early adolescence, the psychologically inflected norms of personality development are gradually transformed by the introduction of the dialectical norms of ethical self-shaping. So, in a strategy that will be familiar to all those who have learned or taught English, Hourd elicits poems from her students and judges them according to their degree of success in integrating 'form and meaning': that is, according to the degree to which a student's fantasies and ideas have been transformed by something 'freshly seen', and his perceptions informed by valuation.

> Now in the third poem, the imagination is doing its work at top speed. This is the kind of vision which Ruskin called 'seeing to the heart'. The eye has certainly rested on the object—colour, size,

position, texture; all are there in the first four lines. In the second and third verses, the child's eye moves and takes in the snowdrop's world and then relates it to her own. So that when we return to the breathing, nodding flowers of the last two lines, it is with our vision of them enlarged and deepened. Nothing is seen with the eye of the imagination which does not produce an accompaniment of feeling. The child may or may not moralise the scene–that is not the point. The question is whether she has felt with her senses awake; if she has, then the morality which follows will be an intrinsic part of the whole vision, as is the exquisite morality of this little piece. (Hourd, 1949, p. 84)

In another production, however, Hourd (ibid., p. 83) judges that 'there is not one word which gives an indication that [the student's] eyes were open', it betrays a 'composing legalism' and is both 'dishonest' and 'immature'. Transposing developmental norms into the aesthetic register, she decides that such failures are either didactic ('oversublimated') or sentimental ('undersublimated'), unlike the successful poem which achieves a perfect reconciliation of the psycho-ethical antinomies in the 'fusion of idea and image'.

The echoes of Schiller and Coleridge, Arnold and Pater are, of course, unmistakable. But equally unmistakable is the fact that their virtuoso aesthetic discipline has undergone a decisive and irrevocable transformation. Resumed on the interior of a psyche developing according to socially administered norms, it is not the relation to the self that is shaped in the play of thought and feeling, form and meaning, but the relation to another. As Hourd herself remarks:

The relation between this form of authority [i.e., the teacher's] and the authority of form is a very interesting one. The teacher's integrity stands to the child's creativeness in much the same relation as the form of a work of art stands to the meanings within it. (Ibid., p. 128)

In short, the formerly esoteric discipline of ethical self-shaping has been transformed into a systematically administered test. Focusing and modifying the relation of psycho-moral supervision, the world-historical tasks of aesthetic reconciliation have been transformed into the means by which a teacher can decipher and mould a student's socio-moral sensibility. It was in this form – and not as the harbinger of 'man's' complete development, or its ideological deformation – that culture entered the social sphere.

At the same time this new test marks the point at which the student moves to take over the task of self-culture for himself. This is not, as Hourd thinks, because he has inherited responsibility for the fullness of his own being, becoming conscious for the first time of that which he must become in order to be 'whole'. Rather, it is because this is the form in which the student internalises the function of moral surveillance itself: finding in himself the onerous ethical antinomies and thereby beginning to shape a 'balanced' self as the condition of shaping the selves of others.

This second and final stage of the aesthetic subsumption of a developmental pedagogy is marked by the transition to the practice of criticism: a transition which marks the passage of those entering the 'Sixth Form' literature class and from there the university English School. Hourd remarks that:

> the final aim of the teacher who gives scope for original composition in prose and verse is that ultimately a reconciliation of the form and meaning shall place; the final aim of the teaching of poetry appreciation is that the child shall reach a reconciliation of subjective and objective interpretation. (Ibid., p 115)

Once again this régime of reading is managed by the teacher, who must allow the student to 'find himself' in the poem while remaining the repository of an authoritative interpretation against which the student's response can be corrected. But now the teacher's job is concentrated in determining the precise point at which to withdraw from this mediating position. The aim is to allow the machine of surveillance to work by itself, as the student finds in the reading and teaching of literature the rhythm of empathy and correction in himself.

In fact Hourd has left us a remarkable record of this final transition. It occurs, as we should expect, in the case of a trainee teacher whom she is supervising. Hourd published this student-teacher's exemplary lesson notes, which record the planning and execution of a creative writing class.

> My tutor suggested that I should ask my class to write some poetry. I did not prepare the lesson in any way. I only knew that I wanted the children to write and I had no idea how to make them want to.

While the register was being called before my lesson, I glanced idly through 'Common Sense English Course' and found a poem on Spring. I gave them the page and they read the poem to themselves. After a while I asked what it was about, and they told me. I then told them to close their books and forget all about Spring, because we had not got there yet. In what season were we? Autumn – Winter? These two I wrote up and the majority said it was not yet winter. We then discussed autumn weather. The day was dull and foggy, but the day before had been a lovely one. I reminded them that yesterday was autumn, too: could they think of words to describe that day; or any sentences? . . .

There follows a list of 'impressionistic' words and phrases. She continues:

Everything I was given I accepted and wrote up on the board, . . . I then read through the list and suggested that there was enough material there for many poems. . .

One or two set to work immediately, but the majority cried that they could not make things rhyme. I told them that rhyme was not necessary, . . . To every query on form I answered that they could do as they wished. They were given complete freedom to write. . .

At a later date my tutor came in and suggested that I gave another lesson of the same type. Actually we shared it. The results were not as satisfactory as in the first instance, and for that I consider myself responsible, because I was not prepared *in my mind* for the lesson and it therefore lost its spontaneity and the feeling of the first lesson that we were discovering and making something together. This second lesson did give something that the first had not. One child, who would never do anything at all in any lesson, did in the last few minutes write this line, 'Edgar, Hugo, Mary and John, went for a walk one day'. (Ibid., pp. 180–1)

After comparing this trainee (who may have 'over-identified' with the lesson and thereby lost some variety and individuality in the expression) with a second one (who may have 'under-identified', reaching 'the children's fears and wishes' but sacrificing aesthetic value) Hourd comments:

The first student has understood, however, what she did in a very interesting way . . . she says that in the second lesson she was 'not prepared in mind', and here she has touched on the spring which

leads into much of the argument of this book. She did not know
what she was going to do, nor even *how* she was going to do it.
She had not prepared her first lesson but *she was prepared for it*,
two very different things. She had *refreshed* her mind ready . . .
was resilient, ready to move in any direction. In other words,
Schiller's 'point of nullity' had been reached. She was in an
aesthetic state of mind. (Ibid., p. 185)

In other words, we might rejoin, by the 1940s it had become
possible to incorporate the caste discipline of aesthetic self-culture
into the normalising machinery of a governmental pedagogy, as the
means of forming the English teacher: that exemplary 'lever' who
might 'raise the whole mass'. If this mutation permitted the popular
teacher to acquire the exemplary attributes of the critic this was not
because, in English, culture had found a way of realising its
promise of 'full' human development at the level of 'society as a
whole'. But neither was it because a moralising ideology had
succeeded in institutionalising itself in the educational system,
thereby blocking the social realisation of this promise in the
interests of a particular class. At the centre of these developments
we do not find the great dialectic of culture and society – governed
by the ethical division between thought and feeling or the political
division between consciousness and 'social being' – but a series of
piecemeal changes in a governmental apparatus and a minority
ethical discipline. It was, we can conclude, a series of technical
transformations that enabled literary pedagogy to assume the form
of a knowledge whose object was the psycho-moral development of
the personality. And these transformations simultaneously allowed
the discipline of aesthetic self-culture to enter the pedagogical
apparatus, absorbing at a certain point the techniques of moral
supervision, and permitting them to surface 'inside' the future
teacher where they could 'work by themselves'.

These changes produced neither a body of missionaries capable
of bestowing the promise of culture on 'society as a whole', nor an
ideological élite bent on sublimating the democratic social
realisation of this promise into the moral excellence of the few.
Instead, they produced an ethical technology directed to forming
the moral attributes of a citizenry, but a technology also capable of
forming a stratum of ethical exemplars from this citizenry: the
teachers of English. We have seen that this division is in part
aligned with the economic divisions between the classes. (Hourd

locates the threshold between the developmental and aesthetic aims of English according to age *and* type of school). Nonetheless, the division itself is the product of an apparatus that cuts a tangent through class boundaries and redistributes their contents according to specific governmental imperatives. Establishing a limited continuum between moral apprenticeship and self-cultivation permits popular literary pedagogy to enter the universities, and the popular teacher to assume the exemplary attributes and public standing of the man of letters.

This transitional point in fact marks the centre of English as a complex of administrative, pedagogical, ethical and aesthetic forms. Stretching in one direction, English encompasses the pedagogical functions of expression and correction embodied in the normative space of the classroom. While moving in the other, it incorporates the specialist dialectic of feeling and thought, spontaneity and method, through which criticism shapes the exemplary personages in whom these functions are to be embodied. At the cross-over point – marked by the student-teacher's resumption of the failed lesson as a sign of her own failure to shape a self in which 'the children's fears and wishes' would be opened to aesthetic moulding – we find the fulcrum on which English is balanced: the exchange of functions between an apparatus for the government of populations and a discipline for the culture of the self.

At this point of exchange we have seen that the teaching of literature could itself become a species of criticism: the English lesson providing the ethical antinomies through which the teacher shapes a persona through which his students can disclose themselves to knowledge and correction. But the exchange also worked in the other direction. Through it criticism itself began to assume the form of a special kind of pedagogy or moral training. And this is not just to say that, from the 1920s, criticism as it had been practised by Johnson and Coleridge, Kames and Arnold, began to be taught in colleges and universities as a means of training teachers. It is to indicate that once deployed in the apparatus of a governmental pedagogy, criticism found its own object and function decisively transformed. If under these circumstances teaching could become a species of criticism, then so too could criticism assume the functions of moral supervision. In the second part of this study I indicate some of the consequences of this exchange for the formation of modern criticism.

Part II

Criticism

5
Two Models

It appears that criticism today is in a state of flux. It is pulled in one direction by its role as a moral discipline, and in another by its mission to take its place as a knowledge alongside the other human sciences. It is championed by some who locate its object in the luminous and unsurpassable moment of the literary response. And it is challenged by others who see in this response nothing more than the experience of a 'pre-theoretical' subjectivity: an experience which must be clarified and transcended through a fundamental reflection on its linguistic, psychological or social conditions of possibility.

Recently the word 'crisis' has been applied to this state of the field.[1] Perhaps these uncertainties indicate radical instabilities in a discipline about to undergo a fundamental mutation. But then again perhaps they indicate nothing more than movements between positions built into the field as options from the very beginning. I leave this open for the moment. Certainly the objective of this final part of the study is nothing so ambitious as to resolve these uncertainties, through a magisterial 'return to the text' or a foundational reflection on its abstract conditions. My focus here is much narrower: to describe what happened when the noble life, shaped by criticism as a minority ethical practice, was deployed as a norm inside a governmental pedagogy. At the same time, it should not surprise us if in describing this transformation – which had such profound consequences for the field in which criticism finds its forms and functions – we should also shed some light on the contours of the current debate.

Let us begin by examining two texts representing different but equally characteristic dimensions of modern criticism. The first is a piece of 'practical criticism' by R. P. Blackmur, and in fact cited by John Crowe Ransom as exemplifying the 'New Criticism' in the preface to his book of that name. Ransom's citation begins with

Blackmur making some comparative remarks concerning aesthetic achievement.

> If we may say that in Shelley we see a great sensibility the victim of the early stages of religious and philosophical decay in the nineteenth century, and that in Swinburne we see an even greater poetic sensibility vitiated by the substitution of emotion for subject matter, then it is only a natural step to see in Hardy the consummate double ruin of an extraordinary sensibility that had been deprived of both emotional discipline and the structural support of a received imagination.

But the body of this citation is taken up with Blackmur's explication of the Emily Dickinson stanza:

> Renunciation
> Is a piercing virtue,
> The letting go
> A presence for an expectation –
> Not now.

and I reproduce it in an abbreviated form.

> The words are all simple words, parts of our stock vocabulary. Only one, *renunciation*, belongs to a special department of experience or contains in itself the focus of a particular attitude, a department and an attitude we condition ourselves to keep mostly in abeyance. We know what renunciation is; we know it turns up as heroism or hypocrisy or sentimentality; and we do as little as possible about it. Only one word, *piercing*, is directly physical; something that if it happens cannot be ignored but always shocks us into reaction. It is the shock of this word that transforms the phrase from a mere grammatical tautology into a metaphorical tautology which establishes as well as asserts identity. Some function of the word *pierce* precipitates a living intrinsic relation between renunciation and virtue; it is what makes the phrase incandesce . . . It is – if we may provisionally risk saying so – the physical elements in the word *pierce* and the participal phrase *letting go* that, by acting upon them, make the other words available to feeling, and it is the word *renunciation*

that, so enlightened, focuses the feeling as actuality. (Blackmur in Ransom, 1941, pp. viii-x)

As an exemplification of one of the central forms in which we have come to know modern criticism these quotations are entirely apt. Ransom (ibid., p. x) comments that 'Critical writing like this is done in our time. In depth and precision at once it is beyond all earlier criticism in our language. It is a new criticism. . .'. And allowing for the euphoria of the innovator we can both agree and disagree. If, for example, we were to make a detailed comparison between Blackmur's text and some parallel passages taken, say, from Matthew Arnold's essays on Wordsworth and Keats, we would find continuities as well as discontinuities.

Both critics work with the Romantic dialectic between feelings and ideas, and between the poet's message and the 'received imagination' or poetic form in which it is embodied. For example, Arnold (1888, p. 150) is concerned that in some of Wordsworth's poetry moral ideas are conveyed too philosophically, as 'doctrine', resulting in 'a tissue of elevated but abstract verbiage, alien to the very nature of poetry'. Such verse, Arnold (ibid., p. 151) says, 'has itself not the character of poetic truth of the best kind; it has no real solidity'. Like Blackmur's Shelley, Arnold's Wordsworth is also in part the victim of nineteenth-century 'philosophical decay'. We can compare Arnold's demand for 'solidity' with Blackmur's claim that it is the 'physical' quality of the word 'piercing' in the Dickinson stanza that makes the abstract idea of renunciation 'available to feeling'. And indeed Arnold (ibid., p. 153) avers that Wordsworth's poetry attains greatness because of its capacity to transcend its tendency to abstract assertion in favour of feeling: 'because of the extraordinary power with which Wordsworth feels the joy offered to us in nature. . .; and because of the extraordinary power with which . . . he shows this joy, and renders it so as to make us share it.'

For his part, Arnold's Keats, like Blackmur's Swinburne, reveals the complementary imbalance of displaying too much feeling in a poetry whose sensuousness lacks the discipline of moral ideas. Hence Keats is at his best only when he brings his luxurious feelings before the bench of 'the mighty *abstract idea* of beauty in all things'. In this way, comments Arnold (ibid., p. 116): 'He has made himself remembered as no merely sensuous poet could be; and he has done it by having "loved the principle of beauty in all things".'

On the other hand, a detailed comparison would also verify the signs of a decisive transformation in the deployment of the critical dialectic. We forget how far, in deciphering imbalances in the poetry, the nineteenth-century critic is exhibiting their disfiguring effects in the poet. Not the poet as a biographical individual – Arnold deplored the publication of Keats' letters to Fanny Brawne as 'inexcusable' – but as an exemplary ethical type, the model for the noble life. Criticising one of these letters Arnold remarks:

> We have the tone, or rather the entire want of tone, the abandonment of all reticence and all dignity, of the merely sensuous man, of the man who 'is passion's slave' . . . It is the sort of love-letter of a surgeon's apprentice which one might hear read out in a breach of promise case, or in the Divorce Court. The sensuous man speaks in it, and the sensuous man of a badly bred and badly trained sort. That many who are themselves also badly bred and badly trained should enjoy it, and should even think it a beautiful and characteristic production of him whom they call their 'lovely and beloved Keats', does not make it better. (Ibid., pp. 103–4).

Not even in F. R. Leavis at his most *ad hominem,* and certainly not in Blackmur's criticism, do we find the same propensity to read-off from aesthetic failure the contours of an ethical failure that is simultaneously personal and social. But this is not because, as Ransom would have it, the didactic and moralising tendencies of nineteenth-century criticism have been definitively superceded: cast into pre-history by a disinterested New Criticism whose 'depth and precision' have enabled it to locate the object of criticism in the exemplary topography of the poem itself. In fact, as we have observed, the ethical antinomies of Romantic criticism reappear inside this topography: but their point of application, and hence their function, has shifted. It is no longer the personage shaped or deciphered by the ethical dialectic who is exemplary. This function has now been invested in the magisterial performance of the critical reading. It is in the reading itself rather than in the artist's life that feelings and ideas, form and meaning, must be reconciled. Moreover, this can no longer be achieved through the calm assurance of the Arnoldian example or 'touchstone'. A critic like Blackmur must demonstrate this achievement in a reading in which the idea of reconciliation now functions as a norm, not only for the critic's own performance, but also for his reader's. In short,

Blackmur's criticism bears testimony to the fact that during the early decades of this century the *caste practice* of literary self-shaping was being redeployed as a *pedagogical procedure,* and the *ethical idea* of the balanced self was assuming the functions of a *pedagogical norm.*

We can provide a second co-ordinate for this transformation by turning to our second text, which is taken from I. A. Richards' *Principles of Literary Criticism.* Unlike Blackmur, Richards is not concerned with registering the ebb and flow of the literary response, but with providing it with theoretical foundations. It turns out – the precise reasons need not concern us at the moment – that as a result of the twin theories of communication and of value chosen as foundations, Richards' theory of criticism is organised around a particular crux. Briefly, because he makes communication and value depend upon the organisation of psychological impulses (themselves the traces of stimulus-response situations), and because different individuals may possess different psychological organisations ('attitudes'), nothing intrinsic to the poem or its readers guarantees uniformity of interpretation and evaluation. Richards solves this problem by appealing to 'the normality of the artist': that is, to a 'fineness' of psychological organisation which – achieved through the stabilising modality of poetic form – functions as a norm for other (deviant) organisations.

Richards (1924, p. 194) comments: 'To be normal is to be a standard, but not, as things are and are likely to remain, an average; and to inquire into the characters of the norm or to ask who are normal is to raise a question as to value.' And it is Richards' appeal to the normal and normalising psycho-ethical organisation of the poet as a foundation for meaning and value that provides the focus of our second text.

At any moment, in any situation, a variety of attitudes i.e., impulse organisations is possible. Which is the best is decided not only by the impulses which gain organised satisfaction in the attitude but also the effect of the attitude upon the rest of the organisation of the individual. We should have to consider the whole system and all the possibilities of all probable situations which might arise if we were to be sure that any one attitude is the best. Since we cannot do this, but can only note the most obvious objections to some, we have to be content if we can avoid those attitudes which are most evidently wasteful.

For the normality of the poet is to be estimated in terms of waste. Most human attitudes are wasteful, some to a shocking degree. The mind which is, so far as can be seen, least wasteful, we take as a norm or standard, and, if possible, we develop in our degree similar experiences. The taking of the norm is for the most part done unconsciously by mere preference, by the shock of delight which follows the release of stifled impulse into organised freedom. Often the choice is mistaken, the advantage which leads to preference is too localised, involves losses in the end, losses round the next corner as it were.

Little by little experience corrects such illusory preference, not through reflection – almost all critical choices are irreflective, spontaneous, as some say – but through unconscious reorganisation of impulses. (Ibid., pp. 197–8)

In Richards' work, it would appear criticism had at least taken the first steps towards theorising its own possibility as a knowledge. If the Romantic antinomies remain, they are not as in Blackmur, deployed in the form of an exemplary reading. Instead, their job in Richards' theory is to harmonise and articulate the organisation of impulses – the unconscious structure of subjectivity – on which such a reading depends. In short, it seems that with Richards criticism has entered the realm of the human sciences posing, if not solving, the problem of how meaning and value are given to consciousness.

In fact, however, Richards' theoretical and Blackmur's practical criticism are not related as contraries but as inseparable parameters for the field of modern criticism. To see this it is enough to observe that Richards' fundamental psychological organisation itself – as he says – has the role of a norm. The unconscious reorganisation of the psychological impulses which makes meaning and value possible also assumes the form of the conscious emulation of the exemplary poetic organisation in which they are embodied. And it is this oscillation in Richards' pursuit of foundations that allows it to overlap with Blackmur's practical criticism: the latter providing, of course, precisely the emulable demonstration of poetic organisation required by the former.

In fact, in these two new developments of the Romantic critical dialectic – as the form in which the reader must approximate a normative demonstration of ethical reconciliation in the balanced literary response; and as the form in which the theorist recovers the unconscious foundation of this response in the structure of subjectivity – we have located the central co-ordinates of modern criticism. Now we must ask: What is it that allows a practice of reading, launched as a normative display of the aesthetic response, to return as a description of the unconscious condition which makes the response possible; and, reciprocally, for this foundational description to itself take on the normative function of the exemplary reading? In this final part of our study it is argued that this exchange between the domain of criticism and that of the human sciences – an exchange which rather than fixing criticism as a discipline, sets the parameters inside which it varies as an institution – this exchange, I will argue, could only take place in the apparatus of literary pedagogy whose formation we have just described.

We have seen that it was through its redeployment inside this apparatus that criticism's ethical ideal could take on the role of a norm operative in the cultural regulation of target populations. But we have also seen that inside this apparatus, as a condition of criticism's redeployment as pedagogy, a new object had been formed: the psycho-ethical development of the student, revealed to the teacher's normalising observation on the surface of the literary response. Now we shall see that it was through this object that criticism (whose object is the development of sensibility) and the human sciences (whose object is the unconscious formation of the human subject) could meet. We shall take the structure of Richards' 'experiments' in practical criticism as representative in this regard. For in them the 'reconciliatory' reading, employed as a pedagogical norm or 'task of behaviour', also functions as a means for revealing the state of the psycho-ethical unconscious to the corrective observation of the teacher-critic.

At the close of the last chapter we saw how, in the highly particular circumstances clustered around the cultural qualification of the teacher, it became possible for criticism to enter the pedagogical sphere and for the teaching of English to acquire the ethical functions of criticism. It now remains to round-off this discussion by showing how in these circumstances criticism itself acquired the functions of a special pedagogy. And this does not mean that criticism simply found a new home in the school system where its essential functions remained unchanged. It means, rather, that the techniques of criticism were put to new uses inside a quite new cultural machinery: one which transformed both the object and the subject of criticism by making them inseparable from the régime of norms, the relations of supervision and correction and the instituted strategies of the educational apparatus. This new machinery, whose development depended on the intervention of the human sciences is, I shall argue, the decisive factor in the genealogy of modern criticism.

Today the historian of modern criticism has two major models at his disposal. The first of these derives from the tradition of Romantic criticism and cultural history and takes as its object the historical realisation of an essential aesthetic experience. The second derives from the field of the human sciences and takes as its object the historical discovery of the structures which make aesthetic experience possible. According to the first model – whose modern monuments are Wellek's *A History of Modern Criticism* and Wimsatt and Brooks' *Literary Criticism: A Short History* – the history of criticism is driven by a series of exemplary oscillations between its didactic and aestheticist tendencies. This dialectic leads inexorably to the moment of modern criticism. Modern criticism is the destiny of a history in which the antinomic topographies of the text and the self coalesce in an unsurpassable experience, one that reconciles the will to extract the content of literature for some extrinsic purpose and the desire to take pleasure in its form for its own sake. While according to the second model – which has yet to receive a definitive statement but which we can discern in a number of recent works including Eagleton's *Criticism and Ideology* and Todorov's *Theories of the Symbol* – the development of criticism is marked not by dialectical progression but by the moment of theoretical rupture and historical discontinuity. This moment, which may recur, in fact divides the history of criticism, or poetics, from its pre-history, and is marked by the (final or anticipatory) discovery of the abstract structures of literary subjectivity.

In this chapter we put some questions to both these historiographies. With regards to the exemplary history which the New Criticism has provided for itself, our attention is drawn to its dialectical form. What does it mean when a history of modern criticism employs the same method as its object – dividing criticism's past into didactic and formalist tendencies and arriving at its destiny through a practice of reconciliation? We begin to suspect a illicit intimacy between modern criticism and its New Critical historiography, sharing as they do a method which is first and foremost a technique for performing a particular ethical work on the self.

As far as the historical model of the human sciences is concerned – organised around the moment in which criticism's 'pre-theoretical' calm is shattered by the fundamental discovery of its conditions of possibility – our attention is engaged by a certain normativity in its disposition. What does it mean that this moment, in which the unthought first appears to consciousness, also functions as a 'task of behaviour' inside the educational apparatus? Is there not an equally suspect intimacy between the epochal *moment of problematisation* at the centre of this historical model and the existence of a regimen in which individuals are *required to problematise* their literary responses? In order to explore these questions and develop the lines of an alternative genealogy for modern criticism it is necessary to investigate both of the major historiographical models in a little more detail.

II

It is significant that in the epilogue to their history of criticism Wimsatt and Brooks should express their concern regarding the historicising tendencies of literary research in the American graduate school. This research, by transforming questions of meaning and value into empirical questions concerning the historical deployment of texts, is, they suggest, jeopardising the ethical function of criticism and threatening to turn its history into a directionless catalogue of taste. In forthrightly stating that their history has been written against these tendencies, the authors reveal that it is also an apology for a certain kind of criticism which they deploy as an historical norm or telos.

> We can study the history of changes in opinion, writes T. S. Eliot in his short history of English criticism, 'without coming to the stultifying conclusion that there is nothing to be said but that opinion changes.' The present writers have not written this short history of literary opinion without seeing in it a pattern of effort pointing toward at least a certain kind of goal. (Wimsatt and Brooks, 1957, p. 735)

A little further on they specify the character of criticism's historical goal in terms of the nature of its object: a universal aesthetic experience or meaning arising from the unique relation between 'form' and 'message' in literature.

> Nevertheless our final view, implicit in our whole narrative and in whatever moments of argument we may have allowed ourselves, has been that 'form' in fact embraces and penetrates 'message' in a way that constitutes a deeper and more substantial meaning than either abstract message or separable ornament. In both the scientific or abstract dimension and in the practical or rhetorical dimension there *is* both message and the means of conveying message, but the poetic dimension is just that dramatically unified meaning which is coterminous with form. This is true both in the sense that all verbal discourse, no matter how unpoetic, has this poetic aspect, and in the more special sense that certain instances of verbal discourse are almost unsusceptible of abstractive message reading, and these are poems (in verse and prose) in the most special and excellent sense. (Ibid., p. 748).

The history of criticism has a goal because 'poetry' – the term, significantly, is used as a synonym for literature – has an essence in the imperative reconciliation of form and meaning. It is this essence – aesthetic meaning or the aesthetic experience – that constitutes the absolute horizon of all literary theory, history and ethics. Just in case we are in any doubt about this Wimsatt and Brooks (ibid., p. 745) remark: 'For the theater of poetic conflict is human substance itself, ethical substance, as Hegel put it; the conflict is of man with himself or of good and evil in man.' And they continue that it is for just such a 'literary substance' that 'ontological' New Critics like Allen Tate and John Crowe Ransom have been searching. The goal of the history of criticism lies in an aesthetic language which articulates the full nature of 'man'.

Our authors begin their trek to this historical rendezvous with 'man's' aesthetic being with a more modest attempt to specify the nature of poetry. This they do by differentiating it from what they take to be its eternal opposite: the formulaic utterance or 'cliché'. The cliché fails in both aesthetic dimensions simultaneously. It is an ornamental utterance in which form is emphasized at the expense of meaning. But for precisely this reason it can be used by orators to deliver messages governed by narrow utilitarian purposes, thereby falling short of the ultimate disinterestedness of the poetically embodied imagination.

It is, of course, a familiar opposition and it is no accident that Wimsatt and Brooks find in it the genesis of the modern aesthetic, focused for them in the debate between Wordsworth and Coleridge over poetic diction. According to Wimsatt and Brooks the two Romantics provide different accounts of the cliché or formulaic utterance. For Wordsworth such utterances fail aesthetically because true poetry is rooted in expression of the untutored feelings. While Coleridge puts their inadequacy down to failure to master inherited poetic form: something which demands a good deal of tutoring. Through this dialectical account Wimsatt and Brooks not only find the division of ethical substance given to them in the very nature of poetry, they also find a pretext for the dialectical practice which is at the heart of their history. So, reconciling Wordsworth and Coleridge they argue that formulaic expression is renovated through a return to the transcendental (that is, disinterested) experience of the feelings and nature; but this return, in the case of the Romantics, was only achieved through the innovation of a new poetic form.

We are not yet finished with the problem of the cliché. For the moment, however, we can observe that having thus to their own satisfaction defined an essence for the aesthetic sphere – in the capacity of poetry to reconcile form and meaning, symbol and feelings – Wimsatt and Brooks can deploy it as the goal of the history of criticism. Given this goal criticism can only move in one of two directions: towards content and the heresy of didacticism or towards form and the heresy of aestheticism. And the history of criticism or the 'defence of poetry' can only assume the form of two complementary movements whose dialectic reduces the *differentia* of historical deployments to the realisation of a telos which finally transcends history altogether. Both the pattern of this history and its goal, as Wimsatt and Brooks 'discover' them in nineteenth-century criticism, are made clear in the following remark:

> The later romantic development in the theory of creative 'imagination' afforded, however, a more complex and ambiguous base from which the English defence of poetry during the 19th century could proceed. For one thing, the defence might and did continue along the line of autonomy oriented toward pleasure – art for art's sake – . . . But it might also . . . wax into the

assertion of a new, autonomous, didacticism (more or less revolutionary). And this didacticism had at least two main phases, the rhapsodic (Shelleyan) and a later more calmly classical and cognitive (the Arnoldian. . .). The dual defence of poetry during the 19th century – the hedonistically autonomic, and the didactically autonomic – was a thoroughly plausible outcome and illustration of the ambivalent poise achieved in the continental defence of poetry by the end of the 18th century and taken over by Coleridge and Wordsworth. (Ibid., p. 425)

Perhaps so: but only if this poise – this reconciliation of meaning and form – is, as our authors claim, the universal form of literature, discovered by the Romantics and the object of criticism ever since. That this is not the case can be very quickly demonstrated by returning to Wimsatt and Brooks' discussion of the cliché and its difference from poetry. In fact here we find not one account of the difference, but two.

The first, as we have seen, works by playing-off Wordsworth's emphasis on feeling against Coleridge's stress on form, and produces an account of poetry as the renovation of cliché through the formal embodiment of personal feeling and experience. The second account, however, is quite different because it has to deal with an important and potentially unmanageable fact. This fact, as Wimsatt and Brooks acknowledge it, is that one cannot at all times and in all circumstances tell the difference between the formulaic and the truly poetic expression. On the one hand, one of Shakespeare's sonnets submitted today to a popular magazine under another name is likely to be rejected as hackneyed. On the other, it is difficult to detect clichéd writing because it may consist of new and original expressions. 'The logic of the situation', they comment (ibid., p. 356), 'would suggest that even ingenuity and originality are no sure proofs against the cliché.' The problem with clichés is not that they have been used before, but that they are words 'out of place'. 'The real character of their offensiveness (or presumable offensiveness) does not lie in their newness or oldness, but in the difficulty one has in conceiving an excuse for them' (ibid., p. 356).

The importance of this second account, with its unexpected echoes of the rhetorical doctrine of decorum, is that it opens the door on a possibility that Wimsatt and Brooks otherwise attempt to keep firmly closed. This is the possibility that 'poetry' or the aesthetic experience is not a universal given to 'man' by virtue of his ethical substance, but is in fact a limited and contingent phenomenon whose recognition is the outcome of specific historical *conditions* or *techniques*. Recognition of the 'truly poetic' in this second account is not a timeless experience of the human subject available in all contexts. It depends on the practical mastery of a certain discriminatory routine – to respond in this way rather than that – and hence on the cultural regimen in which this is a required practice. It is possible to suggest, therefore, that despite its mortgage on transcendental disinterestedness and its claims to universality, the Romantic dialectic of form and meaning is in fact a special cultural technique. We thus arrive by a route appropriate to the domain of criticism at a point already made in our investigation of the concept of culture. By providing the reader with the *imperative* to divide 'literary substance' into a designing message and an autonomous form, and the *readerly techniques* for playing-off each against the other, the Romantic dialectic established definite and limited historical conditions of possibility for the 'aesthetic experience'.

That this is so is suggested by historical and anthropological research into literary and cultural systems in which the Romantic distinction between the formulaic and the truly aesthetic does not pertain. For example, Albert Lord's investigation of the Yugoslav oral epic, in his *The Singer of Tales*, shows that in this case we are confronted by a poetry that is thoroughly and demonstrably formulaic. Using materials provided by a surviving oral culture, Lord sets out to verify Milman Parry's hypothesis that the recitative powers of the Homeric bards lay not in their possessing prodigious memories, but in the fact that they were trained in the use of a set of compositional formulas. These formulas, Lord deduced from his analysis of the training and techniques of the illiterate Yugoslav poets, permitted the bards to compose as they performed, like jazz musicians. Lord describes the young singer-bard's acquisition of the formulas as the imitative absorption of the poetic 'building-blocks' which are simultaneously rhythmic, syllabic and ideational units.

> These 'restrictive' elements he comes to know from much listening to the songs about him and from being engrossed in their imaginative world. He learns the meter ever in association with particular phrases, those expressing the most common and oft-repeated ideas of the traditional story. Even in pre-singing years rhythm and thought are one, and the singer's concept of the

formula is shaped though not explicit. He is aware of the successive beats and the varying lengths of repeated thoughts, and these might be said to be his formulas. (Lord, 1960, (p. 32)

'The most stable formulas', says Lord (ibid., p. 34) 'will be those for the most common ideas of the poetry. They will express the names of the actors, the main actions, time, and place.' And he exemplifies formulas of time (replete with Homeric overtones) by 'When dawn put forth its wings', and 'When the sun had warmed the earth'.

After a long apprenticeship in learning to manipulate these poetic building-blocks, the singer-bard gradually acquires the capacity to compose with them while performing: a capacity which includes the ability to improvise by substituting alternative elements within the syllabic, rhythmic and grammatical contexts established by the formulas. It should be clear that the pleasure taken by the audience of such a performance is not in the transformation of the formula by the personal experiences of a great individual. It is a pleasure in recognising the formula itself and then, subordinate to this, a pleasure in picking the improvisations made on it by a virtuoso performer: improvisations which, needless to say, never transform the formula itself, which remains the technical basis of the composition-performance.

Similarly, work by Walter Ong (1972) and Stephen Orgel (1971, 1975, 1978) on Renaissance rhetorical and courtly literature suggests that the Romantic opposition between the formulaic and the aesthetic is equally out of place in these contexts. Ong treats the rhetorical commonplaces and *sententiae* as part of a cultural system in which knowledge in personal and public life was fundamentally dependent on techniques of citation and commentary. Classical texts, proverbs, known truths and appropriate figures of speech recorded in the orator's commonplace book provided him with a repertoire of verbal possibilities. Furthermore, as Curtius (1948) has shown, the use of this repertoire was determined by the practical demands of private and public life: by the demands of law (the plea), diplomacy (the eulogy), government (the defence or apology) and of sovereignty (the court masque).

Under these circumstances the idea that literature should not serve practical purposes – that it should eschew the formulaic or renovate it through a profound return to personal experience – is not simply unknown, it is unintelligible; its conditions of possibility do not exist. And when these conditions do arrive they are not donated by the great historical dialectic whose goal is the synthesis of 'man's' divided ethical substance. Instead, they are built up gradually through local and contingent transformations. They are typified by such things as the invention of moveable type and the printing press, which helped to displace the compositional function of the rhetorical formulas and commonplaces by mass producing the varieties of literature in standard forms. These were amongst the circumstances in which the rhetorical commonplaces could become 'commonplace', and in which the Romantics could stage their revolt against poetic diction.[2]

But Wimsatt and Brooks have inadvertently allowed us to see that the Romantic dialectic can itself be placed amongst these local historical conditions for the appearance of the 'truly poetic'. If the aesthetic experience is not simply given and depends instead on the mastery of a discriminatory practice, then we must refer this experience not to the 'universal' relations between meaning and form but to the special aesthetico-ethical practice which puts these relations into play. And this shift of perspective allows us to posit a relation between the arts of criticism and poetry unlike the one in which it is imagined that the former have evolved to represent the relation between form and meaning embodied in the latter. If the dialectic of form and meaning is not given in the human ethical substance, and is in fact dependent on a special cultural practice, then it is posssible to suggest that Romantic poetry is itself read *and* written from within the parameters of this practice. In short, we can begin to see criticism and poetry as dual components of a single cultural regimen: criticism transmitting the imperatives and techniques of an ethical practice which resurface on the different (but no more fundamental) terrain of poetry. (We can note in passing that Coleridge's Conversation Poems, for example, are all concerned with reconciling the implacably alien forces of nature with the imperatives of the moral will. In this way they function as devices for a particular aesthetico-ethical exercise; and so too, it is worth noting, did non-verbal phenomena like waterfalls, gorges and mountains.)[3]

Needless to say, Wimsatt and Brooks move to close the door on this line of analysis as quickly and as quietly as possible. They do so, as one might expect, by removing the practice of the dialectic from its home in a specific cultural regimen, identifying it instead with a series of privileged universals: principally with the 'human psyche', the 'complexity of reality' and the 'nature of poetic language'. This strategy fails, however, as the unmistakably historical and contingent character of the aesthetic experience reasserts itself in a series of embarrassing moments in their historical narrative. We can take brief note of two such moments.

The first of these we owe to Leo Tolstoy. Tolstoy, it will be remembered, objected to certain aspects of the Romantic aesthetic. In particular he objected to its difficulty: to its interest in the more recondite formal features of literature which demanded a special education for their appreciation. The aesthetic interest, he declared, was the bauble of a socially privileged class of 'erudite, perverted people destitute of religion', and should be abolished in the name of comprehensibility. Armed with this criterion Tolstoy proceeded to lay waste to large tracts of classic European literature, sweeping away Shakespeare, Dante, Milton, Goethe and even 'Tolstoy' himself. In short, Tolstoy had the temerity to insist that one could not talk about art or the aesthetic without asking the question: 'Art for whom?'

Reformulating his argument for our own purposes, we can say that Tolstoy pointed out that the Romantic aesthetic with its difficult dialectic was not a universal feature of 'man's ethical substance'; it was the reserved discipline of a specially-trained social caste. Of course, Tolstoy did not push his argument to the point of rejecting the idea of a universal aesthetic, as the following quotation shows:

> Art is differentiated from activity of the understanding, which demands preparation and a certain sequence of knowledge. . ., by the fact that it acts on people independently of their state of development and education, that the charm of the picture, of sounds, or of forms, infects any man whatever his plane of development. (Tolstoy, 1930, p. 178)

Remaining firmly within the Romantic aesthetic, Tolstoy simply wanted to transfer the locus of its universality from the Great Works to the simple religious poetry of peasants and children. The significance of this populist project is that it shows, firstly, how tenuous is the claimed universality of classic art and, secondly, that the idea of a universally accessible art presupposes a transcendental ground for the aesthetic experience. Tolstoy (loc. cit.), at least, is quite candid about this: 'Such art should be, and has actually always been, comprehensible to everybody, because every man's relation to God is one and the same.'

But Tolstoy's initial onslaught reminds us that every man's relation to poetry and the aesthetic experience is not the same: that this relation is contingent on the acquisition of special cultural techniques differentially distributed across time and social strata. This is what embarrasses Wimsatt and Brooks. In responding to the charges of élitism and aestheticism, however, Wimsatt and Brooks seek a guarantee for the universality of the aesthetic experience in semantics rather than in God. They argue that the aesthetic is universal in principle (if not in social fact) because poetic language has a 'cognitive' relation to experience, presumably based on the structure of the 'human psyche'; and this means 'poetry' itself must be a 'cognitive' object open to universal enjoyment. Armed thus with semantics, Wimsatt and Brooks can dissolve the problem of the uneven social and historical distribution of the aesthetic. They do so by describing the groups and classes who have not been trained in the use of aesthetic techniques not as 'differently educated', but as 'uneducated'. In other words, they convert *differences* in social competences into *deficiencies* in relation to a 'human' norm.

Our authors cannot press too far in this direction, however, without running into a second equally embarrassing problem. If the language of poetry is universal by virtue of its semantic structure, or its 'cognitive' relation to experience then, presumably, it is a discourse like any other and is subject to the same general criteria of meaning and truth – assuming for the sake of the argument that there are such things. In fact this is precisely what Yvor Winters argued in his *In Defence of Reason,* much to the discomfort of the literary fraternity, however. Like Tolstoy's, Winters' overall project need not detain us. All we need to note is his argument that if the language of poetry does share in a universal semantic structure, (that is, if it is to be subjected to general criteria for meaning and truth), then it must have a paraphrasable content or structure of statement open to 'external' validation. As a consequence, Winters (1947, pp. 35-74) argues, we must reject the Romantic doctrine of the unity of form and content as well as the modernist poetry that puts into practice.

In other words, in seeking to universalise 'poetry' by investing it with a semantic structure, Wimsatt and Brooks jeopardise its privileged standing as the only discourse capable of uniting form and meaning and hence reconciling 'man's' divided ethical substance. Unlike Winters, however, they are not prepared to sacrifice the aesthetic prerogative. Hence they are forced to argue against him that although (in some sense) semantic, aesthetic meaning and the aesthetic experience remain 'internal' to the structure of the 'poem itself' and cannot be paraphased and tested in the usual way. But in thus preserving the uniqueness of the aesthetic mode they forfeit its universality; because the 'organic' unity of form and meaning is not, *pace* Tolstoy, open to all readers, only those in possession of the Romantic dialectic.

Wimsatt and Brooks' desire to employ an essential aesthetic experience as the universal goal towards which all forms of criticism have been evolving thus lands them on the horns of a dilemma. *Either*, they can universalise 'poetry' by investing it with a general semantic structure – in the form of a 'cognitive' relation to reality in principle open to any subject – and hence with a meaning open to paraphrase and validation. But in this case poetry loses its privileged aesthetic standing, which consists precisely in the unparaphrasable unity of form and meaning. *Or*, they can retain the unique privilege of poetry in relation to other merely didactic discourses, by affirming that the aesthetic meaning and experience are 'internal' to the organic form of the poem. But once they thus affirm that the truth of the aesthetic experience cannot be asserted in all discursive contexts – indeed, that it cannot be asserted at all, only 'embodied' or 'dramatised' in poetic form – then the reader of poetry is no longer the (putatively) universal subject of semantics. The aesthetic experience appears once more as the result of a special ethical discipline, lacking general provenance or justification.

It is significant in this regard that when defending the organic character of aesthetic meaning, Wimsatt and Brooks (ibid., p. 604) do so in terms that recall the role of the Romantic dialectic as just such a discipline: 'An argument is the subject to refutation. The noble life, the song, the poem, are none of them subject to refutation. For the poem, like the life of the saint, does not state a proposition but embodies a meaning.' But, without necessarily disagreeing with this remark, we can rejoin that the question of *how* we are to lead the 'noble life' and, more importantly, *who* is to do so and to *what ends*, are not purely aesthetic questions concerning 'man's' ethical or semantic being. They are 'governmental' questions concerning the distribution of cultural techniques.

In short, Wimsatt and Brooks' argument remains poised on this dual condition: if 'poetry' is aesthetic it is not universal, and if it is universal then it is not aesthetic. This dilemma is inescapable for modern criticism and its historiography, because it is generated by their founding strategy: that is, by the attempt to universalise a specific historical deployment of criticism and literature. We have seen that neither of the two tactics – circular in any case – employed to resolve this dilemma will do the job. On the one hand, there is the idea that the Romantic dialectic is universalised in the organic structure of the 'poem itself' or, as Wimsatt and Brooks (ibid., p. 677) would have it: 'the notion that the developing poem furnishes the poet (and thence the critic) with certain norms for its own nurturing.' But this will not work because the Romantic poem, as we have seen, is not a natural object but an artefact of the very cultural practice whose norms our authors are attempting to justify.

On the other hand, Wimsatt and Brooks acknowledge that the aesthetic meaning is, as they put it, inseparable from the person who experiences it. In this case they attempt to move in the opposite direction by transforming the Romantic dialectic into something like a categorical imperative embedded in the figure of the 'ideal reader' or 'human psyche'. According to Wimsatt and Brooks (ibid., p. 677) the Romantic specifications of poetry 'suggest that the imagination obeys laws implicit in the human psyche. They even seem to demand the assumption that all human experience is finally one.' But this tactic is doomed to failure too because, as our authors themselves acknowledge in their discussion of the cliché, the capacity to reconcile form and meaning, ideas and feelings – and thereby discriminate the aesthetic from the formulaic – is not God-given, nor indeed bestowed by semantics, but is an artefact of the Romantic dialectic itself.

Wimsatt and Brooks' (ibid., p. 678) own comment on the consequences of abandoning the assumption of the unity-in-consciousness of all human capacities – 'Unless we can assume it, we necessarily abandon any concept of an aesthetics of poetry in favour of a tabulation of various kinds of social and personal expressions' – falls just wide of the mark, however. Abandoning the attempt to write a history of criticism in terms of the universal goal of the aesthetic experience does not entail accepting the subjectivity of taste or slipping into some imagined chaos of critical opinions. (A 'taste' for the aesthetic, we have argued, is anything but subjective.) Rather, it entails taking as the object of such a history (or genealogy) the specific *dispensation of cultural techniques* – the techniques of the Romantic dialectic itself, for example – which make the 'aesthetic experience' possible.

In other words, our aim must not be to dismiss the aesthetic experience as an ideological fiction or as the chimera of a naive empiricism awaiting theoretical clarification. Instead, it must be to map its emergence and deployment; to describe the *degree* of its generality; to uncover in what régime of life it functions, and whether as an ideal or as a norm. In satisfying these objectives we will be drawn back, slowly but surely, to the domains of pedagogy and government.

III

Our rejection of aesthetic experience as the goal for a history of criticism does not entail, however, that we accept the historiographical model provided by the human sciences: that is, the model in which this history is punctuated by a fundamental break with criticism based on experience and representation, and the theoretical recovery of their 'structural' conditions.

We have already noted that, in comparison with Wimsatt and Brooks' model of dialectical evolution towards the goal of aesthetic experience, this model of theoretical rupture is less monolithic and exists in a number of variant forms. So, we find accounts of criticism in which not only linguistic but also social, historical and pyschological structures are suddenly discovered beneath the apparent immediacy of literary experience. In all these accounts, however, the linguistic and semiotic enjoy a certain privilege: either absolute, as in Todorov (1977) or partial, as in Eagleton (1976) and Jameson (1981) – where linguistic structure functions as the agency through which social and historical imperatives are realised in the subject. Hence we will draw our main example of the history of criticism as a human science from the sphere of linguistics and the theory of the sign, commenting in passing on its relation to variant sociological and historical accounts.

In any case, Tzvetan Todorov's *Theories of the Symbol* probably contains the single most important history that we have of criticism as a human science. Todorov provides us with the key to this history in an earlier work in which he specifies the object of literary theory or poetics.

> It is not the literary work itself that is the object of poetics: what poetics questions are the properties of that particular discourse that is literary discourse. Each work is therefore regarded only as the manifestation of an abstract and general structure, of which it is but one of the possible realisations. Whereby this science is no longer concerned with actual literature, but with a possible literature in other words, with that abstract property that constitutes the singularity of the literary phenomenon: *Literariness*. The goal of this study is no longer to articulate a paraphrase, a descriptive resume of the concrete work, but to propose a theory of the structure and functioning of literary discourse, a theory that affords a list of literary possibilities, so that existing literary works appear as achieved particular cases. (Todorov, 1973, pp. 6–7)

We can treat Todorov's *Theories of the Symbol* as essentially a transposition of this moment of theoretical recovery into the register of history. And this is why his history of criticism is dominated by moments of break with those accounts of literature which treat it empirically, in terms of the experience it supposedly represents.

Significantly for our larger argument, the central moment of rupture, anticipating that of structuralist poetics and making it possible, is located, according to Todorov, precisely in German Romantic criticism. Here, he describes this moment in another text written around the same time as his *Theories:*

> It is with the advent of (German) romanticism that the notion of literature is established in its autonomy, and this is also the beginning of literary theory in the strict sense . . . The concepts of representation and imitation no longer play a dominant role, being replaced at the summit of the hierarchy by the concept of the beautiful, and those related to it: the absence of external finality, the harmonious coherence among the parts of the whole, the untranslatable character of the work of art. All these notions point towards the autonomy of literature and of its works, and lead to an inquiry into their specific properties. (Todorov, 1981, pp. xxv–vi)

Before passing on to examine Todorov's account of this transformation in more detail, it is worth observing that breaking with the critical interpretation of texts in favour of a semiotic description of their structural conditions does not entail dispensing with criticism altogether. The latter undergoes a mutation that gives it a new function, rather than a theoretical annihilation. According to Todorov, criticism's historical necessity is registered in the fact that it was responsible for rescuing literature from a variety of 'extrinsic' (rhetorical) deployments and establishing 'literary discourse' as a single autonomous object: that is, as the potential object of a general theory. If the historical relation between critical interpretation and semiotic description is thus one of mutual dependency, their theoretical relation is – again significantly for our larger argument – dialectical.

> *Poetics* breaks down the symmetry thus established between interpretation and science in the field of literary studies. In contradistinction to the interpretation of particular works, it does not seek to name meaning, but aims at a knowledge of the general laws that preside over the birth of each work. But in contradistinction to such sciences as psychology, sociology, etc., it seeks these laws within literature itself. Poetics is therefore an approach to literature at once 'abstract' and 'internal'. (Todorov, 1973, p. 6)

Or, as Todorov (1977, p. 278) puts it elsewhere: 'only formal relations (including those among meanings) can be *described* in coherent, unchallengeable language; individual semantic contents do not lend themselves to metalanguage, but only to paraphrase – which remains the business of the critic.'

We shall have cause to return to this remarkable conception of a paraphrase of 'individual semantic contents' which is simultaneously a recovery of 'the general laws that preside over the birth of each work'. Perhaps for the moment we can content ourselves with the remark that the idea of seeking the laws of literature 'within literature itself' seems, at first glance anyway, not entirely dissimilar to Wimsatt and Brooks' idea that the poem provides the poet and the critic with 'norms for its own nurturing': even if the dialectic between interpretation and structural description that permits the former is not identical with that between 'feeling and form' which permits the latter. Already it appears that our chief problem will be to map the circumstances of a convergence – taking place on the ground of the autonomy of literature – between two otherwise distinct dialectics.

In fact Todorov concludes his historical survey of *Theories of the Symbol* with his own account of such a convergence, as he finds it in the poetics of Roman Jakobson. In discussing the great Formalist's definition of the poetic function as a use of language not governed by an external object or a utilitarian purpose, but instead by 'the set toward the message as such, the focus on the message for its own sake', Todorov cites the following autobiographical remark from Jakobson:

> The controversial notion of *self-regulation (Selbstgesetz-massigkeit) of form*, to use the poet's language, underwent an evolution in this [the Russian Formalist] movement, from the earliest mechanistic stances to an authentically dialectical conception. This latter had already found a fully synthetic incitation, in Novalis's famous 'Monologue' – which had from the beginning astonished and bewitched me. (Jakobson, in Todorov, 1977, p. 272)

In other words, while Wimsatt and Brooks find in the Romantic idea of the organic and autotelic structure of poetry the form of an experience able to heal the split in 'man's' ethical being, Jakobson and Todorov for their part find a self-regulating structure. This form of language – in which signification is not derived from the purposes of a speaker or the representation of an object – Todorov calls 'symbolic'. And it is on the ground of the symbol that he gives his history of Romantic aesthetics as the revolutionary anticipation of modern structuralist poetics:

> Without exaggerating, we could say that if we had to condense the romantic aesthetic into a single word, it would certainly be the word 'symbol' . . . The entire romantic aesthetic would then be, in the last analysis, a semiotic theory. Conversely, in order to understand the modern meaning of the word 'symbol', it is necessary and sufficient to re-read the romantic texts. (Ibid., pp. 198–9)

Todorov begins his own re-reading of the Romantic aesthetic by constructing its break from a literary pre-history dominated by the principle of imitation and by the didactic intentions of the speaker: that is, by constructing its break from rhetorical poetics. (Todorov remarks in passing that his book could have been called *Rhetoric and Aesthetics*.) According to Todorov (ibid., p. 112) the principle of imitation 'is incompatible with the romantic outlook, in that it subjects works of art to a consideration that is external (anterior, superior) to them, namely nature'. And although he notes a number of variations in the doctrine of imitation – for example, the imitation of classical models and the imitation of a higher (neo-Platonic) model for nature itself – he treats these as 'confusions' in relation to the fundamental idea of imitating nature, because they smuggle in norms of beauty. Indeed, it is in this alleged incoherence that Todorov (ibid., pp. 111–28) locates the 'crisis' in rhetoric out of which aesthetics was supposedly born.

There is no need to dispute this rationalist account in detail. We can simply observe that if this 'incoherence' in imitation was indeed the crisis which marked the beginning of the end for rhetoric, then it was a long time coming. After all, the doctrine of imitation had included the imperatives to imitate Homer and the Heavenly City as well as nature – indeed, to imitate the latter *by* imitating the former – for some eighteen centuries before Romanticism. As Stephen Orgel (1978, p. 485) remarks of the arts of poetry and painting during the Renaissance: 'Both were said to imitate nature, but were in fact throughout the age primarily concerned with imitating models. Scaliger summed it up neatly by observing that we can best imitate nature by imitating Virgil.' And this is only a 'confusion' if one takes 'imitating nature' to mean representing the empirical contents of experience, or the empirical structure of reality – which of course eighteen-century rhetoricians did not. Todorov, on the other hand, has no option but to construe imitation in this anachronistic manner because he locates the object of poetics in the move from empirical representation to its theoretical conditions.

If the system of rhetorical poetics and its doctrine of imitation were being displaced during the eighteen-century – recall our earlier remarks on the transition from the commonplaces to the commonplace – it would be rash to attribute this to the doctrine being in error, or untrue to the nature of art. But this is precisely what Todorov (ibid., p. 128) does. He concludes his discussion of the rhetoricians by claiming that they used the principles of imitation and the beautiful without understanding their incompatibility or, 'if the conflict is noted, it is resolved unhesitatingly in favour of imitation. The latter, moreover, bears up rather badly under this favouritism: too much coddling makes it sickly. Aesthetic theory is at an impasse, and the nature of art eludes its grasp.' But 'art', we have already had cause to observe, does not signify a universal norm to which all literary systems must measure up, but a loose array of historical phenomena varying according to cultural régimes and cultural techniques.

In short, if Todorov locates the theoretical rupture which launches criticism as a human science in the 'Romantic revolt' against rhetorical poetics then, like Wimsatt and Brooks, he can only do so by privileging the Romantic aesthetic as the absolute horizon of historical development. In fact, in this he is both like and unlike the New Critics: *like*, in that he finds in the rhetorical tradition the didacticism and 'externality' that modern poetics must overcome if it is to be born true to 'literature itself'. *Unlike*, in that New Criticism finds in rhetoric one side of the dialectic whose reconciliatory movement issues in a transcendent aesthetic experience; Todorov finds it in the empirical relation to experience and social purpose which modern poetics will transcend through a sudden withdrawal from representation into the 'purely internal' relations which make it possible.

In describing the Romantic anticipation of this moment, Todorov lays his central emphasis on the familiar ideas of expression and organic form; not, however, without subjecting them to a thorough re-working. According to Todorov, the Romantics responded to the 'crisis' in rhetorical poetics – that is, to the putative incoherence of the principles of imitation and beauty – by abandoning the idea of representing 'external reality', concentrating instead on beauty conceived of as an internal disposition of parts. On the one hand, says Todorov (ibid., p. 154), this change of focus 'explains why, in the romantic aesthetic, the accent no longer falls upon the relation of representation (linking the work and the world) but upon the relationship of expression, the one that links the work and the artist'. Todorov labels this new relationship *productivity*. On the other hand, it launches the conception of the work of art as the manifestation of a set of purely internal relations: 'Like the world, the work of art is a self-sufficient totality; precisely to the extent that the work resembles the world, the former no longer needs to assert its relationship to the latter. The central concept of Mortiz's aesthetics is in fact, totality, and this is what he prefers to call the beautiful' (ibid., p. 155). And this fundamental shift from representation to systematicity Todorov describes under the heading of *coherence*.

Arranged around the central *topoi* of productivity and coherence are three other concepts through which Todorov completes his account of the genesis of structuralist poetics in the Romantic aesthetic. These are the concepts of *intransitivity, the inexpressible* and *syntheticism*, only the first two being important for our purposes. Under the heading of intransitivity, Todorov describes the autotelic or (as Arnold would have said) disinterested character of aesthetic discourse. If it is defined by the relation of expression rather than representation, and if expression is not governed by an imposed purpose or intention but instead by a group of 'purely internal' relations, then aesthetic discourse will not be 'transitive' to its didactic uses. Poetry is thus revealed as *sui generis*: an autonomous object and hence the object of a general theory. In the Romantic idea that art 'finds its purpose in itself' – that is, is transcendent in relation to its social deployments – Todorov locates the genesis of Jakobson's account of a universal poetic function characterised by 'the set toward the message as such, the focus on the message for its own sake'.

By the same token, if the poetic message is intransitive – that is, if it is the product of the internal relation of form and content – then its meaning will only be accessible in exactly *that* internal organisation. In short, it will not be expressible or paraphrasable in any other discourse: 'The poem is the only expression of that which it says,' At the same time, because it is not translatable into any other discourse, aesthetic discourse, it is argued, can embody or show the form of them all. By this construction Todorov can find in the 'unparaphrasable' poem the image of two central features of structuralist poetics. First, the idea that the poem is its own metalanguage, because it displays the 'laws that preside over its own birth': 'The work of art signifies itself, through the interplay of its parts; thus it constitutes its own description, the only one that can be adequate' (ibid., p. 160). Second, the idea that interpretation must be 'infinite', because what is offered to description is not any particular meaning but a relational totality in which all possible meanings are contained.

Todorov summarises the inter-dependencies of this set of concepts in the following manner:

This set of assertions – what art expresses cannot be rendered by the words of everyday language; such an impossibility gives rise to an infinite number of interpretations – can be found again intact among the members of the *Athenaeum* group. This should not surprise us: the affirmation of poetry's untranslatability goes hand in hand with that of its intransitivity; to assert that its meaning is inexhaustible is entirely compatible with asserting that its nature is a perpetual becoming and that its character is organic. (Ibid., p. 193)

And in this group of relations he sketches the genesis of modern poetics: that fundamental moment in which by withdrawing language from its 'extrinsic' relation to representation, the Romantic aesthetic was able to constitute for the first time a discourse that represented nothing but itself, but in doing so revealed the laws underlying all discourses.

Clearly in this history we are confronted by a shift in register from the problematics of criticism to those of the human sciences, in this case structuralist semiotics. Todorov is well aware of this, but his own account of the transposition is, it seems to me, less than adequate, because it assumes that the Romantic problematic is foundational for the developments that follow it. Todorov describes both the transposition and the fundamental continuity between Romantic aesthetics and structuralist poetics when discussing Humboldt's linguistics. Significantly, he begins by noting the change of object, from art to language:

However, Humboldt remains, and remains entirely, within the romantic tendency, in the sense in which I am using this term. That does not mean that there are no differences: the most important comes from the change of object that I have just mentioned. No longer seeking to oppose art to other activities, still less to demand of one form of art (modern art) what would be lacking in another (that of antiquity), Humboldt passes from prescription to description, from the optative to the constative. He does not demand that language be production rather than product: he observes that this is the case and asks rather that the science of language take this fact into account. . .

Humboldt thus rediscovers, transposed to another level, the principal affirmations of the romantics on the subject of the work of art. Language is a living being: its production counts more than the product. It is an uninterrupted becoming. One cannot describe linguistic forms accurately without going beyond them: to give an exact description one would have to reconstitute the mechanism of which they are the product. The concrete utterance is at once an instance and an image of the act of production in general, the one that has as its product not the particular sentence but the entire language. (Ibid., pp. 170–1)

But, we must rejoin, Todorov can only establish a genetic continuity between Romantic aesthetics and structuralist linguistics by making the change 'from prescription to description, from the optative to the constative' retrospective. Romantic criticism, as we have already described it, is not a theory or proto-theory of art but an aesthetico-ethical discipline of the self. It is irrevocably optative and prescriptive. And in demonstrating this point we shall have cause to reconsider those major categories on which Todorov has hung his genetic history, beginning with the central pair of productivity and coherence.

To be sure, in comparison with rhetorical poetics, Romantic aesthetics is characterised by a shift from a concern with the didactic specification of imitative form to a concern with the artist's imagination. But this shift cannot be understood as a prefiguration of some fundamental break with empirical representation in favour of its theoretical conditions in the 'process of production'. It was not motivated by the alleged failure of the doctrine of imitation to provide a true knowledge of 'the nature of art', but by the appearance of a split or 'wound' in 'man's' ethical substance. According to Schiller:

It was civilisation [*Kultur*] itself which inflicted this wound upon modern man. Once the increase of empirical knowledge, and more exact modes of thought, made sharper divisions between the sciences inevitable, and once the increasingly complex machinery of State necessitated a more rigorous separation of ranks and occupations, then the inner unity of human nature was severed too, and a disastrous conflict set its powers at variance. The intuitive and the speculative understanding now withdrew in hostility to take up positions in their respective fields, whose functions they now began to guard with jealous mistrust; and with this confining of our activity to a particular sphere we have given ourselves a master within, who not infrequently ends up suppressing the rest of our potentialities. While in the one a riotous imagination ravages the hard-won fruits of the intellect, in another the spirit of abstraction stifles the fire at which the heart should have warmed itself and the imagination been kindled. (Schiller, 1975, pp. 33–5)

No doubt – despite its astonishing contemporaneity – this account of the 'dissociation of sensibility' is, as we have already argued, entirely mythopoeic. This fact has no effect, however, on its power to organise a particular relation to the work of art, when deployed as part of an aesthetico-ethical discipline. The shift from the relation between the work and the world to that linking the work and its writer or reader is not the product of an epistemological concern. It is, rather, framed by the fact that the latter relation became the focus of an ethical practice in which the individual shapes a relation to his self by overcoming its divisions. In the divisions of the work of art – its elements of form and meaning, feelings and ideas – the individual finds echoes of his own ethical imbalances, and in reconciling the former he moderates the latter. In doing so, however, he is neither acting in accordance with a universal structure, nor merely reflecting the empirical strengths and weaknesses of his nature. Schiller comments that:

the relaxing of the sense-drive must in no wise be the result of physical impotence or blunted feeling, which never merits anything but contempt. It must be an act of free choice, an activity of the Person which, by its moral intensity, moderates that of the senses and, by mastering impressions, robs them of depth in order to give them increased surface. It is character which must set bounds to temperament, for it is only to profit the mind that sense may go short. In the same way the relaxing of the formal drive must not be the result of spiritual impotence or flabbiness of thought or will; for this would only degrade man. It must, if it is to be all praiseworthy, spring from abundance of feeling and sensation ... In a single word: Personality must keep the sensuous drive within its proper bounds, and receptivity or Nature, must do the same with the formal drive. (Ibid., p. 93)

In other words, the object of aesthetics is not the work of art as such, or its conditions of intelligibility in the 'process of production', but the formation of a certain kind of 'character'.

Neither is this formative aesthetico-ethical practice deployed on the basis of a more fundamental knowledge; because, owing to the division in 'man's' being, knowledge itself is compromised.

> It is not, then, enough to say that all enlightenment of the understanding is worthy of respect only inasmuch as it reacts upon character. To a certain extent it also proceeds from character, since the way to the head must be opened through the heart. The development of man's capacity for feeling is, therefore, the more urgent need of our age, not merely because it can be a means of making better insights effective for living, but precisely because it provides the impulse for bettering our insights. (Ibid., p. 53)

Translating this into our terms we can say that in the relation between the work of art and its reader or writer the Romantics did not discover theoretical conditions, they imposed an autonomous aesthetico-ethical practice.

Under this dispensation criticism does not have the functions of a theoretical or proto-theoretical knowledge of literature, or 'literariness'. In Friedrich Schlegel's view:

> Only what is quite new and individual requires commentary – but of the sort which should by no means make everything clear for everybody. It deserves the name of excellence only when the reader who understands *Wilhelm Meister* completely finds it utterly familiar and when the reader who does not understand it at all finds it as stupid and empty as the work it is supposed to elucidate. On the other hand, the reader who only half-understands the work would find such a commentary only half-comprehensible; it would enlighten him in some respects, but perhaps only confuse him the more in others – so that out of this disturbance and doubt, knowledge might emerge, or the reader might at least become aware of his incompleteness. (Schlegel, 1800, p. 66)

And this is to say that the functions of criticism for the Romantics are primarily exemplary and educative and, indeed, remain so for us. Their job is to induct the individual into a certain mode of ethical subjectification: to secure the recognition of a specific kind of ethical obligation in relation to the shaping of a self. Criticism is to bring the reader into that relation to the work in which he 'becomes aware of his incompleteness', and is thus forced to begin the endless task of self-culture. In short, in framing its aesthetic in terms of the 'process of production' (and consumption, we might add) Romantic criticism was not seeking knowledge of the 'laws that preside over the birth of each work'. Rather it was installing the practical means of forming a certain kind of person.

Reconstructing Todorov's historical account of 'productivity' in this manner has cognate effects on his version of 'coherence', or the internality of aesthetic relations. Briefly, recognising this internality is not discovering a fact about 'the nature of art', a fact that the rhetoricians with their doctrine of imitation might simply have overlooked. Rather, it is responding to an *obligation* not to refer content to an 'external' or didactic meaning, and instead to discuss it in terms of a set of formal categories: irony, balance, play, etc. And this is one obligation that rhetorical life was mercifully free of. Hence, the presence or absence of the internal unity of form and content in the work can always be referred to its contingent presence or absence in the reader or writer. Schiller is quite explicit about this in a remark that we have already cited, and which we repeat here for the reader's convenience:

> But it is by no means always proof of formlessness in the work of art if it makes its effect solely through its contents; this may just as often be evidence of a lack of form in him who judges it. If he is either too tensed or too relaxed, if he is used to apprehending either exclusively with the intellect or exclusively with the sense, he will, even in the case of the most successfully realised whole, attend only to the parts, and in the presence of the most beauteous form respond only to the matter . . . The interest he takes in it is quite simply either a moral or a material interest; but what precisely it ought to be, namely aesthetic, that it certainly is not. (Schiller, 1795, pp. 158–9)

This returns us to our earlier remark that the work of art does not in fact have a 'nature' or fundamental 'laws' whose discovery might separate the history of poetics from its pre-theoretical past. It is characterised only by contingent and practical conditions of existence, open to description but not to discovery. The Romantic work of art and its criticism exist as different modalities of a cultural regimen focused in the reconciliation of the divided ethical substance, one of whose avatars is the division of form and meaning. For this reason, as we saw with Wimsatt and Brooks, no appeal to an essential 'literariness' can justify the deployment of aesthetic criticism. Such an appeal is always only a symptom of the deployment.

Moreover, because the internal unity of form and content appears in the form of an obligation to moderate each by appealing to the other, it is always incomplete.

> Since in actuality no purely aesthetic effect is ever to be met with (for man can never escape his dependence on conditioning forces), the excellence of a work of art can never consist in anything more than a high approximation to that ideal of aesthetic purity; and whatever the degree of freedom to which it may have been sublimated, we shall still leave it in a particular mood and with some definite bias. (Ibid., p. 153)

The work of art is not the manifestation of a virtual system but the target of a positive practice. This practice does not terminate in a totality whose internal relations constitute the poem's conditions of intelligibility. It ends, rather, on one side of a dialectical practice which, in revealing the individual's ethical incompleteness, only serves to mark the point at which he must resume the exercise.

It now remains to briefly spell out the implications of these remarks for the concepts of 'intransitivity' and 'the inexpressible'. Intransitivity, it will be remembered, is the term Todorov uses to describe the Romantic idea that the work of art 'finds its purpose in itself', and to transpose this idea into Jakobson's definition of the poetic function as 'the focus on the message for its own sake'. It should now be clear, however, that it is not particularly revealing to speak of a poem 'finding its purpose in itself'. This is simply a less than perspicuous way of referring to the fact that it exists in an aesthetico-ethical practice, one of whose imperatives is to cease interpreting poetry in terms of its didactic uses. In providing the dialectic between form and meaning, and the imperative to read each only in its relation to the other, the Romantic aesthetic deploys a *technique* that requires us to refrain from reading a poem in terms of any particular didactic purpose. Nothing about the form or structure of poetry tells us that we must use this technique, however. It is not in the nature of poetry to be non-instrumental and self-regulating, as eighteen or more centuries of hortatory, eulogistic, didactic, etc. poetry would seem to indicate anyway.

The correct formulation for this aspect of the aesthetic, then, is *not*: Poetry transcends all the purposes we have for it (and is hence self-regulating, autonomous, open to a general theorisation, etc.), *but*: In these circumstances we remove the question of purposes from the criteria for 'reading'. Hence, it makes as little sense to say that the poem 'finds its purposes in itself' as it does to say that it finds them elsewhere. As for *why* we withdraw the criterion of didactic or social purpose, this is purely and simply a question of the obligations imposed on us by a specific ethical practice.

Finally, what are we to make of 'the inexpressible'? – perhaps a dubious notion at the best of times. It will be remembered that Todorov uses this term to name the consequences of the unity of form and meaning: namely, that poetry cannot be paraphrased; is itself 'the only expression of that which it says'; and is thereby 'its own description'. In these formulations he finds the Romantic anticipation of the structuralist ideas that the poem is its own metalanguage, and that while thus providing a reflexive description of its own 'becoming', it can never be exhausted by interpretation. But clearly, if the 'unity of form and meaning' is the outcome of an ethical practice in which one is obliged not to paraphrase meaning (but to refer it instead to formal principles), then it is misleading to say that poetry cannot be paraphrased. The Romantic aesthetic has bequeathed us an *imperative* and a *technique* that permit us to withdraw from the practice of paraphrase in favour of a different kind of (aesthetico-ethical) activity.

Hence, the formulation that we need is *not*: Poetry *cannot* be paraphrased (and hence constitutes its own metalinguistic description), *but*: Under these circumstances (that is, in obedience to this regimen, using these techniques etc.) we *do not* paraphrase poetry. And this means that it is nonsensical to say that the poem 'describes its own meaning', because the question of describing meaning does not arise in these circumstances: as long as we accept that paraphrasing is one of the activities that we usually call 'describing meaning'. (This by no means commits us to the view that meaning exists independently of the form of language: only to the view, as Wittgenstein phrased it, that 'Meaning is what is explained in explanations of meaning'.) As for the putative inexhaustibility of interpretation under these conditions, the correct formulation is *not*: Interpretation is *endless* (meaning is always in a state of 'becoming', etc.), *but*: Under these conditions we *do not end it* (for example, in an acceptable paraphrase). Once again, the question of *why* we do not end interpretation can only be answered with reference to the dialectical technique that abrogates the *institution* of the acceptable paraphrase, and to the cultural regimen in which we are required to use this technique.[4]

IV

We can conclude, then, that the account in which the history of criticism is punctuated by a fundamental theoretical rupture – one which reveals the foundations of its object once and for all – is inadequate for our purposes. Todorov attempts to locate the object of structuralist poetics in the 'Romantic revolt': in the idea of a break in the representational surface of poetry which reveals an underlying structure not in itself representational but containing the form of all possible representations (significations). But this attempt, we have argued, is unsuccessful.

First, the notions of productivity, coherence, intransitivity and the inexpressible, which Todorov uses to characterise the Romantic aesthetic, do not in fact mark the forms in which literature reveals its universal conditions of possibility. Instead, in the focus on the imagination, the reconciliation of form and meaning, and the withdrawal from didactics and paraphrase, we find the contours of a specific aesthetico-ethical practice: a practice, moreover, not governed by 'that abstract property that constitutes the literary phenomenon, literariness', but by the prescriptive techniques of a thoroughly normative cultural regimen. Second, the object of this practice is not to recover a formal knowledge of poetic discourse from beneath a deceptive representation; it is to form a certain kind of person: to reconcile the oppositions of the ethical substance and thereby shape a self capable of moral action and knowledge.

The problematic of 'foundations', which Todorov borrows from the field of the human sciences, and which provides the goal of his history, is characterised by the passage from not knowing to knowing in which 'the subject' comes to describe the unconscious (formal) conditions of its own (literary) consciousness. But the subject of Romantic aesthetics is not someone who does not know. In fact, it is someone who knows too much (because disembodied consciousness is without limits), but knows in the wrong way (lacking sensuous resistance the abstract consciousness either remains nascent or else imposes itself violently and tendentiously on the world of the senses). The object of Romantic criticism, therefore, is not to know the hidden conditions of literary experience, but to reconcile the antagonism of intellect and senses and thereby shape the special ethical sensibility in which the *right kind of knowledge* would be formed: 'The development [*Ausbildung*] of man's capacity for feeling is, therefore, the more urgent need of our age, not merely because it can be a means of making better insights effective for living, but precisely because it provides the impulse for bettering our insights.'

No doubt we are ill-prepared to countenance a discipline in which knowledge is not (even potentially) given to a universal subject, and is instead the prerogative of a specially formed ethical personage. But this was indeed the case for Romantic criticism and, so I shall argue, remains so for criticism today. In borrowing this discipline as a model for this theoretical recovery of 'foundations' – even in simply accepting it as a source for the 'literary phenomenon' on which theory goes to work – Todorov transposes the prerogatives of the ethical virtuoso onto 'the subject' of the human sciences. This, as I shall argue below, is not necessarily a bad thing, as long as it is done with open eyes. It does, however, make for bad history when it is used to provide an absolute horizon for the history of criticism by transforming a particular ethical episode into the theoretical recovery of a general 'poetic function'.

In adopting this strategy Todorov seeks to provide structuralist poetics with historical necessity, by anchoring the otherwise unstable pursuit of foundations in an unsurpassable aesthetics and ethics. In so doing he behaves in an opposite but complementary fashion to Wimsatt and Brooks. They seek to universalise the aesthetico-ethical discipline of the Romantics by putting it to work as a foundation of critical judgement. It should come as no surprise, then, that at this point – marked by rival but converging attempts to organise the history of criticism around the absolute autonomy of literature – the project of the human sciences should overlap with that of the Romantic ethical discipline. On the one hand, Todorov motivates the self-regulating productive form of structuralist poetics by appealing to the ethically imperative 'organic form' of the Romantic regimen. On the other, when New Critics like Wellek and Warren (1949, pp. 149–58) attempt to explain the conundrum of a poem whose structure is the result of certain norms of reading – norms nonetheless nascent in the structure itself – they appeal to

Saussure's conception of *langue* in order to convert norms into foundations.

In fact, as we shall see below, this exchange between the noble self of criticism and the self-clarifying subject of the human sciences lies at the very heart of modern criticism and – sobering thought – delineates the field of possibilities for all who inhabit this space. Neither the historiography of the human sciences nor that of the New Criticism can describe how this exchange became possible, because both are symptoms of it. Each in fact evades the task of genealogy by invoking a mythopoeic moment of historical revelation which, in setting an absolute horizon for historical development, preserves the (literary) subject from the scattering winds of historical contingency.

Significantly, for both historiographies, this unsurpassable moment is provided by the 'Romantic revolt' against rhetorical poetics. For Wimsatt and Brooks the rhetorical stress on imitative form and didactic deployment shows that rhetoric embodies only one side of 'man's' divided ethical substance. It is 'man's' dialectical completion that provides the history of criticism with its universal goal: the reconciliation of form and meaning, aesthetics and didactics, reader and text in a transcendent aesthetic experience. As far as Todorov is concerned, these elements of rhetoric are a sign of its pre-theoretical servitude to representation and the empirical work. It was up to Romanticism to restore to 'the subject' a knowledge of what it was that made representation possible, thereby making history coterminous with 'the subject's' self-clarification.

But the system of rhetoric was neither incomplete nor in error. Its deployment of formulaic imitation and epideictic didactics signified neither an ethical imbalance nor a naive empiricism in relation to literary representation. And the history of modern criticism cannot be understood either in terms of an ethical dialectic evolving slowly towards the cancellation of this imbalance, or in terms of a sudden break with literary representation that reveals the latter's formal grounds. Neither the historiography of the New Criticism, nor that of the human sciences, can comprehend the emergence of modern criticism: the former because it seeks to universalise a limited ethical discipline by deploying it as a foundation; the latter because it attempts to authorise a specific régime of problematisation by rooting it in an unsurpassable aesthetics and ethics.

In fact, all that the Romantic aesthetic provided was a contingent set of techniques for shaping a moral self and a normative regimen, in which this activity was required conduct for a special caste. For their part the human sciences provided a discourse on 'man's' unconscious and the (linguistic, psychological and social) structures which both determined this unconscious and revealed it to knowledge. Now, the important point is that for that almost the entire nineteenth century, criticism and the human sciences remained separate: parallel and often rival cultural strategies. One only has to think of Matthew Arnold and Ferdinand de Saussure whose careers, while overlapping on the calendar, belong to different histories. What we must describe are the circumstances that permitted their convergence.

In order to comprehend the emergence of modern criticism we must be able to describe how the normative techniques of aesthetic self-culture came to be deployed as a foundations of literary judgement and, conversely, how the scientific recovery of the literary unconscious came to assume the functions of an aesthetico-ethical discipline. Is it surprising to learn that at the heart of this transformation we should find the apparatus of an emerging national education system? Only here could the ethical techniques of a particular caste be re-deployed as structural norms; and only here could the recondite recovery of 'man's' structural unconscious be operationalised as a strategy for 'training the sensibility'.

6

The Pedagogical Imperative

I

In 1762 Lord Kames published his *Elements of Criticism*. His object, like Hume's (1757) a few years earlier, was to describe and justify the principles of taste by showing their origins in human nature or 'the sensitive part of man's being'. The following paragraph is representative of his method:

It now appears that we are framed by nature to relish order and connection. When an object is introduced by a proper connection, we are conscious of a certain pleasure arising from that circumstance. Among objects of equal rank, the pleasure is proportioned to the degree of connection: but among unequal objects, where we require a certain order, the pleasure arises chiefly from an orderly arrangement; of which one is sensible, in tracing objects contrary to the course of nature, or contrary to our sense of order: the mind proceeds with alacrity down a flowing river, and with the same alacrity from a whole to its parts, or from a principal to its accessories; but in the contrary direction, it is sensible of a sort of retrograde motion, which is unpleasant. And here may be marked the great influence of order upon the mind of man: grandeur, which makes a deep impression, inclines us, in running over any series, to proceed from small to great, rather than from great to small; but order prevails over that tendency, and affords pleasure as well as facility in passing from a whole to its parts and from a subject to its ornaments, which are not felt in the opposite course. Elevation touches the mind no less than grandeur doth; and in raising the mind to elevated objects, there is a sensible pleasure: the course of nature, however, hath a still greater influence than elevation; and therefore the pleasure of falling rain, and descending gradually with a river, prevails over that of mounting upward. But where the course of nature is joined with elevation, the effect must be delightful; and hence the singular beauty of smoke ascending in a calm morning. (Kames, 1762, I, pp. 25–6)

Kames' theme is that while as a matter of fact taste varies between men and between nations, it nonetheless has rational foundations and universal standards provided by the conformity between 'the course of nature' and the mind's 'sense of order'. Taste – or the feeling of pleasure and displeasure that we have in the presence of the fine arts – registers or duplicates the order of things in the order of the mind and is based in the fact that 'we are framed by nature to relish order and connection'. Hence, the pleasure or displeasure we feel when listening to oratory and poetry is by no means subjective. It arises from the degree to which their structure succeeds in duplicating the order of nature in the order of the mind's ideas and feelings, or in duplicating the movement of the mind in the action of nature. This doubled order is so strong that it even allows us to take pleasure in contrary movements like that of the sublime, drawing together in a single structure of taste the pleasures of rhetoric and the picturesque.

In the relatively short time between Kames' outline of the principles of taste and the publication of Schiller's essay 'On the Sublime' in 1801, criticism underwent a transformation that abolished the very idea of universal faculty of taste rooted in human nature. This decisive shift is registered in Schiller's essay in the fact that nature has lost its benign aspect. Human nature, says Schiller, cannot find a pattern and a sanction in the divinely ordained universal order of nature. Indeed, 'physical nature' is pitted against 'man's' 'moral being', which is at every moment threatened with violence and annihilation. And Schiller's treatment of the sublime concerns how 'man' may deal with the threatening antagonism of nature by transcending its violence through 'aesthetic education'.

But though nature as a sensuous activity drives us to the ideal, it throws us still more into the world of ideas by the terrible. Our highest aspiration is to be in good relations with physical nature, without violating morality. But it is not always convenient to serve two masters; and though duty and the appetites should never be at strife, physical necessity is peremptory, and nothing can save men from evil destiny. Happy is he who learns to bear what he cannot change! There are cases where fate overpowers all ramparts, and where the only resistance is, like a pure spirit, to throw freely off all interest of sense, and strip yourself of your body. Now this force comes from sublime emotions and a frequent commerce with destructive nature. Pathos is a sort of artificial misfortune, and brings us to the spiritual law that commands our soul. Real misfortune does not always choose its time opportunely, while pathos finds us armed at all points. By frequently renewing this exercise of its own activity, the mind controls the sensuous, so that when real misfortune comes, it can treat it as an artificial suffering, and make it a sublime emotion. Thus pathos takes away some of the malignity of destiny, and wards off its blows. (Schiller, 1801, pp. 140–1)

Here it is clear that the guarantees of a universal taste – in which the mind's order and nature's find themselves mirrored in the pleasures of the rhetorical figures – have been forfeited. In Schiller's *mythos*, the 'wound' in 'man's' ethical being has been inflicted. Now 'man' is confronted by an implacably alien sensory world, and a moral will whose dictates find no echo there, or else impose themselves in an equally tyrannical fashion. In deliberately seeking out the *sturm und drang* of nature the artist finds the 'infinite manifested in the sensuous' (the sublime), and through this reconciliation can himself internalise the alien being of nature while transcending his own didactic morality. In works of art the critic finds a more accessible form of pathos on which he, nonetheless, performs the same reconciliatory exercise. In short, with Schiller we pass from criticism as a minor branch of eighteenth-century philosophies of human nature, to criticism as an autonomous ethical exercise. Its task is no longer to produce 'clear and distinct' ideas of taste, but the more momentous one of forming a relation to the self which would make right action and right knowledge possible.

Our third and final text is taken from I. A. Richards' *Practical Criticism*. No doubt it seems odd to place this work – which presents itself as an experiment in literary psychology and has been used as a pedagogical manual – in the same series as Kames and Schiller. Kames perhaps: but if Richards' text seems remote from Schiller's enthusiasm for the terrible in nature we should note, nonetheless, that it is focused precisely on the problems of reading figurative language. Drawing on the 'protocols' (readings provided by his Cambridge English students) to poems IX and X in his series, Richards illustrates responses that are either too literal (demanding of metaphor the same coherence and meaning that one finds in non-literary language) or too figurative (eschewing all criteria for coherence and meaning in metaphor). This, of course, recalls Schiller's discussion of the way in which lack of form in a poem often betokens the same imbalance in its reader. The reader may read solely for meaning or solely for form, and in thus failing to reconcile his didactic and sensuous impulses fails in his 'aesthetic education'. Richards himself is looking for (but not finding) 'instances of a middle kind when both a legitimate demand for accuracy and precision and a recognition of the proper liberties and powers of figurative language are combined'; and he offers to sum up this discussion of some instances of figurative language as follows:

> All respectable poetry invites close reading. It encourages attention to its literal sense up to the point, to be detected by the reader's discretion, at which liberty can serve the aim of the poem better than fidelity to fact or strict coherence among fictions. It asks the reader to remember that its aims are varied and not always what he unreflectingly expects. He has to refrain from applying his own external standards. The chemist must not require the poet to write like a chemist, nor the moralist, nor the man of affairs, nor the logician, nor the professor, that he write as they would. The whole trouble of literalism is that the reader forgets that the aim of the poem comes first, and this is the sole justification of its means. We may quarrel, frequently we must, with the aim of the poem, but we have first to ascertain what it is. We cannot legitimately judge its means by external standards (such as accuracy of fact or logical coherence) which may have no relevance to its success in doing what it set out to do, or, if we like, in becoming what in the end it has become. (Richards, 1929, pp. 203–4)

But here we can see that the differences from Schiller are no less important than the evident continuity. The reconciliation of meaning and form is no longer simply the goal of a practice of the self that the individual voluntarily performs on his ethical substance. 'Aesthetic education' has taken on a quite new meaning and the task of reconciliation has undergone a double displacement and change of function: it is now fully inside the poem where it functions as the autotelic 'aim' against which the reader's tendency to literalism or aestheticism can be measured; and it marks the point where the reader's responses open the state of his (psycho-ethical) sensibility to the inspection of another. This relation is simultaneously one of observation and correction. Richards (ibid., p. 202) comments in relation to one of the literalists that he is 'tempted to suspect some incapacity of visual meaning': the ethical telos has become a pedagogical norm.

Moreover, if the 'aim of the poem' marks the redeployment of the ethical discipline as a pedagogical technique, it also signifies that the aesthetic reading has acquired a second major new function: not just to reveal the 'poetic meaning' but to restore to consciousness the hidden laws which allow the subject to read this meaning. Richards' comments in a note on 'the aim of the poem':

> I hope to be understood to mean by this the whole state of mind, the mental condition, which in another sense *is* the poem. Roughly the collection of impulses which shaped the poem originally, to which it gave expression, and to which in an ideally susceptible reader it would again give rise. . . . I do not mean by its 'aim' any sociological, aesthetic, commercial or propagandist intentions or hopes of the poet. (Ibid., p. 204)

Here we have entered the same realm in which Jakobson and Todorov locate the self-regulating form of the poem: a form which is simultaneously instance and description of the hidden laws which make it possible.

In other words, with Richards, Schiller's minority aesthetic education has been redeployed as a technique in the governmental training of sensibility. At the same time it has acquired the role of a science of the foundations of critical judgement. Moreover, it seems that both these things have happened on the basis of a single unprecedented deployment: that deployment in which the 'critical response' reveals a sensibility which is both incomplete and unconscious to another sensibility which is both exemplary and 'scientific'. It is the aim of this chapter to show how the ethical function of criticism and the epistemological function of the human sciences entered into an exchange inside the apparatus of a governmental pedagogy. I wish to describe how in this normatised space the discipline of the noble life came to overlap with the theoretical clarification of the 'literary unconscious' giving birth to modern criticism.

II

We have noted that at the centre of the eighteenth-century project to provide a rational foundation for taste lies the conception of a common order linking nature and human nature. Nature has an intrinsic pattern consisting of the relations between parts and wholes, substances and their attributes. But so too does the mind, whose 'trains of ideas' naturally move from wholes to parts and from things to their properties when performing the tasks of analysis and synthesis, which were in the eighteenth century the privileged forms of knowledge. Similarly, 'man's sensitive being' – his emotions and passions – are framed in accordance with the 'course of nature'. Like the river they flow, for example, from immediate events to the web of affective circumstances surrounding them. As a result, that 'man' should take pleasure in the movement of the river, and in oratory that imitates this movement, is not accidental or arbitrary, but is a universal fact concerning his nature.

The fine arts – oratory, poetry, music, painting, architecture and landscape-gardening – are located at precisely that point where the order of nature is *duplicated* in human nature. 'Duplicated' not 'signified'; because the fine arts, like language at this time, do not transmit nature's order indirectly through the 'third party' of meaning. They do so directly through things *seen* and *felt*: through the chains of ideas and emotions in which this order is literally doubled or *re-presented* in the order of the mind. The common order linking nature and human nature is the order of representation, and Kames' analysis of taste takes place wholly in the sphere of representation.

This is why Kames' criticism does not take the form of a hermeneutics. Signification is not hidden in the enigmatic opacity of words but assumes the form of representation: a doubling of the pattern of nature immediately present to the mind's eye and ear.[1] (Kames describes painting and poetry as 'pleasures of the eye and ear'.) Taste in the fine arts, therefore, is the sensitive registration of this doubling on an 'internal' eye, ear or palate; and works of art may be infallibly judged agreeable or disagreeable depending on how successfully they fulfil the function of duplication or representation.

Every work of art that is conformable to the natural course of our

ideas, is so far agreeable; and every work of art that reverses that
course, is so far disagreeable. Hence it is required in every such
work, that, like an organic system, its parts be orderly arranged
and mutually connected, bearing each of them a relation to the
whole, some more intimate, some less, according to their
destination: when due regard is had to these particulars, we have
a sense of just composition, and so far are pleased with the
performance. (Kames, 1762, I, p. 27)

Despite certain attempts to treat Kames as a precursor of the
Romantics, it should be clear that 'organic' in this context is far
removed from its Romantic meanings. For Kames, the order of a
work is organic not because it is an autonomous union of form and
content, but because it imitates a natural order lying on either side
of it, in the mind and nature. Hence he is quite happy to use the
rhetorical maxim that 'language is the dress of thought', and to
judge works precisely on the grounds of the fitness of expression to
the 'conjunctions and disjunctions' of thought.

To find these conjunctions and disjunctions imitated in the
expression, is a beauty; because such imitation makes the words
concordant with the sense. This doctrine may be illustrated by a
familiar example. When we have occasion to mention the
intimate connection that the soul hath with the body, the
expression ought to be, *the soul and body*; because the particle *the*,
relative to both, makes a connection in the expression,
resembling in some degree the connection in the thought: but
when the soul is distinguished from the body, it is better to say
the soul and the body; because the disjunction in words resembles
the disjunction in thought. (Ibid., II, pp. 24–5)

In fact, it would be quite accurate to describe Kames – together
with other eighteenth-century men of taste like Campbell, Blair and
Alison – as writing a 'philosophical rhetoric', in exactly the same
sense in which Arnauld and Lancelot wrote a 'philosophical
grammar' in the previous century. Neither is the connection
fortuitous. Kames draws on the same model of representation
deployed by the universal grammarians. According to Lancelot and
Arnauld (1660, pp. 122–29) the copula of predication ('is') does not
signify the meaning of the relation between a thing and its property.
It is in fact the very form in which the mind performs the action of
predication on its 'chain of ideas', thereby duplicating or

re-presenting the order of nature. Similarly, for Kames, rhetorical structure is not arbitrary, but the form in which the 'course of nature' is represented in the movements of the ideas and the emotions. What judgement is in classical philosophical grammar and logic, taste is in eighteenth-century criticism: the recognition of the true order of representation in which nature is folded-over in human nature.

How, then, are we to understand the distintegration of the harmony of representation which is signalled in Schiller's anxieties concerning the hostility of 'physical nature', and the arbitrariness of the 'moral will'? Here I draw on the 'archaeology of the human sciences' provided in Michel Foucault's *The Order of Things*. According to Foucault (1966, pp. 217–94) this disintegration is heralded by the rise of the positive sciences of philology, biology and economics. It must be observed at the outset that Foucault is not offering an explanation of the eclipse of representation: at least not an explanation of the sort found in the history of ideas where philosophical grammar is replaced by philology because the latter is truer to the nature of language, or because (contrawise) the latter is a vehicle for new social interests. Foucault's archaeology is in one sense 'shallower' than such explanations. He simply describes the fact of the rise of the empirical sciences and shows in what way they were incompatible with the model of representation without attempting to provide a general answer to the question of 'why' the transformation occurred. In another sense, however, his account is anything but shallow. In resisting the temptation to explain the change via modern conceptions of truth or ideology, Foucault avoids writing history backwards and is in a better position to respect the historical specificity of the eclipse.

Taking the example of philology, Foucault shows that its emergence displaced the representational conception of language found in eighteenth-century philosophical grammars and rhetorics. Philology is concerned with the phonetic and morphological structures of words, but it does not trace these to a representational function, as Lancelot and Arnauld do for the copula and Kames does for the rhetorical *figura*. Instead, philology describes these structures in terms of the purely formal relations they have with parallel structures in other languages (Comparative Philology), or in terms of their progressive historical derivation and differentiation from more primitive root forms (Historical or Indo-European Philology).

Under these circumstances, argues Foucault (ibid., pp. 294–302), language becomes 'opaque'. It is no longer the place in which nature and human nature duplicate or represent their common structure of ideas. It is no longer the surface on which this representation is itself represented to a judgement or a taste which finds in language the transparent form of human nature's fundamental ideas and emotions. In philology language itself becomes an *object* of knowledge instead of its universal medium. And knowledge of language – together with knowledge of labour and (biological) life – can no longer be gained through a philosophical analysis of the mind's representations or ideas. These knowledges must now be searched for amidst empirical regularities that owe nothing to the function of representation.

At the same time, under these new circumstances it became possible to constitute an autonomous philosophy of knowledge in the form of the Kantian analytic. Prior to this point, Foucault argues, philosophy could not separate itself from the analysis of representation carried out in philosophical grammar. It was in language that the mind's ideas of nature received their fundamental reflection and analysis; and it was in the analysis of the representational function of language that 'clear and distinct ideas' could be formed. It is for this reason that the chapter on the verb in Arnauld and Lancelot's *grammar* is reproduced verbatim in Arnauld's *logic* as an analysis of predication. And it is for this reason that Hume regarded his 'Essay of the Standard of Taste' as a topic in his philosophy, while Kames regarded his *Elements of Criticism* as a contribution to the philosophy of human nature. Given this, it should come as no surprise that when an autonomous philosophy of knowledge did emerge, on the far side of the fissure that now divided the empirical sciences from the inspection of consciousness, it was by posing a question literally unthinkable prior to the split occurring: On what basis can 'man' have knowledge of empirical reality given that it is not a datum of his consciousness?

It is this splitting apart of knowledge from representation and nature from human nature that signals the end of the 'classical episteme' in Foucault's account. But isn't it precisely this split that we find registered mythopoeically in Schiller's image of a 'wound' in 'man's' ethical substance? – A wound dividing 'physical nature' from 'man's' 'moral being', the world of his senses from the world of his thoughts and feelings, and bringing with it the whole set of antinomies clustered around the division between culture and society?

This seems to me, at the very least, to be a good working hypothesis. It permits us to treat the Romantic aesthetic as an attempt to side-step the effects of the split by reconstituting the unity of nature and human nature in another register: not that of representation, but of ethics. If 'man' was constituted by the wound dividing his physical from his intellectual being, then there was no point in him attempting to know nature directly (the hubris of the sciences), nor in him attempting to put knowledge to work in social action (the hubris of politics). His pre-eminent duty from this point on would be to reconcile the division in his ethical substance and thereby shape a self in whom right knowledge and right action would be the fruits of ethical discipline. This was the task of culture and criticism, not the sciences and politics.

In fact, Foucault does not mention culture and criticism in his archaeology of the human sciences. Here I am extrapolating from his work to indicate how an ethical practice – which in Shaftesbury's time was an esoteric discipline for the ethical virtuoso – could have been transformed into a powerful means of 'aesthetic education' and redeployed in the place vacated by the eighteenth-century philosophy of human nature. But we have already said enough about that. Foucault is concerned with a second, different and later response to the break-up of the system of representation: the response which gave birth to the human sciences. All that we need keep in mind for the moment is the likelihood that in the *Romantic aesthetic* and the *human sciences* we are confronted by two quite different compensatory strategies emerging from this disintegration.

III

If nineteenth-century criticism turned its back on the new sciences in favour of culture – or else acknowledged them only in so far as they could be reconciled with culture's ethical imperatives, as in Humboldt's (1836) 'Romantic philology' – the strategy which led to the human sciences was of a quite different sort. This strategy embraced the sciences of philology, biology and economics and affirmed the consequence of their existence: that knowledge of language, life and labour could not be derived from an inspection of the mind's ideas, and had instead to be gleaned from study of the empirical laws and forces acting on man as a speaking, living and productive being.

However, this strategy was also shaped by a question that it *put to* the positive sciences, a question which originated in the space that separated them from the newly emergent critical philosophy: Given that knowledge of language, life and labour was thus dependent on empirical laws operating blindly through 'man' as an empirical being, on what basis could this knowledge be represented in his consciousness? In fact this question was not a sign of any incompleteness in the empirical sciences themselves, but of the fact that the human sciences were derived from them via a particular interrogation performed, as it were, in another place. This interrogation – the question of how it was possible for 'man' to know his speaking, living and labouring being now that it was no longer open to inspection in the form of 'ideas' – was not the result of the delayed discovery of a fundamental phenomenon: the human subject. It was purely a function of the historical gap which had been opened between the empirical sciences and the philosophical interrogation of consciousness.

It was in this contingent and historical space that 'man' could be projected under an unprecedented double aspect. As a creature whose speech, life and labour were the result of empirical laws owing nothing to his consciousness, 'man's' being like the rest of nature's was limited and conditioned: subject to what Foucault calls 'finitude'. But because he was the only being in which these laws could be represented to consciousness, he was set apart by his capacity to develop a reflexive knowledge or 'analytic' of his empirical being. The precise methodological locale of the human sciences, then – their uncertain proximity to the positive sciences and to the discourse of philosophy – is marked by what Foucault (ibid., pp. 312–18) calls the 'analytic of finitude'. This is the undertaking to represent those laws in 'man' that make his empirical consciousness possible while themselves escaping knowledge; but to derive this representation from the very operation of the empirical laws themselves.

It is on the basis of this undertaking that the human sciences of sociology, psychology and 'structuralist' linguistics have been able to give themselves a rationale distinct from that of the positive sciences of economics, biology and philology, on which they nonetheless remain entirely dependent. Saussure (1916, pp. 1–17), for example, inaugurates his *Course in General Linguistics* with the allegation that although historical philology draws on the speaking subject's pre-theoretical knowledge of sounds and meanings, it has failed to discover the laws that make this knowledge possible. And on this basis he formulates his project to recover for consciousness the purely formal or unconscious laws of sound and meaning which reside in the very 'mechanism of language' itself. In Marxist sociology the project to discover the laws of capitalist production receives a parallel motivation: that is, to restore to 'man's' consciousness as a productive being the forces and relations which make this consciousness possible, even while eluding it in the smokescreen of ideology – and so on.

Now Foucault's point about this strategy is not that it is illegitimate, but that it *is* a strategy: that is, that the human sciences are not formed on the basis of a fundamental discovery or an exhaustive formalisation, but on the basis of a highly specific and contingent operation that they perform on their 'parent' sciences.

> This is why what characterises the human sciences is not that they are directed at a certain content (that singular object, the human being); it is much more a purely formal characteristic: the simple fact that, in relation to the sciences in which the human being is given as object (exclusive in the case of economics and philology, or partial in that of biology), they are in a position of duplication, and that this duplication can serve *a fortiori* for themselves. (Foucault, 1966, p. 354)

Saussure (1916, pp. 126–35), for example, does not discard the morphological word-lists compiled by the philologists. He *redeploys* them under a new philosophical sign: this time not as descriptions of the empirical form of words, but as recoveries of the abstract mechanism which supposedly makes the recognition of empirical form possible. This operation of duplication, which is precisely the undertaking announced by the analytic of finitude, has a number of consequences important for understanding the role of the human sciences in modern criticism.

First, because 'man' is a projection of the analytic of finitude he acquires a complex yet familiar double aspect. In so far as his speech, life and labour are the result of laws determining his empirical behaviour – of the vital processes that connect his life to his environment; of the economic and linguistic laws which he must obey – 'man' is an empirical being satisfactorily described by the methods of the positive sciences. At the same time, because he is the being in whom these empirical laws will be represented to consciousness he, unlike other natural beings, is blessed with the capacity to comprehend his own determination, and hence transcend it. So perhaps 'man' is the object of a special reflexive knowledge ireducible to that of the positive sciences. From this duality 'man' emerges as the ambivalent figure that Foucault (1966, pp. 318–22) calls the 'transcendental-empirical couple'. Having this genesis means – as Cousins and Hussain (1984, pp. 63–5) remark in their important exposition of Foucault's work – that knowledge in the human sciences is from the outset pulled in two different directions: towards the empirical and positivistic and towards the reflexive and hermeneutic. And this gives rise to characteristic 'debates' between 'positivist' and 'reflexive' tendencies in all the human sciences – like those between Popper and Adorno (1969) in sociology; generative grammar and 'continental' semiotics in linguistics; and 'text-linguistics' and 'reader response' criticism in literary theory: debates which are quite literally interminable because they simply reproduce the ambiguous space in which the human sciences come into being.

Second, under these circumstances the human sciences acquire a highly distinctive function or project. Because they are addressed not to the laws of 'man's' empirical being as such, but only to these laws in so far as they escape the consciousness which they make possible, the project of the human sciences is to 'think that which is unthought in man'. Their project is nothing less than to complete 'man' by recovering for the *cogito* that which has been lost to knowledges formed independently of it in the unconscious depths of 'man's' biological, economic and linguistic being. As such they attempt to restore the link between knowledge and representation, but in a completely new modality: not through the analysis of ideas but on the axis linking 'the subject's' consciousness to its unconscious being.

Third, because their project is thus to close the gap between unconscious knowledge and conscious representation, the mode of existence of the human sciences is neither that of an ethics nor that of a disinterested empirical investigation. The outcome of their ambivalent conditions of existence is an intense 'will to knowledge'. 'Typically', say Cousins and Hussain (1984, p. 56), 'the social sciences exist as a form of *intellectual action*, in which the object of knowledge is transformed by the act of knowing'. Their mode of existence is therefore 'perennially political' and, in a remark we shall return to, 'compulsively pedagogical'.

We can now see why Foucault argues that the human sciences are not characterised by a particular 'content' or object of knowledge – the human subject. The human subject – Saussure's 'speaking subject', for example – is an artefact of that operation of duplication performed on a 'parent' science in which it does not exist. It is a projection formed according to the figures of the analytic of finitude, the transcendental-empirical couple, and the unconscious. We shall see that when criticism borrowed from the human sciences the imperative to restore to consciousness the subject's unthought literary experience, it also inherited the radical instability of a field marked by blurred frontiers and interminable competition between rival 'foundations'.

This is what it means to describe the human sciences in relation to the Romantic aesthetic as a quite different, but nonetheless parallel response, to the disintegration of representation which attended the rise of the positive sciences. Instead of turning their back on the problem of representation in favour of culture and ethical discipline, the human sciences attempt to reconstitute the link between knowledge and thought (representation), but in a manner quite unlike the old 'classical episteme'. Representation in the human sciences is not a transparent surface on which the *cogito* finds the ideas of nature re-presented in the ideas of words. It is that complex and ambiguous 'intellectual action' in which the human sciences themselves complete 'man' by recovering from his empirical being the unconscious laws that make consciousness possible.

It is a consequence of the preceding analysis that when confronted by the spectacle of competition between the ethical strategy of criticism and the clarificatory strategy of the human sciences – as we were in our discussion of Wimsatt and Brooks and Todorov – we are forced to admit that neither is any more fundamental, or closer to the truth of 'man', than the other. Of course, the human sciences gives themselves the mission of providing a foundational clarification of the subject's unconscious being. But we have seen that the pretext on which they do this – the alleged unconscious immediacy of the knowledge of life, labour and language provided by the empirical sciences – is no less mythopoeic (but no less effective) than Schiller's pretext of a split in 'man's' ethical substance. This 'pre-theoretical' immediacy, like the figure of 'man' itself, is an *effect* of the operation performed on the positive sciences when they are suspended (Wittgenstein would say: prevented from doing their proper jobs) in the space that separates them from philosophy. As such, it cannot function as a *justification* for the project of the human sciences, which we must regard as an historical strategy no more deeply rooted in the order of things than the parallel strategy of ethical self-culture.

IV

We observed in the preceding chapter that criticism today attempts to indemnify itself against the historical contingency of its domain – the aesthetic – by deploying two sorts of history. According to the first sort, the history of criticism is distinguished by an oscillation between two aesthetico-ethical tendencies – the didactic and the formalist. It is said that the reconciliation of these tendencies in modern ('New') criticism not only generates an unsurpassable aesthetic experience – which thereby functions as the absolute horizon of literary history – but also reveals the hidden forms on which this experience is based. While according to the second, this history is marked by a sudden breach in the pre-theoretical immediacy of literary representation. This breach, it is said, not only reveals the unconscious or formal laws which make literary representation possible, but also anchors these in an equally unsurpassable 'autonomous' aesthetic form.

We soon discovered, however, that in Romantic criticism we are dealing with a special aesthetico-ethical discipline which – by imposing the obligation to reconcile the ethical imbalances reflected in literature – seeks to shape a particular relation to the self as the subject of ethical action and knowledge. While in the human sciences we are confronted by a specific 'intellectual action' which – through an oblique redeployment of the positive sciences – seeks to complete 'man' by recovering for consciousness that which makes his experience possible while escaping it.

The point is that while both in different ways appeal to 'man' or the human subject as the object and horizon of their undertakings, this figure can neither justify them nor provide the ground on which they might meet in modern criticism. The Romantic aesthetic and the human sciences are, we have seen, not characterised by a given 'content' or object – 'man' – but by a contingent ethical practice (in the first case) and the equally contingent 'intellectual action' of self-problematisation (in the second). This means that if we wish to comprehend the emergence of modern criticism, then it will not be enough to appeal to the achievement of a latter's unthought conditions of possibility. Instead, we must describe the specific historical deployment or apparatus through which an ethical discipline directed at the formation of the exemplary life could be articulated to an intellectual exercise aimed at the problematisation and clarification of (literary) experience.

We can begin this description by returning to a passage in Kames' *Elements*.

> There is here an analogy between our internal and external senses: the latter are sufficiently acute for all useful purposes of life, and so are the former. Some persons indeed, Nature's favourites, have a wonderful acuteness of sense, which to them unfolds many a delightful scene totally hid from vulgar eyes. But if such refined pleasure be confined to a small number, it is however wisely ordered that others are not sensible of the defect; nor detracts it from their happiness that others secretly are more happy. With relation to the fine arts only, that qualification seems essential; and there it is termed *delicacy of taste*. (Kames, 1762, I, pp. 111–12)

This passage is noteworthy because its stress on the recondite character of taste seems to sit oddly with the proclaimed universality of the faculty. We can resolve this puzzle by observing that eighteenth-century philosophical rhetoric is not organised by a pedagogical imperative.

This is not to say that it was not, as a matter of fact, taught. It was; but only in a marginal way, to one side of mainstream classical education, in the English Dissenting Academies and the Scottish Universities. Dominated by the metaphor of sense-perception and the God-given faculties of judgement and taste, the philosophy of representation was premised on the universality of human nature and its discriminatory powers. But – notwithstanding those who seek origins for democracy in this philosophy – it was precisely their presumed universality that removed any need to secure the dissemination of these powers through universal education. Culture for the eighteenth-century man of taste was an essentially voluntary activity, undertaken by a minority of virtuosi. Mysteriously blessed with sharper faculties than the multitude,

'Nature's favourites' chose to sharpen them still further in pursuit of a 'refined pleasure ... confined to a small number'. This is another way of saying that at this time the refinement of taste was not the object of any developed system of social discipline or government.

If we compare this dimension of eighteenth-century taste with the deployment of the literary response in modern criticism, a striking contrast soon emerges. We have seen that as far as Wimsatt and Brooks are concerned, any restriction on the generality of the aesthetic experience or aesthetic meaning threatens its very existence. Tolstoy's denunciation of aesthetics as the preserve of an élite 'whose taste has been perverted by false training', shows that the flaw in the 'formalist' position – in the desire to take pleasure in art for its own sake – is the lack of a didactic dimension. And Wimsatt and Brooks describe those in society who do not have access to the aesthetic experience as 'uneducated'. For modern criticism, unlike eighteenth-century taste, it is not enough that the aesthetic is universally accessible in principle. All individuals must in fact undergo the discipline of the aesthetic because their completion as human beings depends on it. Modern criticism is thus driven by a powerful pedagogical imperative: even if, as we have seen, it attempts to disguise this imperative by relocating it in the 'poem itself', the 'theatre of poetic conflict' or the 'human psyche' – in short, in 'man's' divided ethical substance.

How did this change come about? In fact we have already noted two aspects of it. By reconstituting the division in the field of representation which accompanied the emergence of the positive sciences as a 'wound' in 'man's' ethical substance, the Romantics transformed the function of culture. Culture ceased to be a leisurely nurturing of faculties already given in an unproblematic human nature: a nurturing typified in the formation of 'clear and distinct ideas' of the rules of taste. Redeployed as a means of reconciling his divided ethical being, culture imposed an ethical obligation on the individual to conduct himself in a certain way. Culture became the site of a specific mode of ethical subjectification. And human nature was no longer the starting point of culture, but its indefinitely deferred goal. It became the telos for a practice of the self which could never be concluded, because the kind of ethical being one aspired to become receded before each step of the dialectic of culture: each step revealing a new imbalance and a new beginning.[2] The difference in titles between Kames' *Elements of Criticism* and

Schiller's *On the Aesthetic Education of Man* is, therefore, anything but arbitrary. With the Romantic aesthetic the object of criticism and the subject who 'knew' it both became functions of a specific educational imperative or *techne*.

At the same time, we have seen that the emergence of the human sciences witnessed the formation of a different educational imperative, also important for the pedagogical character of modern criticism. The positive sciences of philology, economics and biology are not by nature pedagogical. Once again, clearly, this is not to say that they are not taught. It is to say, however, that they form their objects of knowledge independently of any imperative to transform those individuals who will be the bearers of this knowledge.

In Rask's (1811) philological description of Icelandic, for example, the phonetic and morphological features of this language are described without reference to the figure of the 'speaking subject' as a factor on which the recognition of these features might depend. But Saussure, we have noted, launches his *Course* with the claim that it is impossible to specify the object of linguistics without referring to this being: without referring to the insufficiency of its immediate linguistic intuitions, and to the unconscious 'mechanism' whose theoretical representation will transform these intuitions into objects of knowledge. For Saussurian linguistics, in other words, the object of knowledge is inseparable from a specific pedagogical action performed on or by the subject: the problematisation of 'immediate' linguistic experience and the theoretical recovery of its 'hidden' structure. It is for this reason that Cousins and Hussain describe the human sciences as 'compulsively pedagogical'; even if the sense in which they are is by no means identical with the pedagogical imperative of the Romantic aesthetic.

The pedagogical imperatives of the human sciences and the Romantic aesthetic will not by themselves account for the powerful educative drive of modern criticism, however. Neither – given their quite different functions and orientations – do they permit us to understand the merging of aesthetics and the human sciences in this criticism. The reason is not far to seek. Despite the fact that the human sciences and the aesthetic dialectic are organised by *pedagogical imperatives*, during the nineteenth century neither was systematically connected to an empirical field capable of providing it with an *educable being*. Another way of putting this is to say that during the nineteenth century criticism and the human sciences remained, in a certain sense, 'voluntary', except for special castes and groups. Even if once taken up each was capable of making itself a duty, there were no systematic and widely disseminated means for making sure that either or both would be taken up. In other words, because these pedagogical imperatives were 'internal' – that is, were contingent on a certain ethical practice or 'intellectual action' rather than being founded in the nature of 'man' – each could well have remained a separate and voluntary minority cultural practice.

Of course, the question of the practical circumstances in which the good and the true are realised in actual forms of social organisation is usually something that ethics and epistemology ignore: assuming as they do that these absolutes can be revealed in 'man' simply by virtue of his ethical and intellectual organisation. But it is precisely this assumption that is negated by the pedagogical organisations of the Romantic aesthetic and the human sciences. In them the good and the true are not transparently revealed in 'man's' ethical and epistemic being; they are achievements of a special ethical practice and a local intellectual action. The 'ground' of 'man's' ethical and intellectual being is in these instances the product of contingent practical activities and is, therefore, inseparable from the practical circumstances in which these activities are carried out.

Now it is possible to say that the ground on which Romantic criticism and the human sciences could meet – the empirical field which provided their pedagogical drives with an educable object, simultaneously making them mandatory for whole populations – was produced quite outside the two minority activities themselves. It was synthesised in that governmental apparatus which sought to subject the cultural attributes of human beings to a single formative regimen: the system of public education. More precisely, this ground – the ground of modern criticism – was formed by the disciplinary organisation of the school. By attaching the formation of the cultural attributes of a citizenry to the formation of a corrective knowledge of the individual citizen, this organisation made 'man' available as a systematically educable being.

This is *not* to say that the aesthetics and the human sciences that came together to form modern criticism are reducible to the pedagogical functions they serve in the system of public education. We have spent some time showing that the Romantic aesthetic and the human sciences were in fact able to generate distinctive and irreducible pedagogical imperatives as responses to the disintegration of the sphere of representation. And we have noted that these two cultural strategies might easily have gone on in their own separate spheres quite independently of the school system. (Indeed, to a certain degree the human sciences at least have gone on in this way.) What we *have* argued, however, is that nothing in either of these strategies dictated that they should or would be operationalised in any general way, or that they had to meet on the ground of modern criticism. The 'man' that each addressed was a figure of its own internal organisation, which is not to say that special groups of individuals did not make themselves over in the image of this figure. By themselves, however, aesthetics and the human sciences could not appropriate 'man' as an educable being.

On the one hand, they *found* this being in the space of the school and its adjacent 'social' apparatuses: the hospital, the reformatory and the policed environments of the family and the neighbourhood. These apparatuses for the first time made a particular organisation of life normative for a whole population, and did so through the manner in which they formed a corrective knowledge of each individual member. 'Man' as a systematically educable being is the artefact of these new forms for administering and investigating the 'social' sphere. On the other hand, aesthetics and the human sciences helped *shape* this sphere.[3] They provided it with the ethical and intellectual co-ordinates which permitted modern criticism to emerge as a distinctive pedagogy: one combining the ethical discipline of the cultivated man and the clarificactory practice of the social scientist.

V

The field of modern criticism, then, is not formed by the topography of 'man's' divided ethical being, nor by that of his unconscious subjectivity. In fact, it takes the form of a contingent historical space in which the educative imperatives of a special ethical practice and a local 'intellectual action' were able to appropriate 'man' as an educable being made available by a powerful pedagogical apparatus. The space in which this meeting could occur was bounded by four intersecting surfaces. We have already described three of these in some detail; but we will quickly traverse them again in order to resume the main themes of Part I and align them with the fourth surface – modern criticism – which completes our genealogy of literary education.

First, there is the surface formed by popular literary pedagogy. Outstripping its nearest rivals, the literature lesson had, by the turn of the nineteenth century, been able to emerge as the privileged embodiment of the disciplines of 'supervised freedom' and 'correction through self-expression' which characterised the school as a site of moral training. These disciplines were at the heart of the technology through which new norms for the attributes of a citizenry were realised at the level of individual desires. They were the means by which the 'self' that the individual brought in from a problematic social environment could be exposed to a normalising regimen embodied in the teacher's 'moral observation': an observation which the child learned to take over and internalise as conscience. It was by absorbing these disciplines that English was able to emerge as a powerful ethical technology, characterised by four attributes: a special ethical privilege which it acquired as the inheritor of the socio-moral disciplines ('closeness to life'); a pedagogical strategy characterised by correction through self-expression; a purpose-built teacher-student relationship combining identification and correction ('detached warmth'); and a new relation to the literary text in which the immediacy of its surface lured the reader into the unfathomable depth of the norms he was corrected by.

Second, there is the surface formed by 'culture' or the aesthetico-ethical practice of criticism itself. Criticism, we discovered, first entered the pedagogical domain not as the (true or false) vehicle of 'man's' cultural realisation, but as the source of a special social personality – the ethical exemplar – required by the tactics of moral administration. This figure was first seen in the person of Her Majesty's Inspector, but with the rise of literary pedagogy was soon being deployed as a model for the English teacher. Literary pedagogy was, however, organised by the normalising tactics of the classroom and was inseparable from the relations of identification and correction embodied in the teacher-student couple. This meant that initially the still voluntary practice of ethical self-shaping could not be integrated into the classroom or the teacher-student relationship, except as a 'knowledge subject', which both disrupted the tactics of 'moral observation' and destroyed the ascetic powers of criticism.

In the event, criticism was only able to join up with literary pedagogy by first intersecting with a *third* surface: that formed by the special *savoirs* of progressive education and educational psychology. It was the latter knowledge in particular which – by capitalising on the powers of observation and correction produced in the classroom – was able to redeploy socio-moral norms as norms of individual psycho-ethical development. In short, through 'experimental pedagogy', the student acquired a sensibility. This sensibility provided the 'hook' which allowed the ethical practice of criticism to be attached to the disciplinary functions of the classroom. In Marjorie Hourd's account, it is through the figure of 'personal growth' that the relations of empathy and correction sustained by the teacher-student couple are gradually displaced onto the relations of the ethical dialectic lodged in the authority of the literary text. In this manner the exemplary practice of the critic is redeployed as a 'task of behaviour' in the training of sensibilities. Through the instituted relations between 'surface' and 'depth', meaning and form, the student is not only exposed to observation and correction, he is made to assume responsibility for his own ethical discipline: internalising his relation to the teacher in order to become one.

In other words, it was through the special *savoirs* of experimental pedagogy that the pedagogical imperative of the Romantic aesthetic could take as its object the educable individual produced by a governmental pedagogy. In so doing it became mandatory for an important social stratum: those individuals selected for the position of ethical exemplar defined by the machinery of moral training.

At the same time, however, these special *savoirs* also opened the school to the pedagogical imperative of the human sciences, allowing this imperative to overlap for the first time with that of the Romantic aesthetic. This meeting produced the *fourth* and final surface of the literary apparatus: the surface on which modern criticism appeared. In resuming the disciplinary relations of the school on the interior of the individual's sensibility – that is, in transforming the school's 'tasks of behaviour' into tests of psychological functioning – the *savoirs* of experimental pedagogy *produced* a division between the students' overt behaviour and a level of unconscious developmental structure subtending it. We have already seen that this division, and the knowledge of the pedagogical unconscious that it gave rise to, remained inseparable from the normalising relation of 'moral observation' connecting teacher and student. Nonetheless, in overlaying this relationship with the division between observable behaviour and unconscious functions, experimental pedagogy made it possible to align the individual as the object of a disciplinary pedagogy with the figure of 'man' in the human sciences. 'Man' in the human sciences, we have observed, is characterised precisely by a division between his empirical behaviour or consciousness and the unconscious laws which make this behaviour or consciousness possible.

So, if the 'psychologisation' of the pedagogical disciplines provided the educative imperative of the Romantic aesthetic with its object, then it simultaneously achieved the same end for the educative imperative of the human sciences. It made available for the first time in a systematic fashion an individual whose responses were governed by laws which escaped his knowledge, and an apparatus in which the clarification of these laws would be made obligatory for an important social stratum.

The important point here, however, is that the 'psychologisation' of the pedagogical disciplines faced in the two directions at the same time. To the ethical imperative of criticism it offered an individual defined by an immature sensibility. But this sensibility was one whose maturation criticism might allow the individual himself to become responsible for: reconciling his ideas and feelings, his didactic and his sensuous impulses, on the testing surface of the literary text. To the clarificatory imperative of the human sciences it offered an individual defined by his unconscious subjectivity. But this was an unconscious that the individual might himself bring to consciousness through the self-problematising regimen of a human science. In short, modern criticism emerged in the unstable space between an aesthetico-ethical practice deployed as a pedagogical norm, and a reflexive intellectual action deployed as a pedagogical discipline.

In this space the inaugural act of modern criticism was not the reconciliation of its earlier didactic and formalist imbalances, bringing 'man' face to face with the unsurpassable aesthetic experience of the 'poem itself' for the first time. But neither was it a theoretical incision in the empirical surface of the text which revealed to the subject the unconscious laws of literary representation. Instead, we can say that modern criticism was inaugurated when I. A. Richards presented his undergraduate classes with thirteen unseen poems, and found in their responses both the traces of ethically incomplete sensibilities and the symptoms of the unconscious laws which made such responses possible. This is not to make any claim of absolute priority for Richards. It is only to say that in his work the formerly distinct imperatives of the Romantic aesthetic and the human sciences entered into an exchange of functions. And we can see that this exchange took place through the 'immature' and 'pre-theoretical' individual made available by the pedagogical apparatus.

We saw in Part I that this individual was the artefact of the dense network of observation and correction produced by the pedagogical disciplines and embodied in the relation between student and teacher. Now we can see that in this disciplinary environment or, more precisely, in that special branch of it dedicated to the formation of the English teacher as an ethical exemplar, the mythopoeic pretexts of the Romantic aesthetic and the human sciences could find correlates in the tactics of a governmental pedagogy. The 'wound' in 'man's' ethical substance, through which the Romantics had displaced the split in representation, could now become the site at which the teacher supervised the formation of the exemplary sensibility required by the machinery of moral training. While the subject's 'pre-theoretical intuition', which had provided the human sciences with their pretext for pursuing unthought being, could now provide the 'man who observed' with signs of behaviour open to modification according to unconscious norms. Moreover, because each of these tactics was made possible by precisely the same organisation of corrective observation, the individual's (instituted) failure to achieve aesthetico-ethical reconciliation could immediately appear as the sign of a pre-theoretical intuition. While on the same basis the individual's (instituted) failure to recover the unconscious laws of the literary reading could be treated as a correlate of his failure to reconcile form and meaning in an appropriate aesthetic response.

It should not surprise us, then, that Richards' diagnosis of the defective sensibility of the 'literalist' should be made at exactly the point where these two co-ordinates of failure meet. The 'aim of the poem' which eludes the literalist is the reconciliation of form and meaning which the reader must also achieve in order to become ethically complete. But it is also the unconscious 'mental condition' or 'collection of impulses' which made the poem possible and that the reader must restore to consciousness.

It is possible to say, then, that *modern criticism* is the artefact of a special kind of *literary pedagogy* and is therefore inseparable from it: the two together making up the field of 'English'. Of course, it is possible for criticism to function as a form of voluntary self-culture independently of the relations of surveillance and correction embodied in the classroom and the teacher-student couple. But under these conditions self-culture can have no pretensions to generality. It lacks systematic access to 'man' as an educable being. Neither could it – as Wimsatt and Brooks would wish – do double service as a theory of literature; because only through the correctional force of the pedagogical disciplines can the individual's ethical imbalance be redeployed as a pre-theoretical intuition in need of 'structural' clarification.

Similarly, we have seen that it was possible for the human sciences to emerge in the space between the positive sciences and philosophy without any help from the pedagogical apparatus. But we have also seen that the resultant imperative to restore 'man's' unconscious being to consciousness can have no claims to generality either: being internal to the 'intellectual action' that opens this space in the first place. Neither can the literary affiliates of the human sciences – literary psychology and semiotics, myth criticism, literary sociology – attach themselves to the aesthetic domain except through the school. Only through the corrective force of the pedagogical disciplines can the subject's 'failure' to reconcile form and meaning in the aesthetic experience be represented as a failure to make conscious the unconscious laws which make the experience possible. (This, the reader will re-member, is precisely the manner in which Todorov represents the 'crisis' in rhetoric.)

Today criticism is characterised by two overlapping tendencies: the tendency to push the aesthetic reading to the point where it doubles as its own foundations (New Criticism); and the tendency to locate the theoretical recovery of the subject's 'literary unconscious' in a fully reconciled (self-regulating) aesthetic structure (semiotic, psychological, archetypal and sociological poetics). We know that these two tendencies set the stage for a vociferous and interminable argument within modern criticism between its 'practical' and 'theoretical' wings. It should now be clear, however, that – like the debate between the 'positivist' and 'reflexive' arms of the human sciences – this debate is constitutionally unresolvable, marking as it does the historical space in which modern criticism comes into being. This is the space in which the pedagogical imperatives of the Romantic aesthetic and the human sciences were able to meet, in a being characterised by a divided ethical substance and a pre-theoretical consciousness. These attributes of the subject of modern criticism are not, of course, attributes of 'man'. Rather, they mark the exact point at which the pedagogical disciplines allow social norms to take root in the depths of 'man's' educable being, which is their artefact.

Like the Romantic aesthetic and the human sciences, modern criticism is not anchored in a particular empirical content (the 'poem itself', the aesthetic experience) or a particular theoretical object (aesthetic form, the 'subject of literary discourse'). Instead, its mode of existence is characterised by the co-deployment of a specific ethical practice and a local 'intellectual action' inside an apparatus aimed at forming a special kind of personage – the teacher-critic. Embodying the non-coercive disciplines of the modern school, and combining the attributes of the cultivated man and the social scientist, the teacher-critic in fact personifies the patchwork historical field in which modern criticism emerges. In describing modern criticism, then, we cannot take as our object either an autonomous aesthetic experience or a set of fundamental laws which make such an experience possible. Instead, we must describe the contours of the unstable historical field which sets the limits inside which the forms and functions of criticism can vary. This description will complete our genealogy of modern criticism.

7

Exemplary Knowledge

I

For ease of exposition we can imagine the space of modern criticism as a field formed between two poles. At one end is the pole of the Romantic aesthetic characterised by the practice of reconciling the ethical antinomies – of form and meaning, feeling and thought, tradition and vision, the aesthetic and the didactic – in an exemplary reading of the literary text. At the other stands the pole of the human sciences, around which is clustered a whole swarm of 'foundational' literary theories. All of these, however, are characterised by a single intellectual action – the restoration to consciousness of literary representation's unthought conditions – differing only over whether these conditions are to be looked for in 'man's' speaking, living or labouring being.

Modern criticism does not exist at either pole. It is neither a pure aesthetico-ethical discipline nor a pure human science (perhaps a contradiction in terms anyway), nor can it aspire to be such. Instead, as we have seen, it comes into being between these poles in the unexpected exchange of functions between the discipline of the ethical exemplar and the clarificatory practice of the 'rational man'. The ground on which this exchange takes place – the very substance of the forces organised into a field by the polar imperatives – is constituted by the supervisory strategy of a governmental pedagogy. And in describing the forms assumed by criticism in this field we must keep to the forefront that it is this strategy that provides criticism with an individual characterised by a divided ethical substance and an unconscious being.

This is where our genealogy differs from a number of recent anatomies of modern criticism; for example, those provided by Krieger (1969), Polletta (1973a), Belsey (1980), Hartman (1980), Jameson (1981), Todorov (1981) and Cain (1984). These too characterise criticism as bipolar, consisting of practical criticism or the 'close reading' at one end, and literary theory or 'structural

220

poetics' at the other. However, because they derive either from the New Criticism, or from the literary appropriation of the human sciences, they assume that the poles mark the two dimensions of a single figure: 'man' or the human subject. It is thus characteristic of these anatomies that they are driven to posit a continuity between, or to call for a reconciliation of, practical criticism and literary theory. It should come as no surprise that this continuity or reconciliation comes in only two forms: one in which a theory which has abstracted itself from the act of reading is recalled to the unsurpassable aesthetic mediation of the 'text itself' (Krieger); and one in which the 'naive empiricism' of the close reading is subsumed within a theoretical recovery of its structural conditions (Belsey, Jameson and Todorov). There is a hybrid of these two forms which attempts to combine them in an ecumenical gesture (Polletta, Hartman and Cain), but this only produces an oscillation hedging all bets.

It should be clear from the argument of the preceding chapter that these anatomies which posit a continuity or call for a reconciliation, of either sort, are in fact quite misleading. At one level, it is simply a misunderstanding of the conditions which brought modern criticism into being to seek a continuity between practical criticism and literary theory. 'Theory' in this instance is not related to practical criticism as an abstraction from a fundamental experience to which it must be recalled. Rather, it derives from the autonomous self-problematising regimen of the human sciences and is only contingently related to the techniques of the 'close reading'. Moreover, the close reading is not based in 'the subject's' pre-theoretical intuition; it is the outcome of an irreducible aesthetico-ethical practice in relation to which the intellectual action of the human sciences can exercise no 'foundational' prerogative. (The domain of reason is a patchwork.)

At another level it is simply beside the point to call for a reconciliation of the aesthetic dialectic and the theoretical analysis of structures, because this has already been achieved as the condition of modern criticism's emergence. However, this continuity was established neither on the grounds of 'man's' ethical nor his unconscious being, but in the educable being offered to criticism by the pedagogical disciplines. Hence, in describing the forms assumed by modern criticism in the space between the 'close reading' and literary theory, we must resist the temptation to posit an ethical or an epistemological continuity where none exists. But even more importantly we must resist an even stronger temptation: to ignore the entirely historical and contingent continuity that does exist. In describing the exchange of functions between an aesthetico-ethical discipline and the sciences of man that defines the field of modern criticism, it is the formation of this historical and contingent continuity in the pedagogical disciplines that is crucial.

II

Approaching the *first* pole – that of Romantic critical practice – but remaining at one remove from it, is the activity of practical criticism. We have already looked at an example of this activity in the Blackmur text discussed at the opening of Chapter 5. In the following remarks we find F. R. Leavis specifying it as the 'essential discipline' of the English School by, significantly, distinguishing it from 'mere knowledge'.

> Are the principles that should govern a School of English so hard to grasp? Here, to begin with, is a negative formulation: there is no more futile study than that which ends with mere knowledge *about* literature . . . The study of a literary text about which the student cannot say, as a matter of first-hand perception and judgement – of intelligent realisation – why it should be worth study is a self-stultifying occupation. . .
>
> It is plain that in the work of a properly ordered English School . . . the training of reading capacity has first place. By training of reading capacity I mean the training of perception, judgement and analytic skill commonly referred to as 'practical criticism' – or, rather, the training that 'practical criticism' ought to be. . .
>
> In pointing to [the words on the page] what we are doing is to bring into sharp focus, in turn, this, that and the other detail, juncture or relation in our total response; or (since 'sharp focus' may be a misleading account of the attention sometimes required), what we are doing is to dwell with a deliberate, considering responsiveness on this, that or the other node or focal point in the complete organisation that the poem is, in so far as we have it. (Leavis, 1943, pp. 67–70)

Equally, we might cite a more recent description of the activity to the same effect; this time made in the more generalising and trans-Atlantic accent of Cleanth Brooks, who wrote in 1962 that:

> it is possible to restate the history of criticism in our time thus: We have been witnessing a strenuous attempt to focus attention upon the poem rather than upon the poet or the reader. Along with this stress upon the poem as a structure in its own right, has come the attempt to fix the boundaries and limits of poetry. Modern critics have tried to see what was meant when one considered the poem as an artistic document . . . Poetry has a characteristic structure and yields a characteristic knowledge. It does not compete with, but exists alongside of and complements, scientific knowledge and historical knowledge. (Brooks, cited in Polletta, 1973a, p. 3)

In fact, despite Leavis' stress on the unsurpassable concreteness of the literary text and Brooks' on the autonomous character of the literary experience – and, we might add, despite the misnomer 'close reading' – it is misleading to treat practical criticism as an attempt to get 'closer to the text': either closer to an irreducible aesthetic experience, *or* to a naively empirical intuition. It is not difficult to show the incoherence of practical criticism if pursued in its own terms. On the one hand, its advocates affirm that the poem is 'a structure in its own right' which 'as a matter of first-hand perception and judgement' can be 'pointed to'. On the other, the knowledge of this structure is not the same as 'scientific knowledge and historical knowledge' because 'We can have the poem only as an inner kind of possession; it is "there" for analysis only in so far as we are responding appropriately to the words on the page . . . What we call analysis is, of course, a constructive or creative process' (Leavis, 1943, p. 70). So, the poem is an irreducibly concrete structure whose availability to 'perception and judgement' justifies the 'first-hand' autonomy of the aesthetic response. But this peculiar structure is not given to ordinary knowledge and is 'there' only because it is the object of the aesthetic response. The aesthetic response must therefore function as a justification for the poetic structure that justifies it.

Showing this incoherence is of no particular importance, however. In fact, it is a variant of the same circularity that we found in Wimsatt and Brooks' attempt to install the aesthetic experience as the goal of the history of criticism. It will be remembered that they attempted to universalise the normative regimen of the aesthetic dialectic by locating it in an objective semantic structure, but that because this threatened the ethical specificity of the dialectic they had to simultaneously locate 'semantic structure' in the aesthetic reconciliation of form and meaning. The reader will also recall that the resolution of this circularity is not to invoke the 'hermeneutic circle' or to treat criticism as a 'special kind of knowledge'. It can be achieved simply by observing that criticism is not a knowledge at all, but a different kind of activity: a practice of ethical self-shaping.[1] In this regard, the phrase to emphasise in Leavis' account is 'responding *appropriately*'. To say that poetic structure justifies a special kind of (aesthetic) response which is also the only justification for poetic structure, is simply to say that this response is being deployed as a *norm*. The correct formulation is thus: we only say that we recognise *poetic* structure when we respond in *this* way. And, indeed, this is the case. When Leavis completes his specification of practical criticism by 'pointing to' poetic structure, he does so by reconciling the tendencies to didacticism and sentimentality (the work of the 'unrealising mind') in a reading of Shakespeare.

In other words, despite Brooks' claim that modern criticism is characterised by 'a strenuous effort to focus attention on the poem', the poem in practical criticism is not the object of a knowledge but the vehicle for a specialised ethical practice, whose real target is the ethical organisation of the reader. We can recall Schiller's (1795, p. 53) remark that not knowledge but 'the development of man's capacity for feeling, is . . . the more urgent need of our age'. And we can note that in Leavis' handbook it is not its theoretical breadth that wins the English School its unquestionable pre-eminence as the co-ordinating hub of the humanities. It is, rather, the fact that it contains a discipline for the integration of 'intelligence' and 'sensitiveness' on which right knowledge and right action depend.

> It is of the essence of the scheme that the work of all kinds would be done by the 'literary mind'. . .; by, that is, an intelligence with the sensitiveness, the flexibility and the disciplined and mature preoccupation with value that should be the product of literary training. It is an intelligence so trained that is best fitted to develop into the central kind of mind, the co-ordinating consciousness, capable of performing the function assigned to the class of the educated. (Leavis, 1943, p. 55)

Practical criticism, then, is not characterised by an (unsurpassable or naive) perception of the text, but by a normative technique or practice for shaping a particular relation to the self as a moral subject. Practical criticism, like Romantic criticism before it, is the site of a particular mode of ethical subjectification. The mode is not the same in the two cases, however. In practical criticism the aesthetico-ethical dialectic through which the individual constructs the relation to the self has been subordinated to its deployment as a means for focusing the individual's relation to another, the teacher. At the heart of practical criticism we do not find an irreducibly concrete (or stupidly empirical) perception of literature. Instead, we find a specially-instituted relation between one who teaches and one who is taught: between an individual who corrects and shapes and an individual whose ethical incompleteness – revealed in his 'first-hand' responses – opens him to correction and moulding. Leavis himself comes close to realising this when he affirms that criticism is inseparable from the teaching relation, and in fact takes the form of the dialogue: 'This is so isn't it? . . . Yes, but . . .' Here we glimpse the form of the disciplinary relation in which the individual's response draws forth the agreement and then the correction of an ethical superior. 'The more experienced the teacher is in these matters, the more he is able to draw from the pupil the certainties (first) and later the doubts' (Dixon, 1967, p. 8).

In fact the sedulous manner in which practical criticism scours the body of the text – but always seeking and finding precisely the same antinomies (ideas and feelings; structure and texture; form and meaning) and reconciliations (embodiment; metaphor; irony; paradox; ambiguity) – is the product of the redeployment of the Romantic dialectic as a pedagogical norm. In the first place, the text is open to 'first-hand perception and judgement' – requires no preparatory historical or philological knowledge – because it is deployed as the means by which the student's problematic 'social' experiences can be freely affirmed: not just affirmed, of course, but corrected according to norms invested in the teacher's 'moral observation'. But for this very reason, as we have already noted, the 'immediate response' is never finished with. The reader must return again and again to the text – not because of a will to knowledge, but because it is the point where his 'social soul' is opened to observation and correction. This is the first reason why modern practical criticism is much more 'searching' than its Romantic forebear.

In the second place, at a more advanced (tertiary) stage in the formation of the 'class of the educated', the text is 'concrete and immediate' because – according to one imperative of the ethical dialectic – it must resist all my efforts to derive its meaning from some 'external' didactic system or intention. It challenges me to transcend 'stock responses' through a spontaneous perception or play of consciousness. At the same time – according to the second imperative – that final ineffable perception will always elude my consciousness. I cannot help, at the last minute, falling back on meanings derived from ordinary language and morality. The enormous energy with which Leavis seeks to fix the poem in an apodictic insight is, in fact, only a sign that in this new deployment it is impossible for reading to come to rest in 'touchstones'. 'Commonly', Leavis (1943, p. 74) says, 'one can call attention to this, that or the other detail by way of making the nature and force of one's judgement plain. And in a case as simple as the present one can very often, putting a finger on something in the text, make an observation that is irresistable and final.' But this finality, which Arnold claimed, is no longer available. In practical criticism the dialectic of reading has the role of demonstrating the state of my sensibility: either to someone positioned to diagnose and correct its imbalance, or to 'myself', who is the outcome of internalising the tactics of observation and correction. Hence the second reason for the often compulsive intensity with which practical criticism addresses the text: each reading, even when performed in solitude, marks the point where the individual is required by the pedagogical relationship to register his ethical incompleteness, and to begin again.

A number of the central features of practical criticism became easier to understand when viewed in this light:

● *First*, the minuteness and incompleteness of its analysis. These now appear, we have observed, not as the sign of an (irreducible or naive) perception of the text, but as the functional outcome of the redeployment of the Romantic ethical practice as a pedagogical discipline.

● *Second*, the anti-theoretical tendency of practical criticism, which must not be treated as a symptom of obtuseness or ideological obscurantism. This tendency too flows directly from the pedagogical use of the Romantic dialectic, which is from the outset an ethical practice and not a knowledge.

● *Third,* we can now see why practical criticism is inseparable from a specially instituted teacher-student relation: because it is the outcome of the redeployment of the Romantic aesthetic as a vehicle for this relation.

● *Fourth,* for all these reasons we can see why 'knowledge' in practical criticism remains dependent on the critic's possession of a special public ethical status or persona and, hence, why disputes in criticism tend to take the form of unresolvable clashes of ethical personality.

III

Approaching the *second* pole of the critical field – that of the human sciences – but always at one remove from it, we find the domain of literary theory or structural poetics. It will be remembered from Todorov's history that this domain is formed according to a particular project: that of breaking with criticism as a pre-theoretical field based on an empirical conception of literary representation, and reconstituting it through a scientific recovery of its unthought conditions. This strategy is, of course, precisely what literary theory borrows from the field of the human sciences. And because this is in fact the defining strategy of that field it brings with it the central features of the human sciences, even if transposed into a new register. Any of the contemporary forms of literary theory would do to exemplify this transposition of the structure of the human sciences into the register of criticism, but we can begin with Northrop Frye's 'literary anthropology', which is both widely known and representative. For the sake of exposition, we will draw mainly on Frye's seminal essay 'The Archetypes of Literature' – described by the author as 'to some extent a summarised statement of the critical programme' developed in his *Anatomy of Criticism* – supplementing it with reference to the *Anatomy* where necessary.

Frye launches his programme – just as Saussure begins his *Course* – by lamenting the pre-theoretical disunity of the field. Criticism, like linguistics, cannot become a science until it has an autonomous object. The study of literature embraces positive sciences like phonetics, prosody and philology, but each of these has its own object which is not (aesthetic) 'literature'. It also embraces commentary or criticism, but this consists mostly of unexamined value judgements and subjective intuitions. Hence Frye suggests that:

> what is at present missing from literary criticism is a co-ordinating principle, a central hypothesis which, like the theory of evolution in biology, will see the phenomena it deals with as parts of a whole. . .
> The first postulate of this hypothesis is the same as that of any science: the assumption of total coherence. (Frye, 1951, p. 602)

Before discussing what is involved in the 'total coherence' of criticism as a science, it is worth commenting on the strategy by which Frye arrives at this postulate. In the first place, there is a use of the 'transcendental argument' which need not detain us because it is evidently circular: 'Criticism cannot be systematic unless there is a quality in literature which enables it to be so, an order of words corresponding to the order of nature in the natural sciences.' But at the same time, 'A belief in an order of nature is an inference from the intelligibility of the natural sciences' (ibid., pp. 604, 602). In fact, the real motivation for the postulate of 'total coherence' is provided by Frye's characterisation of the 'pre-theoretical field'. This field demands a systematic foundation not simply because it is fragmented and hence fragments 'literature', but because this lack of unity is a sign that the study of literature has not yet recovered the unthought conditions of its object. In other words, Frye's literary anthropology' emerges in precisely that space, opened between the positive sciences and a new philosophical discourse, where the human sciences first appeared; and it does so by asking the 'foundational' question asked by every human science: On what basis are the representations given to man by virtue of his empirical being represented to his consciousness?

Frye's answer, of course, is given in terms of the recurrent ritual structures which he calls archetypes or myths, because the human science he happens to alight on is anthropology. But the important thing for us to note is that like all the other (linguistic, psychological, sociological) structures constructed in answer to this question, Frye's ritual structures are double-sided. They root 'man' in the world of nature with its great seasonal rhythms and hence determine his empirical 'finitude'. But they also function as the means by which 'man' can master these forces, obtain an 'analytic' knowledge of them through them, and hence realise all that he might become.

> Rhythm, or recurrent movement, is deeply founded on the natural cycle, and everything in nature that we think of as having some analogy with works of art, like the flower or the bird's song, grows out of a profound synchronisation between an organism and the rhythms of its environment, especially that of the solar year. With animals some expressions of synchronisation, like the mating dances of birds, could almost be called rituals. But in human life ritual seems to be something of a voluntary effort (hence the magical element in it) to recapture a lost rapport with a natural cycle ... In ritual, then, we may find the origin of narrative, a ritual being a temporal sequence of acts in which the conscious meaning or significance is latent: it can be seen by an observer, but is largely concealed from the participators themselves ... We should notice too the regular tendency of ritual to become encyclopedic ... most of the higher religions are equipped with a definitive body of rituals suggestive, if we may put it so, of the entire range of potentially significant actions in human life. (Ibid., pp. 605–6)

This set of moves is disarming in its very audacity. However, there is no inherent reason why Frye's location of the fundaments of literary representation in the dancing of peasant farmers should be found any less plausible than Todorov's unconscious semiotic system, or Richards' organisation of mental impulses. All we need note for the moment is that the archetypal structure of literature, like its semiotic and psychological cousins, takes the form of the 'analytic of finitude': that is, a double-sided form which both links 'man's' being to the empirical world and sets limits to it (the 'organism'); while also functioning as the form in which this empirical being gives birth to a consciousness which contains all possible forms of being (the 'encyclopedia'). And we can see in the preceding quotation that this central figure of the human sciences draws in its train the two other figures which Foucault isolates as characteristic.

First, the ambivalent figure of 'man' as a 'transcendental-empirical couple': that is as a being determined by the blind laws of his natural being, yet able to deploy these laws in a reflexive modality and hence transcend them. Second, the figure of the unconscious: that is, of the unthought character of these archetypal structures, and hence of the imperative to 'think' them. Frye (ibid., p. 603) comments that 'every poet has his private mythology, his own spectroscopic band or peculiar formation of symbols, of which he is quite unconscious', and it is the central task of poetics to bring these to consciousness by recovering their archetypal forms.

It should now be clear that the foundational strategy permitting Frye to postulate the 'total coherence' of critical science is in fact governed by the three figures that characterise the deployment of the human sciences. *They* provide the motivation and the blueprint for Frye's construction of a single 'total form' underlying all literature and literary history: a form based on the rhythmic structure of the seasons, recapitulated in the quest myth which assumes the role of a universal genre-grammar for all literature. But in describing Frye's monumental undertaking in this fashion, what becomes apparent is its radical instability. After all, we have seen that the three figures of the human sciences – the analytic of finitude, the transcendental-empirical couple and the unconscious – are not signs that the human sciences were born with the discovery of a fundamental object – 'man'. They are, rather, signs that these knowledges have their genesis in a highly particular and contingent intellectual action: that oblique duplication of the positive sciences in the space of representation which separates them from philosophy. And we have seen that no appeal to the topography of the 'human subject' – to its pre-theoretical empirical experiences or its unthought constitutive structures – can motivate this action, because this topography is in fact its *outcome*.

Frye (ibid., p. 602), for example, attempts to motivate his postulate of criticism's 'total coherence' and his search for literature's 'total form' by redeploying practical criticism (which he calls 'rhetorical or structural analysis') as a partial 'first effort' at a full critical analysis. Practical criticism is necessary but deficient, according to Frye, because it is the spontaneous expression of the 'subject's' pre-theoretical intuition, which must therefore be purified through a theoretical clarification of its unthought general laws. But, as we have just seen, practical criticism is *not* an expression of the subject's pre-theoretical intuitions. It is the contemporary form of an irreducible aesthetico-ethical discipline in which the text is not the object of a knowledge but the target of a practice. (The domain of reason is a patchwork.) Practical criticism is not pre-theoretical or incomplete. (It may have outlived its usefulness and it may be disintegrating under its own weight, but these are quite different questions.)

In other words, Frye's structural poetics, like the human sciences whose model it borrows, is not characterised by the recovery of the unconscious laws of 'man's' literary being. Rather, it is governed by the repetition of an entirely historical and contingent intellectual action: that action in which the positive sciences (philology and rhetoric) are suspended in the space which separates them from philosophy, where they are forced to go proxy for 'the conditions of literary representation'. Frye is in no way unique in this regard. After all, Todorov rehearses precisely the same action in order to construct the 'crisis' in rhetorical imitation, which he then solves by appealing to the Romantic aesthetic as a semiotics *avant la lettre*. From the fact that structural poetics is not based in a specific object, and is instead the outcome of a contingent intellectual action, two important consequences follow.

First, because this action is entirely historical, there is no limit to the number of times it can be performed, except perhaps that determined by the permutations of the positive sciences that it draws on. Hence, Frye's literary anthropology was preceded by Richards' (1924) literary psychology and the literary semiotics of the Russian and Czech formalists. And it has been succeeded by further developments of these earlier initiatives, like Greimas' (1966) literary semantics; by new initiatives obeying the same fundamental strategy, such as the use of Lacanian psychoanalysis to develop a literary psychoanalytics; and by an endless proliferation of hybrid combinations of these 'sciences': for example, Jameson's (1981) amalgamation of Greimassian narrative semantics and the Marxian theory of ideology into a hybrid aimed at recovering literature's 'political unconscious'. This riot of foundations mocks the very idea of a 'foundation' for criticism. It certainly casts an ironic light on Frye's (ibid., p. 605) prophecy: 'A minor result of our new perspective is that contradictions among critics, and assertions that this and not that critical approach is the right one, show a remarkable tendency to dissolve into unreality.'

Anything but this has been the outcome of the pursuit of critical foundations. But we are now in a position to see that this is not the outcome of the 'pre-theoretical' irrationality of critics as a group; nor of some transcendent aesthetic property of art that defies theorisation. Rather, the uncontrollable pursuit of foundations results from the fact that this pursuit has no final object – 'man's' literary unconscious – only the contingent intellectual action that generates the will to think the unthought conditions of 'man's' being. The competition between a profusion of rival critical foundations is thus an inescapable and hence permanent feature of modern criticism: a congenital malady. It cannot be resolved or adjudicated by literary theory because it marks the space where literary theory comes into being.

Second, because it is thus dominated by the will to bring to light that which in 'man's' empirical literary representations makes them possible while eluding consciousness, literary theory inherits the pedagogical imperative of the human sciences. It cannot address its supposed object – literature's structural conditions – except as a function of the problematising and clarificatory action it performs on 'the subject'. However, we have seen that the being on whom this action is performed today is not the figure of 'man' projected by the three co-ordinates of the human sciences. It is the 'educable being' made available by the supervisory tactics of public education and their privileged embodiment, the teacher-student couple. It is the correctional force of these tactics that operationalises the distinction between overt responses and underlying developmental norms on which the human sciences can go to work as a pedagogy, as we can quite clearly see in the pattern of response and correction recorded in Richards' *Practical Criticism*.

At the same time, we have seen that it was in this same disciplinary organisation that the Romantic aesthetic discovered the being whose ethical incompleteness justified *its* deployment as a pedagogy. In short, the pedagogical imperative of literary theory finds its object in the disciplinary transformation of an individual, who is simultaneously the object of an aesthetico-ethical shaping. And this has meant, as we have noted, that the theoretical project to recover 'man's' literary unconscious has from the outset been inseparable from the aesthetico-ethical imperative to reconcile his divided being through the literary reading. This is why literary theory, or structural poetics, has no choice but to remain at one remove from the domain of the human sciences whose model it borrows. It should come as no surprise, then, if we discover that, inside the 'scientific' domain of literary theory, all the old themes of 'criticism and culture' resurface: the clarification of the subject's literary unconscious going proxy for 'man's' cultural apotheosis.

IV

We can now see why the major tendencies of modern criticism cannot be identified with either of its polar forms, and instead take shape in a dense network of exchanges between the *exemplary reading* of practical criticism and the *reflexive reading* of structural poetics. Through the 'educable being' of modern pedagogy the 'close reading' is always pushing toward an aesthetic reconciliation of the text which, by revealing its governing norms, will allow the reading to double as 'theory of literature'. At the same time, through this same being, the theoretical project to reveal literature's unconscious laws finds itself driven to demonstrate these laws through exemplary readings of aesthetic organisation. It is in the overlap of these two practices of criticism that most critical activity and critical dispute occurs today. Let us examine each in turn.

First, the drive of the 'close reading' to become reflexive to its own conditions of possibility: we can find a well-known and representative example of this tendency in Cleanth Brooks' exemplary New Critical reading of Keats' 'Ode on a Grecian Urn'.

Significantly, and typically, Brooks begins his essay by posing the problem of the aesthetic reading itself, in a semi-explicit fashion. T. S. Eliot has pronounced that the 'Ode's' climactic lines – 'Beauty is truth, – truth beauty, – that is all/Ye know on earth, and all ye need to know.' – are a 'serious blemish on a beautiful poem', because they are either meaningless or make a false statement. In other words, Eliot has raised the problem of didacticism or, as Brooks would have it, the problem of truth in poetry, and hence the problem of the truth of poetry for criticism. Brooks' strategy for dealing with this problem will be quite familiar, given our previous discussion of his and Wimsatt's attempts to universalise the aesthetic reading. He argues that the famous aphorism is not a statement about beauty and truth in any ordinary sense, but a 'dramatisation' of such a statement motivated by a series of 'ironies' and 'paradoxes'. These, Brooks (1947, p. 126) claims, confine the meaning of the poem to the relation between its own form and content; and he suggests: 'the "Ode on a Grecian Urn" provides us with as neat an instance as one could wish in order to test the implications of such a manoeuvre.'

He then proceeds to demonstrate that the poem (and 'poetry') does meet the 'test' of this strategy, by performing a reading which shows that the central statement is indeed contained within a 'context' of motivating ironies and paradoxes which dramatise it. These latter are of a fairly familiar Romantic kind: art represents and immortalises life's pleasures and beauties, but in doing so puts them beyond ordinary human use and enjoyment. They are only significant because they duplicate at the level of the poem's *content* the same 'paradox' which Brooks is posing at the level of its *reading*: art makes beautiful statements about life, but these cannot be used (interpreted) for ordinary human purposes. Neither should this surprise us if, as we have argued earlier, Keats' poetry and Brooks' criticism are simply alternative vehicles for the same aesthetico-ethical regimen.

Brooks' strategy is, of course, to show through his reading that the ironies and paradoxes of content are in fact generated by irony and paradox as formal principles of poetic structure, so that the poem can be regarded as 'enacting' its own statements. In other words, Keats' aphorism is not meant to be didactically true (so it is neither stupid nor a 'blemish'), but has its own special (aesthetic) truth (so is not merely a private frippery). In this way the poem can apparently itself tell Brooks that he is reading it in the right way, because it both enacts and states the truth of the aesthetic reading – unity of form and experience – through the voice of the urn.

> What will it say to them [the other generations]? Presumably, what it says to the poet now: that 'formed experience', imaginative insight, embodies the basic and fundamental perception of man and nature. The urn is beautiful, and yet its beauty is based – what else is the poem concerned with? – on an imaginative perception of essentials. Such a vision is beautiful but it is also true. The sylvan historian [i.e., the urn] presents us with beautiful histories, but they are true histories, and it is a good historian. (Brooks, 1947, p. 134)

At the same time, because these truths are not contained in ordinary statements but are generated from the internal organisation of the poem, they are in fact truths of a 'statement' that the poem makes about its own structure. In other words, the aesthetic reading is driven to locate the 'imaginative perception of essentials' in the poem's reflexive recovery of its own formal conditions. In the 'dramatisation' of the aphorism the 'close reading' is made to go proxy for a 'theory' of its own possibility.

> If we have been alive to these items [of irony and paradox], we shall not, perhaps, be too much surprised to have the urn speak once more, not in the sense in which it tells a story – a metaphor which is rather easy to accept – but, to have it speak on a higher level, to have it make a commentary on its own nature. If the urn has been properly dramatised, if we have followed the development of the metaphors, if we have been alive to the paradoxes which work throughout the poem, perhaps then, we shall be prepared for the enigmatic, final paradox which the 'silent form' utters. But in that case, we shall not feel that the generalisation, unqualified to be taken literally, is meant to march out of its context to compete with the scientific and philosophical generalisations which dominate our world. (Ibid., pp. 134–5)

In short, the aesthetic reading, in demonstrating the unity of form and meaning wins from the poem a 'theoretical' reflection on that unity, but one entirely contained in the 'special knowledge' of literature provided by the aesthetic reading.

We can best unravel this 'enigmatic and paradoxical' reading by returning to Matthew Arnold's essay on Keats, which we discussed in Chapter 5. It will be remembered that in this essay Arnold is not concerned about the problem of the 'Ode's' didacticism, nor about its 'special kind of truth'. Neither does he undertake a 'close reading' to make his points. Why is this so? It is certainly not because Arnold is unaware of the problem of didacticism as such. After all, he has just finished taking Wordsworth to task for this very tendency. It is, rather, that in this essay the target for the dialectic of didacticism and senuousness is not the poem but the 'life of the poet'. In this context the 'Ode's' famous aphorism is unproblematically true in the 'ordinary sense' for Arnold, because it shows that Keats had been able to moderate his disfiguring tendency to sensuousness through the discovery of a moral principle: 'the principle of beauty in all things'. This does not mean that Arnold is any less sensitive than Brooks or, as Wimsatt and Brooks claim, that he himself was disfigured by a tendency towards didacticism. (Note the ethical terrain on which critical discussion is typically carried out.) It simply means that at this juncture the reconciliation of the ethical antinomies achieved by the aesthetic reading is being carried out through a work performed on the exemplary *life*, rather than one performed on the exemplary *text*.

But what this shows is precisely the *variability* of the investments which criticism is subject to. It shows again that the real target of criticism is not the structure of the poem, but the aesthetico-ethical organisation of its reader, for which the exemplary poem – but equally the exemplary life – provides the pretext for the practice of self-shaping. And this returns us to the point which we reached by another route in Chapter 5: To say that the poem does not make a (verifiable, 'ordinary', etc.) statement, is not to say that it makes a special kind of statement, or that it states only its own structure. It is simply to say that under certain special circumstances we do not attempt to use its utterances as statements: that is, to paraphrase them, verify them, etc. And for this reason it is quite misleading to claim that poetry provides access to a special kind of truth – 'the imaginative perception of essentials' – and that we must therefore read it in such a manner as to preserve this truth. Reading it in *this* manner – that is, refusing to paraphrase; referring meaning to formal features like irony and paradox – is simply what we *call* 'having access to a special kind of truth'.

Now we can see that Brooks' real problem is not whether the 'Ode' is didactic, or whether poetry and criticism have their own special kind of truth. It is the problem of how to ensure that the poem's expressions will not be *used as statements*, and will instead always be referred to its formal organisation. It is the problem, in short, of how to impose a particular aesthetico-ethical obligation – or mode of subjectification – on his reader: the student. This diagnosis is confirmed by the observation that when Brooks addresses his reader directly it is not to equip him with descriptive techniques; it is, rather, to impose an obligation on him.

> Yet there are some claims to be made upon the reader too, claims which he, for his part, will have to be prepared to honour. He must not be allowed to dismiss the early characterisations of the urn as merely so much vaguely beautiful description. He must not be too surprised if 'mere decoration' turns out to be meaningful symbolism – or if ironies develop where he has been taught to expect only sensuous pictures. Most of all, if the teasing

riddle spoken finally by the urn is not to strike him as a bewildering break in tone, he must not be too disturbed to have the element of paradox latent in the poem emphasised. . . (Ibid., pp. 126–7)

But, as Arnold's reading shows, nothing about the poem justifies the imposition of this obligation or prevents us from taking its central aphorism as a somewhat quaint Romantic statement open to paraphrase. Again: it is not that we *cannot* paraphrase the poem, but that under certain special circumstances we *do not*. These circumstances are precisely those obtaining under the normative obligation to use the poem as a device in a particular aesthetico-ethical practice. Brooks' practical criticism is in fact a demonstration of such a practice and its primary function is to be exemplary. It shows us how not to take the poem as a didactic statement, and it exhorts us not to take it so; but it cannot show that the poem as an object of knowledge requires that we address it and ourselves in this manner.

In other words, Brooks' reading of the poem is a pedagogical action performed on *its* reader who is also, amongst other individuals, Brooks. This shows the manner in which the aesthetic reading functions as a surface on which the reader is opened to a pedagogical supervision, imposing an ever-more sedulous attention to the aesthetic balance of the text as a means of operationalising norms for the reader's own ethical formation. It shows how inside the school the Romantic aesthetic is redeployed as a pedagogical discipline – practical criticism. But it also reveals how under these changed conditions practical criticism has also acquired a theoretical function: to reveal the 'formal conditions' of poetry, but to do so through the reconciliatory action of the aesthetic reading itself.

We can now turn to the *second* major form assumed by criticism today. This is the form arising from the tendency of literary theory to locate literature's unthought laws not in a theoretical statement, but 'dramatised' in the aesthetic form of the text. Here our task is to show how a theoretical strategy which begins by cancelling the privilege of the aesthetic can end by reinstating it in another register: that of the clarification of the literary unconscious. We have seen that for all its drive to reconstitute criticism on a systematic basis, the domain of theoretical criticism cannot help but be characterised by a chaos of competing foundational gestures.

For this reason it is impossible to find a *locus classicus* for this type of criticism. The best we can do, therefore, is to choose as an example a foundational gesture which condenses a number of others, drawing our conclusions from it while acknowledging that the example is indicative rather than exhaustive.

Fredrick Jameson's *The Political Unconscious* serves these purposes well enough. Characteristically enough, Jameson (1981, pp. 9–14) announces that his project entails suspending the privileges of literary representation ('realism') and its spontaneous critical reflection (practical or 'ethical' criticism) and reconstituting them as functions of unthought structural conditions. These unthought structures are in fact the 'political unconscious' of his title. It is not in 'man's' psychology, nor his ritual life, nor his language as such that Jameson locates the literary unconscious; but in the history of class society. 'It is in detecting the traces of that uninterrupted narrative, in restoring to the surface of the text the repressed and buried reality of this fundamental history, that the doctrine of the political unconscious finds its function and necessity' (ibid., p. 20).

This is not the whole story, however, because history – as we shall see in the final section of this chapter – plays a very problematic role in relation to the model of the human sciences on which Jameson relies. In Jameson's case, doubly problematic, because his 'political unconscious' is in part derived from the Marxian theory of ideology, and Marxism is now riven by two different conceptions of history. One is based on the model of culture and the dialectical evolution of 'man' towards historical self-consciousness, and society towards totality, which we examined in Chapter 3. The other is based in the model of the human sciences, with its quite different stress on a sudden rupture in 'man's' historical consciousness and the scientific recovery of its formal conditions. These two models – the one conceiving of society as a totality able to reflect itself on the privileged surface of literature; the other conceiving of it as a ('de-centred') structure of semi-autonomous instances which are not transparently reflected on the single surface of consciousness – are associated with the writing of Georg Lukacs and Louis Althusser, respectively. Our only interest in them here is to see how Jameson deploys them to specify the figure of the political unconscious. He does this not by choosing one over the other, but by playing each off against the other and producing a kind of reconciliation.

From the 'Lukacs' model – with its stress on the way in which historical (class) structure is reflected in the other instances of the social totality – Jameson derives a method of interpreting literature as the expression of socio-historical structures and conflicts. This allows him to parry what he considers to be the 'formalistic' implications of Althusserian structuralism which, in some hands, has gone so far as to suspend history itself as a pre-theoretical construct of the textual systems used to represent it. For its part the structuralist model – with its insistence on the unavailability of historical reality (the 'Real') to consciousness – teaches the lesson that history is only given to consciousness as the product of certain formal structures or processes ('textualisation' or 'narrativisation'). And this allows Jameson to keep at bay the Lukacsian tendency to read-off historico-political reality as if it was transparently reflected in literary structure. As a result of this trade-off Jameson specifies his manner of dealing with the political unconscious – that is, his version of literary theory – in the following way:

> We would therefore propose the following revised formulation: that history is *not* a text, not a narrative, master or otherwise, but that, as an absent cause, it is inaccessible to us except in textual form, and that our approach to it and to the Real itself necessarily passes through its prior textualisation, its narrativisation in the political unconscious. (Jameson, 1981, p. 35)

There is no question then of reading-off historical structure (the 'subtext') directly from the text itself, because the latter is determined by its own (semantic) processes of textualisation. And, in an exemplary demonstration of the tendency of foundations to multiply in the field of the human sciences, Jameson draws on Greimas' literary semantics – his theory of narrative structure – to describe the process through which history is 'retextualised'. At the same time, the process of textualisation is itself determined by the 'absent cause' of history (class structure) which finds in this process a convenient way to reconcile social contradictions at the symbolic level. Greimas' foundational narratology is thus itself subject to an even 'deeper' foundation in the Marxian theory of ideology.

In fact, through these manoeuvres, Jameson does not manage to reconcile the two models of 'culture' and the human sciences. He simply provides himself with a means of stepping backwards and forwards between them. History thus appears on both sides of the equation. It is a pre-theoretical projection of the purely formal narrative processes of textualisation ('the literary work . . . brings into being that very situation to which it is also . . . a reaction'). But it is simultaneously the underlying form which determines the process of textualisation itself: 'the production of aesthetic or narrative form is to be seen as an ideological act in its own right, with the function of inventing imaginary or formal "solutions" to unresolvable social contradictions' (ibid., pp. 82, 79).

Under these circumstances the process of rewriting or retextualisation which lies at the centre of Jameson's literary theory takes on a strikingly familiar double aspect. As the product of the historical necessities of class society, textualisation embodies the ideological laws which condition 'man's' consciousness and determine his empirical 'finitude'. But as the form in which class structure is itself represented in 'man' the process assumes the form of a reflexive 'analytic', revealing ideological determination to a consciousness that will transcend it. In short, despite the long meditation on history, and the demands to historicise literature and criticism, at the heart of Jameson's poetics we find the tell-tale figure of the 'analytic of finitude'.

> The type of interpretation here proposed is more satisfactorily grasped as the rewriting of the literary text in such a way that the latter may itself be seen as the rewriting or restructuration of a prior historical or ideological *subtext*, it being always understood that the 'subtext' is not immediately present as such, not some common-sense external reality, nor even the conventional narratives of history manuals, but rather must itself always be (re)constructed after the fact. (Ibid., p. 81)

Once again, it is not difficult to show that this attempt to motivate a reflexive description of literature's political unconscious is quite circular. To interpret the text you must have access to the historical subtext which it rewrites; but it is only by interpreting the text that rewrites it that one gains access to the historical subtext. It is futile of Jameson to attempt to escape this circle by claiming for his poetics the status of a special kind of ('dialectical') knowledge. The space between a text which can only be deciphered through the formal laws of a fundamental subtext, and a subtext which can only be approached through a semantic interpretation of the text, is not occupied by an object of knowledge at all. Rather, it is organised by a particular intellectual action, in which the individual is *required* to move between the registration of a problematic response whose laws remain unthought, and the 'thinking' of these laws which can only take place through the response itself.

Jameson's poetic – like Brooks' but in a different way – is thus not descriptive, but exemplary and pedagogical. Its motivation lies not in the 'repressed and buried reality' of class structure, but in the space opened between 'the subject's' empirical intuitions and that which escapes them while making them possible. In short, Jameson's poetic indicates that theoretical criticism comes into being by reproducing that contingent intellectual action – the duplication of the positive sciences in the space of 'representation' – which marks the genesis of the sciences of man. And it is for this reason that theoretical criticism is also marked by the three figures – the analytic of finitude, the transcendental-empirical couple and the unconscious – whose ambivalence only reflects the complex task of mediation they are forced to perform. The difference is that in literary theory these figures are transposed into the register of the literary text – or, should we say, to its reading – on which they impose a complex, but now familiar, topography.

First, as we have seen in the case of Frye and Jameson, because they emerge in the space of the analytic of finitude, literature's unthought laws or processes obey a double imperative. They mark the place where 'man's' literary representations are removed from his will, being determined by inexorable laws which revoke the privilege of the aesthetic experience and root man in the order of things. But, they also indicate the moment at which the 'fixity' of empirical representation will be escaped through the recovery of a formal organisation or process capable of producing an 'infinite number' of such representations. Typically, as with Frye and Jameson, both tendencies are present in the characteristically ambivalent tactics of modern criticism. It is, however, possible to treat them as optional theoretical strategies.

The first, for example, is exploited by empirical 'text-linguistics', which attempts to subject literary representation to an objective description of 'underlying' psycho-linguistic processes. The second tendency marks the site of 'deconstructive' criticism. The deconstructive movement looks to the 'textual process' for a reprieve from representation; finding in its allegedly open-ended character the means to defer 'sense-making' and to redeem subjectivity from finitude.[2] However, it should be clear that from the perspective of our genealogy, these possibilities and their more usual dual articulations are simply equivalent options inside the single field formed by the analytic of finitude.

Second, inside this space, the figure of 'man', or 'the subject' taken over by theoretical criticism, assumes the distinctive form of the transcendental-empirical couple. As a being whose literary consciousness is the product of formal laws or structures, the subject of literary theory is an empirical being open to scientific description: as in Frye's description of ritual structure; Jameson's account of the ideological function; and the descriptions of psycho-semantic processes deployed in text-linguistics. But the literary subject is also the being in which these laws will themselves be represented to a consciousness lying beyond them. Under these circumstances textual laws and processes take on a reflexive character. They are revealed only in the 'the subject's' effort to comprehend its responsibility for the representations that they make possible. 'The subject' of literary theory thus takes on the quasi-transcendental character typified by the figure of the reader in 'reader response' criticism; but also by the reader in Jameson's 'social hermeneutic', who must see through his own ideological determination in the process of textualisation. Here we find the claim that the forms of literary representation elude all scientific description, because they are remade each time the subject attempts to 'make sense' of the work, and hence can only be the object of a reflexive hermeneutics. Once again, it should be clear that these two positions emerge as equivalent options, made available within a single space: that opened between the positive sciences and a philosophy of representation. The 'argument' between them cannot be resolved by literary theory, marking as it does the place where the latter comes into being.

Third, because it is defined by the analytic of finitude and invested in 'man' as a transcendental-empirical being, literary theory reproduces the division between 'the subject's' immediate recognitions and the unthought conditions which make them possible. It is thus a variant of the nineteenth-century project to restore knowledge to representation, but to do so on the axis linking the *cogito* to its grounds in 'man's' unconscious being. Hence theoretical criticism is driven by the imperative to trace the meaning of the text to an unconscious organisation: whether this be a political unconscious; a semiotic one; or one that is fully psychoanalytic, as in the use of Lacan's machinery to stage the 'formation of the subject' in the text.[3]

These, then, are the main forms assumed by theoretical criticism today. We have summarised them here only to show that they are wholly contained within the three figures of 'man' formed in the field of the human sciences. The point that we have made a number of times now is that these figures are not in fact based in the discovery of a fundamental object – 'man'. Instead, they are formed in that contingent and historical space which the sciences of man opened between the positive sciences and a philosophy of representation. They are, as it were, the means of maintaining these two otherwise disjunct spheres in the same orbit, and 'the subject' is their projection: the figure traced by the endless movement between the positive and the philosophical that they make possible.

It is for this reason that the ostensibly autonomous object of literary theory – the formal structure of literary representation – remains inseparable from a particular task of self-problematisation required of the reader: his recovery of that which makes his reading possible, while eluding it. Moreover, as we have seen in the case of Todorov, Frye and Jameson, this task cannot be motivated by pointing to the unconscious character of literary representation and its 'pre-theoretical' reflection in practical criticism. Performing this task is *how* these alleged shortcomings are 'pointed to'.

By these steps we return to the pedagogical imperative that theoretical criticism takes over from the sciences of man. Every time that the theoretical critic 'points to' a flaw or 'fissure' in the surface of literary representation – discovers the unconscious grammar that makes it possible, or the process that promises to annihilate its fixity in a plethora of possibilities – he exemplifies an action which his reader is also obliged to perform. We have seen that nothing about the text as an object of knowledge requires that this problematisation of literary recognition be undertaken. It is a 'task of behaviour'. The ('realist') text which conceals its own structural conditions is not the reason for the act of problematisation, but its outcome. (Such a text is unthinkable, for example, in a literary system like Renaissance rhetoric, characterised by the practical mastery of compositional formulas. But it is equally unintelligible in other systems formed prior to the historical 'split in representation': systems like Kames' philosophical rhetoric, where the order of things and the order of thoughts are duplicated in the order of words without difficulty.) As a result, like practical criticism, theoretical criticism requires a being whose initial literary responses are both immediate and open to correction. It acquires this being, we have seen, through the pedagogical disciplines and their privileged armature – the teacher-student couple.

In the relation of emulation and correction which characterises the teacher-student couple, theoretical criticism finds a being whose responses are marked by an unthought immediacy, but also by underlying norms which can be brought to the 'surface' in a movement which is simultaneously clarificatory and corrective. But – because it is formed according to the imperatives of literary pedagogy – this being is also characterised by a certain aesthetico-ethical incompleteness: in particular by the didactic tendency to subject literary form to an 'extrinsic' content; and the 'aestheticist' tendency to ignore moral content in favour of a purely formal interest in literature. It should come as no surprise, then, that the reading in which Jameson seeks to recover literature's political unconscious achieves its end only by the imperative reconciliation of form and content, thereby reproducing the ethical discipline of practical criticism in the register of literary theory.

> Thus, it can be argued that this type of interpretation, while containing a transcendent moment [i.e., the appeal to an 'extrinsic' historical subtext], forsees that moment as merely *provisionally* extrinsic, and requires for its completion a movement to the point at which that apparently external content (political attitudes, ideological materials, juridical categories, the raw materials of history, the economic processes) is then at length drawn back within the process of reading. (Ibid., p. 57)

In other words, if Brooks' practical criticism is driven to make the discipline of aesthetic reconciliation function as a 'theory of literature', Jameson's literary theory is compelled by the same historical logic to function as an aesthetico-ethical discipline. This exchange lies at the very heart of modern criticism, because it marks the point where the quite different pedagogical imperatives of the Romantic aesthetic and the human sciences could meet in the educable individual of modern pedagogy. This analysis is confirmed by the fact that we find both these tendencies fully realised at the birth of modern criticism, in the work of I. A. Richards: for example, in the discussion of 'sentimentality' in his *Practical Criticism*.

On the one hand, the sentimental poem – as it was for Schiller – is characterised by an imbalance in the relation of form and meaning: by a disembodied feeling that meets no resistance in poetic form and hence tyrannises over experience, quite in excess of its supposed object. But because the poem is only the relay for an ethical balancing act to be performed by its reader, it is the latter who is sentimental:

> there is reason to think that very many people are ready to react emotionally to a 'pathetic' situation merely at this level of abstractness, provided it is put before them in some kind of metre; and, if so, such reactions are certainly 'sentimental' in the sense of excessive. (Richards, 1929, p. 263)

On the other hand, the sentimental poem is not given to experience, but is the projection of an underlying structure: 'A sentiment . . . is not an experience . . . It is not a momentary thing but a more or less permanent arrangement of the mind . . . a persisting, organised system of dispositions' (ibid., p. 260). And a response is sentimental when this structure is allowed to unconsciously reproduce itself – that is, when it is not recovered and transcended in the consciousness that it makes possible.

At the centre of these two conceptions, and organising their exchange, we find the disciplinary organisation of the literary seminar itself. We find, that is, that group of relations in which the responses elicited from Richards' students provide a surface revealing their incomplete sensibilities to ethical invigilation and shaping, while simultaneously revealing the unthought structure of their responses to a corrective consciousness. Richards' pedagogy combines the functions of the ethical exemplar and the social scientist. His criticism is one in which the poem relays the normative reconciliation of the ethical antinomies, while simultaneously imposing the obligation to problematise the 'immediacy' of the literary response in order to recover its unconscious conditions. In this ambivalent space, the 'scientific' clarification of the literary unconscious exchanges functions with the disciplinary formation of the ethical exemplar. From this exchange arise the attributes of the stratum of teachers and critics defined by its – at least until recently – crucial role in the ethical operation of a governmental pedagogy. For all the attempts to go beyond it, this exchange continues to define the possibilities open to criticism today.

V

This completes our genealogy of modern criticism. The reader might be forgiven, however, for feeling that there is something incomplete or ambivalent about this genealogy. Furthermore, it would not be a mistake if this incompleteness or ambivalence were to be located in the role that *history* has played in the present work. History – in the form of the two models for the history of criticism discussed in Chapter 5 – has been implicated in the universalising strategies which have been criticised for obscuring the historical contingency and specificity of English and modern criticism. But, at the same time, these criticisms have themselves been made in the name of history or 'genealogy'. In fact, they have been made to recall the 'founding forms' of English and modern criticism – the dialectics of 'man's' cultural becoming; the figure of 'the subject' projected by the human sciences – to a motley of ethical techniques (aesthetico-ethical self-shaping), 'intellectual actions' (the redeployment of the positive sciences as 'conditions of representation') and forms of social organisation (the disciplinary techniques and relationships embodied in the modern school).

I have argued that it is from such historical ensembles that the attributes of individuals and groups – in this case the special attributes of the teacher-critic – arise as contingent and variable historical achievements. These achievements are governed neither by the dialectic between culture and society that would complete 'man' by reconciling his divided nature; nor by the logic of the human sciences which promises the same goal, to be reached by restoring 'the subject's' unthought being to consciousness. These achievements are, in a certain sense, goal-less and directionless save for the (perfectly respectable) local objectives – for example, to administer the formation of cultural attributes according to the new norms of the 'social' sphere – formed within specific cultural and governmental technologies.

In fact, this ambivalence regarding history is a direct outcome of the stance I have assumed with regard to the contrapuntal histories of 'culture' and the human sciences. The adoption of a 'genealogical' exposition is itself an option made available by the historical transformations already described. In discussing the availability of this option we can, therefore, provide a coda to our twin genealogies and give a summary indication of the kind of historical description that they entail.

The emergence of the positive sciences – as Foucault (1966, pp. 367–73) has shown – witnessed the appearance of a new and unsettling form of historical time. If we look at the role of history in the philosophical grammars and rhetorics of the period prior to this emergence, then we see that it is strictly subordinated to the function of representation. Language is governed by its function of duplicating the order of nature in the order of the mind. Its history can therefore only be a progression towards (or a falling away from) the ideal pattern of this duplication. Hence language could be described as originating in a fully transparent form which men of all races and nations could understand on sight, like Hebrew before the Tower of Babel. Or, it might be thought of as being open to refinement in order to better reflect the order of things in the order of the thoughts. It was on this basis that Kames sought to improve on the classical rhetoricians. Either way, the history of language was the history of the form in which the ideas of nature found themselves reflected in the ideas of the mind.

The emergence of philology (but also biology and economics) towards the end of the eighteenth century changed all this. Philology was historical in a quite new sense. In philology, phonetic forms and morphological patterns change over time, but not in accordance with the logic of representation. They change not in order to better represent the order of nature in their own order, but according to laws (of simplification or differentiation; of derivation from a root form, or homogenisation in relation to parallel verbal contexts) which are immanent to the historical development of language as an autonomous 'organism'.

In short, when philology transformed language from the universal medium of knowledge into one of its objects, it not only divided knowledge of language from the analysis of representation, it also divorced the history of language from the evolution of representation or consciousness. Because of the parallel sunderings that were effected through economics and biology, 'man' soon appeared as a being whose unity and destiny, far from being guaranteed by a single history, were threatened by the autonomous histories of language, production and evolution. These, while acting through 'man', undermined the idea that he was a single being – the unity in consciousness of all his attributes – by turning him into the contingent by-product of the histories of language, production and life: histories not destined to meet in the single goal of self-consciousness.[4]

We have described the Romantic aesthetic and the human sciences as optional strategies evolving in response to these events. The former, we have seen, represented the new configuration of knowledges as a division in 'man's' ethical substance, and thereby attempted to reconstitute the unity of 'man' in the register of culture or ethical discipline. The latter, taking advantage of the space opened between the positive sciences and an emergent philosophy of representation, attempted to reconstitute representation itself through the addition of its unthought conditions. It is hardly surprising, given these circumstances, that the Romantic aesthetic and the social sciences also mark the site of two historiographical strategies responding to the disintegration of history as human history. In fact, we have already discussed these strategies as they apply to the history of culture and criticism in Chapters 3 and 5. But we can briefly recapitulate those discussions here, approaching them from a slightly different angle.

First, inside the Romantic aesthetic there evolved the strategy to rescue 'man' from the fragmentation of different historical times, by positing a Universal History whose goal was to restore him as the 'synthesis of many determinations'. This strategy involved subsuming the different histories of language, production and evolution within the single figure of 'man's' divided ethical substance and the reconciliatory movements of the dialectic. In this way, the practice of shaping a 'complete' self (culture) could be projected as the model for a 'total' historical development (of races, nations, classes, etc.). Hence we have seen Fichte (1794) and Schiller (1795) dividing the ethical sphere into an unrealised moral will (on one side) and an alien physical nature (on the other) and finding in the dialectical movements of culture the stages of progress towards an (indefinitely deferred) final synthesis.

In this synthesis the moral will would be actualised without subjecting nature and society to its abstract violence; while nature and society would attain their full development without subjecting the moral will to their material necessities. Schiller, we observed, identified this historical completion of 'man's' being with his entering the domain of *play*. We also noted that it has been quite easy for 'materialist' cultural histories, like those provided by Raymond Williams, Georg Lukacs and Herbert Marcuse, to take over this figure of completion: the exchange taking place on the ground of an ethical practice quite removed from the competing ontologies (the World Spirit, the modes of production) which have been dragged in to universalise the practice.

We can see, from A. W. Schlegel's *Lectures on Dramatic Art and Literature*, that the Romantics had no difficulty in deriving a literary history from this model. The periodisation of *classic* and *romantic* was formed to mark the divergence between the ancient unity of the ethical substance (the too sensuous ethical paradise of the Greeks) and its modern division (which sets the scene for the antinomic progress of contemporary literature).

> The groundwork of human nature is no doubt everywhere the same; but in all our investigations, we may observe that, throughout the whole range of nature, there is no elementary power so simple, but that it is capable of dividing and diverging into opposite directions. The whole play of vital motion hinges on harmony and contrast. Why, then, should not this phenomenon recur on a grander scale in the history of man? In this idea we have perhaps discovered the true key to the ancient and modern history of poetry and the fine arts. Those who adopted it, gave to the peculiar spirit of *modern* art, as contrasted with *antique* or *classical*, the name of *romantic*. . .
>
> The Grecian ideal of human nature was perfect unison and proportion between all the powers – a natural harmony. The moderns, on the contrary, have arrived at the consciousness of an internal discord which renders such an ideal impossible; and hence the endeavour of their poetry is to reconcile these two worlds between which we find ourselves divided, and to blend them indissolubly together. (Schlegel, 1808, pp. 209, 213)

On this basis – in the successive reconciliations of the ethical substance differentiated according to the factors of race, milieu and epoch – Taine could find a hidden principle of unity which ran through all the elements of historical societies ('religion, art, philosophy, the state, the family, the industries'). This principle was the 'moral condition', which was expressed through these elements and which was embodied in its pure state in the reconciled form of literature. In this manner Romantic historicism saved literature from a philological description that would completely divorce it from the historical vocation of 'man's' ethical being. It did so by deriving a model of history from the practice of ethical reconciliation (self-culture) and by deploying this model as a means of transforming historico-philological documents into sacral sites for the recovery of 'man's' moral unity.

No one has better taught us [than Stendhal] how to open our eyes and see, to see first the men that surround us and the life that is present, then the ancient and authentic documents, to read between the black and white lines of the pages, to recognise beneath the old impression, under the scribbling of a text, the precise sentiment, the movement of ideas, the state of mind in which they were written. In his writings, in Sainte-Beuve, in the German critics, the reader will see all the wealth that may be drawn from a literary work: when the work is rich and people know how to interpret it, we find there the psychology of a soul, frequently of an age, now and then of a race. (Taine, 1863, I, p. 34)

We can locate contemporary histories of culture and criticism in this same transposition of the ethical dialectic into the register of an historical hermeneutic. Compare, for example, these remarks of Raymond Williams (which we have already quoted in part) with those just cited from Taine.

For it seems to me to be true that meanings and values, discovered in particular societies and by particular individuals, and kept alive by social inheritance and by embodiment in particular kinds of work, have proved to be universal in the sense that when they are learned, in any particular situation, they can contribute radically to the growth of man's powers to enrich his life, to regulate his society, and to control his environment. We are most aware of these elements in the form of particular techniques, in medicine, production, and communications, but it is clear not only that these depend on more purely intellectual disciplines, which had to be wrought out in the creative handling of experience, but also that these disciplines themselves, together with certain basic ethical assumptions and certain major art forms, have proved similarly capable of being gathered into a general tradition which seems to represent, through many variations and conflicts, a line of common growth. It seems reasonable to speak of this tradition as a general human culture, while adding that it can only become active within particular societies, being shaped, as it does so, by more local and temporary systems. (Williams, 1961, p. 59)

It is hardly surprising, therefore, that the 'particular kinds of work' in which Williams can read-off the 'meanings and values' of a whole society should be pre-eminently works of literature, and that this process should involve precisely the refusal to treat these works as philological documents. In short, Williams (ibid., p. 63) can say that 'cultural history must be more than the sum of the particular histories', because cultural history is the outcome of a strategy for a particular normative use of the archive and the literary text: one which attempts to forestall the fragmenting effects of philological time by imposing in its place the obligation to read society's 'moral condition', in the same movements of the text that shape the moral condition of the cultural historian himself.

Second, inside the field of the human sciences a quite different strategy evolved for recuperating the fragmentation of historical times. Recall that the human sciences are not characterised by the attempt to displace the positive sciences with 'culture', but by the move to redeploy them in a new modality: that of the 'conditions of representation'. As a result, their historiographical strategy involves taking one of the particular histories – of language, production or evolution – and universalising *it* as the true genesis of the human subject. This strategy is quite evident in the diachronic sections of Saussure's *Course* (for example, the remarks on 'ethnicity' in Chapter IV). Here the redeployment of philological description as 'system' provides the basis of a framework in which *all* of man's social being will be derived from the historical mutations of his system of speech.

This second strategy, as we noted in our discussion of Todorov's historical survey of *Theories of the Symbol*, is not characterised by an historical dialectic that completes 'man's' ethical being by reconciling its imbalances. It is, rather, marked by a sudden rupture in historical consciousness and the recovery of its unthought conditions. It will be recalled that this is how Todorov represents the break between the system of rhetoric and the emergence of the Romantic aesthetic. In doing so he can find in the latter the 'subject's' universal form: the reason being that the Romantics are credited with discovering in literature's 'self-regulating form' a form able to outstrip, and hence unify, all possible uses ('manifestations') of literature.

In other words, by redeploying the positive sciences under the sign of 'conditions of representation' the human sciences provide (competing) models for a single, unsurpassable historical horizon. Inside this horizon 'what man actually is' as a contingency of his empirical being is subsumed within the figure of 'everything that he might become' when one of the positive sciences is redeployed as an open-ended calculus of historical possibility. This process of subsumption and unification is quite visible in Frye's description of literature's 'total form'. Here the typology of genres derived from rhetoric and philology – once it has been aligned with the seasonal myth of the heroic quest – takes on the form of an unsurpassable 'total literary history', which also contains the forms of the entire 'culture'.

Under these circumstances, the genres of comedy and pastoral, tragedy and elegy, satire and irony – which in rhetoric and philology have been deployed as a motley array of practical recipes or compositional formularies – lose their historically fragmentary and fragmenting character. They combine to restore the figure of 'man' in the form of a universal grammar of his cultural being. Moreover, something very similar happens in Jameson's attempt to redeploy the old four-fold typology of biblical exegesis, as a schema linking the (political-allegorical) interpretation of the individual work to its place in a universal history based on the sequence of modes of production. By these unlikely means, Jameson also forms an absolute horizon in which 'man' will be restored to the centre of history as the locus of all that he might become.

In fact, for reasons that we have already discussed in some detail, these two historiographical strategies, despite their different genesis and organisation, are today typically deployed in tandem. The strategy which attempts to escape the fragmentation of human history by imposing a single grammar of historical possibility, and the strategy which achieves the same end by subsuming the positive histories within the general dialectic of 'man's' ethical substance, are made to go proxy for each other. This is particularly clear in Frye's literary and cultural history. After reducing the historical motley of literary deployments to the genre-grammar of the central quest narrative – the organon of a 'total body of rituals suggestive . . . of the entire range of potentially significant actions in human life' – Frye turns his attention to the question of meaning or significance. This, significantly, he locates in dialectical opposition to the repetitive temporality of narrative – in the instantaneous insight: 'the epiphanic moment, the flash of instantaneous comprehension with no direct reference to time' (Frye, 1951, p. 606). Under these circumstances the mode in which the abstract genre grammar is realised in history begins to overlap with the historico-ethical dialectic which completes 'man's' being by reconciling his sensuous and intellectual natures.

The critic would . . . note how popular literature which appeals to the inertia of the untrained mind puts a heavy emphasis on narrative values, whereas a sophisticated attempt to disrupt the connection between the poet and his environment produces the Rimbaud type of *illumination,* Joyce's solitary epiphanies, and Baudelaire's conception of nature as a source of oracles. Also how literature, as it develops from the primitive to the self-conscious, shows a gradual shift of the poet's attention from narrative to significant values, this shift of attention being the basis of Schiller's distinction between naive and sentimental poetry. (Ibid., p. 607)

This overlapping of the two historiographical strategies is by no means unique to Frye. It is at the centre of Jameson's attempt to reconcile the 'Lukacsian' model of a history destined by 'man' as the 'synthesis of many determinations', and the 'Althusserian' model of history as the projection of an a-temporal grammar of modes of production. In Jameson's project the two forms of universal history exchange functions in the figure of 'textualisation'. Here, as in Frye's 'total literary history', the theoretical recovery of a historico-semantic grammar from which the 'whole' history of literature can be generated, is put into a relation of mutual dependence with the ethical practice of reconciling form and meaning: the latter permitting the 'moral condition' of society to be read-off from a text which anticipates 'man's' historical completion. Jameson, like Frye, thus manages to combine Romantic historicism (in which the fragmentation of human history is forestalled by the ethical dialectic) with the 'structural' historiography of the sciences of man (in which it is forestalled by the transformation of one of the particular histories – of production in Jameson's case – into an exhaustive historical calculus). Jameson and Frye thus typify the process by which modern criticism gives birth to an historical criticism that preserves the literary text from the erosive currents of philological time: currents which would otherwise deny 'literature' a single history as the vehicle of 'man's' historical vocation.

These are also the circumstances in which modern criticism attempts to conceive of its own historicity. Frye's deliberations on this topic in the conclusion in his *Anatomy of Criticism* bring all the elements together, and clearly reveal the narrow limits inside which modern criticism can be historical. On the one hand, Frye acknowledges the contingency and disunity of philological time by remarking that:

Nearly every work of art in the past had a social function in its own time, a function which was often not primarily an aesthetic function at all. The whole conception of 'works of art' as a classification for all pictures, statues, poems, and musical compositions is a relatively modern one. (Frye, 1957, pp. 344–5)

This indeed approaches our own remarks on the historical contingency of the aesthetic; although Frye makes no reference to the cultural techniques and forms of social organisation required to enforce the aesthetic as a norm of life. He simply notes that it is the task of 'historical criticism' to record the 'social functions' that literature has served in the past. It is the task of 'ethical criticism', on the other hand, to register literature's contemporary relevance, although 'it is natural that this sense of contemporary relevance should often be confined to a specific issue in the present; that it should be thought of, not as expanding the perspective of present life, but as supporting a cause or thesis in the present' (ibid., p. 346).

Characteristically, the true vocation of criticism is held to lie in the dialectical reconciliation of these two sub-species:

So, just as historical criticism uncorrected relates culture only to the past, ethical criticism uncorrected relates culture only to the future, to the ideal society which may eventually come if we take sufficient pains to guard the educating of our youth. For all such lines of thought end in indoctrinating the next generation, . . . (Ibid., p. 346–7)

Nor, given our preceding remarks, will the reader be surprised to discover that this dialectic is none other than that of aesthetic criticism itself: historical criticism being characterised by the 'naive' or sensuous tendency to read literature in terms of social necessities; and ethical criticism by the 'sentimental' or didactic tendency to make literature serve ideal goals. According to Frye, these tendencies are responsible for the sometimes tendentious and sectional deployment of literature. But their reconciliation in criticism proper transcends all normativities and social divisions to achieve the goal of a disinterested and classless 'liberal education'.

The ethical purpose of a liberal education is to liberate, which can only mean to make one capable of conceiving society as free, classless, and urbane. No such society exists, which is one reason why a liberal education must be deeply concerned with works of imagination. The imaginative element in works of art, again, lifts them clear of the bondage of history. Anything that emerges from the total experience of criticism to form part of a liberal education becomes, by virtue of that fact, part of the emancipated and humane community of culture, whatever its original reference. This liberal education liberates the works of culture themselves as well as the mind they educate. (Ibid., pp. 347–8)

In other words, modern criticism is incapable of comprehending its own historicity or that of 'literature'. In the dialectic between the 'historical determination' and the 'contemporary experience' of literature which 'lifts it clear of the bondage of history' – a dialectic which we find not only in Frye but in Wellek and Warren (1949, pp. 38–46), Williams (1973), Hartman (1973) and Jameson (1981, pp. 9–14) – we discover nothing more than the imposition of a specific historical deployment of literature (the Romantic aesthetic) as a norm. It should now be clear that this historical incapacity is a condition of existence of modern criticism: a direct function of the two strategies by which criticism has attempted to preserve its object from historical fragmentation by historicising it. But these attempts to rescue literature and criticism from philological time must remain permanently tenuous and unstable, because they can never neutralise the disintegrative effects of a time not governed by 'man's' ethical or epistemological being. The best they can do is contain these effects by deploying a history which restores 'man' through a dialectical movement towards his 'complete' form, or one which does so through the figure of a sudden rupture that reveals a 'total' grammar of his historical 'manifestations'.

Neither of these strategies can succeed in its own terms, however. The fact is that modern literary history is the *result* of these strategies for containing the contingency and unevenness of philological time. And this means that this contingency and unevenness is perpetually asserting itself at the heart of modern criticism, threatening to undermine its whole project. Consider, as a brief exemplification, the Renaissance court masque. Frye might well locate this form as a species of pastoral in the mythos of spring, as one phase of the 'total literary form' and 'total literary history' in which 'man's' cultural being is secured. Equally, Hartman (1973) might well locate the masque at the centre of the dialectic between literature's historico-social functions and its permanent relevance (between *genius loci* and 'genius'). The historico-philological description of the masque provided by Stephen Orgel (1971; 1975) does something quite different, however. It does not attempt to uncover in the masque the unconscious grammar which makes it available to 'the subject'. Neither does it find there the ethical antinomies – form and content, 'pastness' and 'presentness' – whose reconciliation makes other literatures available for today's 'liberal education'. Instead, Orgel describes a local ensemble of techniques (the rhetorical formulas for the pastoral); arrangements of social space (the positioning of the courtly audience in relation to the stage and the king who was the real object of the spectacle) and forms of social organisation (the rules of precedence and deference governing the relations between the members of the court, reflected in the sequence of unmaskings). This ensemble – or cultural technology – was organised by the imperative of a definite politico-cultural regimen: to reveal the image of the king at the centre of his kingdom according to a 'pre-governmental' symbolic deployment of power.

Two comments are necessary. *First*, that such a spectacle 'serves a social function' and that it 'teaches a lesson' – the lesson of the sovereign presence of the king – is evident. But this does not mean that we are dealing with an 'interested' or 'didactic' – and therefore with an inferior – kind of art. Such a judgement is quite anachronistic, because it activates the dialectic between the didactic and the pleasurable which only defines the deployment of art from the Romantics onwards. In fact, the court masque is neither didactic nor aesthetic in our senses of these terms. One could begin to show the limits of this opposition by observing that the masque did not so much 'serve the functions' of sovereignty as form part of a larger cultural technology – everything from the minting of coins marked by the king's head to the staging of exemplary public executions – which made such functions possible. But then this technology was not 'literary'.

Second, in describing these elements of a local cultural technology the philologist is not 'neglecting' the problem of representation and its 'unthought' conditions. We have seen that this problem is unthinkable within the positive science of philology, and is in fact an artefact of its redeployment as a human science. Neither was 'representation' a problem for the court dramatists themselves, except in the local and practical sense associated with assembling the spectacle, employing the appropriate *figura*, getting the position of the king right and so on. This is not to say, however, that Ben Jonson was the dupe of the literary unconscious that spoke through him (on the one hand), or that he was reflexive ahead of his time (on the other). It is to say that in historical philology what is to count as a 'representation' has no single general form – for example, the projection of empirical recognition by an unthought formal system – but must be described from case to case in terms of the contingent deployment of cultural technologies. In other words, what counts as a 'representation' in the system of rhetoric is the achievement of a local ensemble of historical techniques and practices (the formula; the commonplace book; the rules of decorum, etc.) possessing no necessary continuity with other things that we might call 'literary representation': for example, the Romantic nature lyric as the vehicle for a new kind of ethical work on the self.

There can be no question therefore of providing a general history or theory of literary representation and its social functions, of the sort attempted by Frye, Todorov and Jameson. Literary deployments can well be political – as in the court masque – but this does not mean that they are always political, or that when they are political they are so in the same way or in the same sense. They no more serve a general social or political function – for example, the abrogation of true consciousness as the condition of reproduction of class society – than they support a general function of representation. For most of the nineteenth century, for example, Romantic criticism remained a voluntary ethical practice, more or less disconnected from the new governmental apparatuses forming the social sphere. And, as we have seen, when it was connected to them through its deployment in the pedagogical apparatus, it was not to complete 'man's' ethical being or to repress his 'political unconscious', but to shape the attributes of an exemplary stratum in the system of moral administration. It is this deployment, I have argued, which not only determines the functions of modern criticism and its historical sense, but also sets the limits of our analysis of it.

We can now see more clearly the manner in which modern historical criticism remains permanently beseiged by historical philology: the Trojan Horse which modern criticism has been forced to admit within its walls as a condition of its existence. Philology perpetually threatens to topple 'man's' ethical being and 'the subject's' unconscious being into the fragmentary and contingent cultural technology which sustains them. The great bulwark against this occurrence is not of course literature's allegedly unsurpassable contemporaneity. The much-vaunted fact that we can still respond to Shakespeare without the elaborate historico-philological apparatus provided by someone like T. W. Baldwin (1949) is simply a sign that we are *required* to respond *without* this apparatus – in the relations of supervision and correction that characterise the disciplinary deployment of literature.

'Literature' is contemporary and 'permanent' because it is not deployed as a philological document registering the motley of cultural technologies, and is instead predominantly deployed as an ethical device inside one such technology: the supervisory apparatus of modern pedagogy. This is why the great works of historical philology – like Auerbach's *Mimesis* and Curtius' *European Literature and the Latin Middle Ages* – play such an ambivalent role in relation to modern criticism. On the one hand, they provide the motley of philological descriptions that are universalised by the historicising strategies of 'culture' and the human sciences. On the other, they never cease threatening to dissolve the unities of 'man' and 'the subject' in the scattering winds of historical contingency. It is in this unsettling space, opened at the heart of the modern deployment of culture and criticism, that the present work has been conceived and written.

8

Conclusion

I wish to conclude this dual genealogy of literary education in a more reflective register, by indicating its bearing on the present state of English and modern criticism. Needless to say I am well aware of the dangers attending any such undertaking. After all, haven't we seen that the 'present' is precisely the place in which the local and contingent episodes of history are overridden, subsumed within the restoration of a lost unity (culture) or the recovery of a hidden truth (science)? Too often meditations on the present have the tendency to transform historical time into something resembling Dante's purgatory: a place where lost wedding rings, the souls of unbaptised infants and the cowls of defrocked monks circulate in limbo, awaiting the final day on which they will be restored to their truth and glory.

The two models of literary education, against whose limits we have charted up our own map of the field, are no exception in this regard. According to the model of ethical reconciliation, the present indicates the place where the lost or anticipated unity of 'man's' ethical substance will be restored, or not. It is characterised by the promised 'full development of human capacities', deriving from the dialectic of intellect and emotions or 'the idea of culture as art and the idea of culture as a whole way of life'. For example, in the conclusion to his *Culture and Society*, Raymond Williams (1958, pp. 285–325) argues that the present state of literary culture must be judged against the possibility of just such a reconciliation. In his account the promise of complete development made by the prophets of culture cannot be fulfilled until it has been removed from its purely literary and ethical forms, plunged into the 'practical democracy' of the working class, and withdrawn transformed into a 'common culture'. It should come as no surprise, however, that this common culture is premised on the figure of unalienated and unrestricted communication: in fact, on the figure of aesthetic communication in which the work of art – by reconciling the didactic and the sensuous; social necessity and moral freedom – provides the model for unalienated social relations. This is the figure – we noted it first in Schiller and Fichte – in which social purpose is not imposed, but freely realised in each individual who becomes the equal member of a true community by participating in the unity of the ethical substance. Here, the unity of the present – despite the fact that it takes the form of a 'programme' for overcoming class differences and socialising the means of production – is quite clearly the anticipated unity of man's divided ethical substance.

Under the model of theoretical clarification, however, the present appears in a quite different guide. Here it appears not as the horizon of the slow process of ethical reconciliation, but as the moment in which the truth of 'the subject' is suddenly recovered from beneath the ancient error of its unconscious being. The present is illuminated in the lightning flash of reflexive consciousness, in which all the fragments of subjectivity are restored to their unity as 'manifestations' of a single underlying 'grammar'. This conception of criticism's present was there at its birth. According to I. A. Richards, the theoretical reconstruction of criticism promises to redeem not only literature but culture in its entirety. The ills of culture derive from the same stock responses, sentimentalities and inhibitions – the same failure of 'the subject' to think its unthought being – that marks the irrationality of 'pre-theoretical' criticism.

For his part, Northrop Frye reaches the same conception while meditating on the analogy between literature and mathematics in the conclusion to his *Anatomy*. Re-activating the old figure of the universal *mathesis* in a new register, Frye considers that both literature and mathematics are languages each of which is able to function as a calculus exhausting the entirety of experience. As the theory of the language of literature, criticism – in this instance, archetypal – might therefore function as a grammar for 'culture as a whole'. Thus Frye (1957, p. 352) finds himself pondering whether it might not be true 'that the verbal structures of psychology, anthropology, theology, history, law and everything else built out of words have been informed or constructed by the same kind of myths and metaphors that we find, in their original hypothetical form, in literature?' Apparently it is so, because Frye (ibid., p. 354) concludes: 'Some such activity as this of reforging the broken links between creation and knowledge, art and science, myth and concept, is what I envisage for criticism.'

Frye and Richards were, of course, merely forerunners in this regard. The recent ascendency of semiotics in 'the pursuit of foundations' has produced a plethora of analyses – Jameson's being one – in which it is language or 'discourse' that holds the key to criticism's apparently boundless present and future. These analyses absorb all forms of social activity into forms of 'sense making', promising to unlock all possible forms with the key of theoretical criticism. In all of these cases, however, the unity of the present is neither more nor less than the unity of 'the subject', achieved through a theoretical recovery of its unconscious being.[1]

Both these conceptions of the present state of literary education are capable of sustaining the figure of 'crisis'. Indeed, in them the idea of the present and the idea of crisis are inseparable. According to one account, English is in crisis because the narrowly literary and moral forms to which it has attempted to confine culture are under seige from the forms of culture as 'the way of life as a whole'. They are under seige, it is said, from the forms of popular culture, third-world culture, or women's culture – or from the return of criticism's own 'hidden history' as a species of ideology – any or all of which threaten to shatter the ethical pretensions of literary education and reconstitute it in the form of a 'common culture'. A second view has it that criticism is in crisis 'today' because the old immediacy of the aesthetic experience has been called into question by a variety of foundational interrogations. These – we are told – reveal the aesthetic experience to be nothing more than the spontaneous or unconscious expression of a subjectivity which has yet to think its own unthought conditions. As such, this experience faces a variety of theoretical abrogations – linguistic, psychological, sociological – to be followed by its reconstitution on the ground of an open-ended calculus of possible 'subject positions'. It should be clear from this description, however, that in these conceptions English and criticism have always been in crisis. The figure of crisis is simply an alternative expression of the unity of literary education in the present. It is, as it were, that unity in the moment just prior to its realisation in the reconciliation of 'man's' ethical being and the theoretical clarification of 'the subject's' unconscious.

If the preceding double-genealogy is correct, however, then it is necessary for us to stop living in the moment of this always-to-be fulfilled promise. It is a consequence of this genealogy that literary education does not have a single logic or 'present' in either of the above senses. The ensemble of historical surfaces and forces which brought modern literary education into being is not, as I have described it, unified by either of the two figures of 'man's' completion. Rather, it takes the form of a purely contingent and provisional configuration or 'programme', whose emergence is not governed by any overarching historical purpose or theoretical goal. I have emblematised these surfaces:

● *first*, in the emergence of a governmental pedagogy aimed at the cultural transformation of populations and organised by techniques of moral supervision, for which the practice of criticism came to provide the exemplary agent – the teacher-critic;

● *second*, in those two strategic responses to the rise of the positive sciences – the Romantic aesthetic and the human sciences – whose twin imperatives of ethical reconciliation and theoretical clarification eventually met in the disciplined individual of the school system.

Modern literary education, I have argued, is a patchwork consisting of an aesthetico-ethical discipline (the Romantic aesthetic), a theoretical discourse (the human sciences) and its own positive sciences (rhetoric and philology), held together by a powerful supervisory technology embodied in a specific apparatus of government (the popular school). The figures of 'man' and 'the subject', far from providing the basis on which the motley of literary education can be reconciled and unified in a single present, are nothing more than the forms in which it takes hold of individuals, subjecting them to the imperative norms of a specific cultural formation. In other words, the various components of English and modern criticism cannot be made contemporaneous through their ethical reconciliation or theoretical clarification, and hence brought within a single ethical or intellectual rationality. The components constitute, as it were, 'regional rationalities' governed by no ethical or epistemological central state. This is why, for example, the practice of ethical self–shaping encompassed in the 'close reading' cannot be subordinated to the imperative of theoretical clarification of literary theory. The fact that these 'regions' of literary education are not unified in the 'poem itself', or in its unconscious conditions, is responsible for the permanent disunity and inescapable instability of the field. But this is also the reason why this instability cannot assume the form of a 'crisis'. The regions set the limits inside which mutations of the field are possible and thinkable, and these mutations can therefore never assume the total forms of an ethical or a theoretical 'revolution'.

In the account I have given, the various literary regions do in fact have a logic of articulation. It is provided by the forms of investigation and administration which compose the sphere of the 'social' as a domain of regulated interventions in the life of the population. It was as an instrumentality of the 'social' sphere that the modern school emerged. The modern school is, we have seen, organised by the technology of moral supervision and is governed by the aim of transforming the cultural physiognomies of whole populations through the forms in which individuals internalise 'social' norms as conscience and as sensibility. And it was in the purpose-built space of the popular school that literary education could emerge, when English absorbed the technology of moral surveillance and called for the exemplary attributes of the critic to be invested in the popular school teacher.

Nevertheless, there are two reasons why this pedagogical articulation cannot subsume the literary regions which it holds together and transform them into functions of a purely pedagogical or governmental logic. *First,* because – unlike 'culture' and 'society' – the sphere of the 'social' is not unified by a single principle of totalisation or completion. It is organised by the local or programmatic imperatives (to school the population; to achieve certain levels of health or literacy; to levy certain norms of conduct. sentiment and ethical demeanour) arising from the forms of investigation and administration which compose it. *Second,* because the imperatives of the Romantic aesthetic and the human sciences are not on another level to these governmental programmes. (They do not play the role of 'consciousness' to the latter's 'social determination'.) Instead, as distinct régimes of technique and practice, they exist at the level of the programme itself, and therefore in part determine the forms in which the sphere of the 'social' is governed. They determine, for example, that through the apparatus of literary education the aims of government will receive an irreducibly aesthetico-ethical formulation and execution.

For these reasons, it seems to me to be unproductive to speculate on the present state of English and modern criticism as if this could assume a single form, governed perhaps by the figure of a crisis to be averted through a single general theoretical or political gesture. The apparatus of literary education confronts us as a patchwork of regional forms, each setting limits to analysis, but each nonetheless articulated into the provisional unities of English and modern criticism in the pedagogical apparatus. To discuss the bearing of our genealogy on 'the present state of literary education' means, therefore, to bring it up against the limits imposed by these 'regional rationalities'. It also means to chart the contours of their pedagogical articulation – which are the lines along which they are open to change – without assuming that this articulation obeys a single logic or that change will occur along a single historical or theoretical trajectory. In order to undertake this discussion we will turn for the last time to the two optional models of literary education. This will permit us to interrogate their twin projects for general ethical and theoretical supercession.

II

We have already referred to Chris Baldick's *The Social Mission of English Criticism* on a number of occasions. It is an elaboration in the specific sphere of English of the general analysis of literary culture first developed by Raymond Williams. It will be remembered that at the heart of this analysis is the idea of an historico-ethical division – between culture and society – which abrogates culture's promised totalisation of human capacities in true community. We have seen that the role of Arnold in this (the 'materialist') variant of the first model is to preside over the withdrawal of culture from its full social-democratic realisation; to sublimate it into ethics; and to revisit it on society, but this time as an ideology of moral improvement passed on to the working class through literary education in lieu of 'real' social improvement. According to Baldick (1983, p. 22), the principles of this division 'which require the partitioning of creation and criticism, of poet and thinker, and of practice and ideas in Arnold's cultural campaigns, form the basis of his whole critical project'.

Ben Knights' *The Idea of the Clerisy in the Nineteenth Century* contributes its own variation on the same theme. For Knights, the division between culture and society is the problematic that frames nineteenth-century conceptions of the social role of intellectuals. As a result, he sees intellectuals faced with the problem of how to actualise their vision of human completion without merely imposing it with abstract violence on the 'embodied imagination' of the rest of the population. This is a variant of Williams' problem – but also Schiller's – of how to reconcile the moral and sensuous tendencies and achieve free communication and true community. The figure of dialectical reconciliation is never far away under these circumstances; 'In conclusion I want to emphasise this sense of a sustained and necessary dialectic between forms of discourse, and (both at a personal and social level) between on the one hand the highly rationalised and highly formed and on the other, the serial activities of day to day living' (Knights, 1978, p. 232).

Finally, the most recent variant of this problematic occurs in discussions of the 'bourgeois public sphere'. In Peter Hohendahl's telling, a domain of open and wide-ranging discussion – allegedly formed when criticism went public in the salon culture of the eighteenth-century middle class – exemplifies the achievement of a limited synthesis of culture and society. This was a synthesis in which culture's promise of universal human development was partially fulfilled in the political and cultural institutions of the (then) 'universal class'. Needless to say, this golden age appears as the background to the historico-ethical split – brought about by the intensification of the division of labour and the crystallisation of antagonistic class interests – which is manifest, again, in the appearance of a distinctively aesthetic and ethical literary culture addressed to an élite. Hohendahl summarises his version of the *lapsus* thus:

The idea of the public sphere maintained that public discussion participated in a process of humanisation, insofar as the reception of art could be converted into social praxis through the mediation of the political public sphere. Yet this essential connection was lost in the later stage of development of bourgeois society. The relationship between the literary and the political public sphere was severed by the middle-class public as it set itself apart more distinctly from the masses. The educated elite withdrew to a 'sacral' reception of art which sought to shelter the work of art from a vulgarised world of reality in order to preserve the human potentials which though repressed by society, were preserved in the work. The lower classes, however, were soon caught in the jaws of the capitalist culture industry, which steadily eroded the concept of autonomous culture. Both of these courses led toward depoliticisation: the social impotence of the elitists, who clutched tightly onto art, corresponds to the subjugation of the masses to the apparatus of the culture industry. (Hohendahl, 1982, pp. 72–3)

It should be clear that all these variants of the 'culture and society' problematic deploy a particular conception of the relation between ethics (and aesthetics) and politics. Ethics is the distorted form assumed by culture when it is cut-off from the possibility of political realisation in 'the way of life as a whole'. Ethics is in fact the ideological form of culture. And in each of the versions just discussed, the appearance of a distinctively ethical and aesthetic literary education is treated as the appearance of a systematic misrepresentation of the true social and political bases of culture. In other words, in literary education, ethics is neither more nor less than the disguised exercise of class power, according to this model. But we should also recall that if this problematic is characterised by the project to unmask aesthetics and ethics as disguised politics, and to return them to the democratic totality of social relations, then this return is always conceived of as fulfilling the original promise of criticism and culture: that is, the reconciliation of 'man's' divided ethical substance and his universal development in unalienated communication and true community.

Let us briefly recapitulate the main consequences of our genealogy of literary education for this conception of its past and present.

First, we have seen that literary education did not emerge from the lost or anticipated synthesis of aesthetic culture and 'the way of life as a whole'. It emerged, rather, from a distinctive governmental apparatus formed not in the consciousness of literary intellectuals, but in an unprecedented investigative and administrative network which made the 'moral and physical' condition of the population into an object of government. It was in this network that the old techniques of pastoral surveillance aimed at the individual soul, and new forms of social discipline aimed at whole populations, could combine to form the technology of moral training which English was to inherit. In these developments administrative intellectuals like David Stow and James Kay-Shuttleworth were incomparably more important than literary intellectuals like

Carlyle, Arnold and Morris; but only because they were the agents of a great historical enterprise: the construction of an apparatus of government inside which the idea of the cultural improvement of whole populations first became thinkable and achievable. Disconnected from this apparatus, the proposal that true education depended on the reconciliation of culture and society was marginal and utopian; and it remains so today.

Second, the Romantic aesthetic and its conception of culture was not the theoretical or practical foundation – it was not the ideal vehicle of 'man's' cultural completion – in relation to which these educational developments were the full or partial realisation. We have just noted that popular education emerged on quite different – 'governmental' – historical surfaces. Moreover, for most of the nineteenth century, the Romantic aesthetic remained a caste 'practice of the self': a practice organised by the figure of the divided ethical substance and the telos of 'complete development' which therefore possessed no intrinsic ethical rationality or universality. Romantic criticism was not élitist by default, as the result of its tendentious withdrawal from 'the way of life as a whole', or of a split between 'the literary and political public spheres'. It was from the outset wholly and positively the province of a special caste, because it did not arise from a division inside the universal form of 'man's' ethical substance – a division that we might live to see overcome.[2] Instead, it was the exercise of a locally deployed ethical practice, initially disconnected from the governmental apparatus in which the idea of a uniform cultural development was made thinkable. Circulating largely through the ethical journalism of the educated middle class, this practice was a ritual for living the noble life – for shaping the self as the subject of moral action and knowledge – characterised by its capacity for withdrawal from 'premature' moral and social commitment.

Third, when the exemplary figure of the critic entered the pedagogical apparatus, giving birth to English, it was not as the (true or false) bearer of a culture on which the apparatus itself depended. Quite the opposite. First, in the persona of the inspector and then in the special personality of the English teacher, the critic became pedagogue in order to support tactics of moral supervision – those of 'correction through self-expression' – defined by the organisation of the popular school. It was here, focused in the remarkable moral career of the popular school teacher, that an exchange became possible between the normalising apparatus of moral supervision and the exemplary discipline of ethical self-shaping. It was at this point of exchange that we discovered the formation of the student-teacher, who perceived her own failure to reconcile the didactic and aesthetic impulses as a failure to shape a self in whom her students would find themselves shaped. That the teaching of English should continue to be organised around the relations of supervision and correction embodied in an ethical hierarchy is hardly surprising. This is not a sign of political failure, but of the fact that the technology of moral supervision provided the conditions for the dissemination of the attributes of the critic in the pedagogical sphere, and continues to do so.

Finally, as a consequence of this genealogy of literary education, we must revise the conception of the relation between ethics and politics lying at the heart of the problematic of 'culture and society'. The central manifestation of ethics in literary education is not that of the code or the moral ideology. Here we meet ethics not as the misrepresentation of the social and political basis of culture, but in the form of normative practices deployed within a purpose-built supervisory machinery. The ethical demeanour of popular education is a function not of the ideas that it purveys, but of the disciplinary techniques around which it is organised. This permits us to understand the fact that, despite the somewhat different ideas they wished to teach, the Chartists projected a school system organised around Stow's playground and the 'moral observation' of the teacher. In the popular school and – as T. W. Laqueur has shown – in the Sunday school which preceded it, it is not as ideas or as ideology that morality takes hold of individuals. Rather, it does so quite directly through an ensemble of practices and techniques: techniques for distributing individuals in supervisable spaces like the playground and the classroom; for passing all their activities through a grid of normalising observation; for making them responsible for their own conduct, sentiments and use of time; and, above all, techniques which embody new 'social' norms in the purpose-built relation to the teacher in whose 'moral observation' each individual finds his own conscience.

In short, the ethics of the popular school – the ethics which literary education has inherited – do not take the form of an ideological misrepresentation of 'real social improvement'. Instead they are present as a quite material ethical technology actually able to raise the cultural level of whole populations – to achieve near-universal literacy, for example – through the normative formation of personal attributes.

To argue that the popular school represents the ideological deformation of 'the complete development of human capacities' is, therefore, to radically misconceive the conditions under which the cultural attributes of populations became objects of systematic development. This did not occur on the basis of a split in 'man's' ethical substance which – in the various projects to reunify culture and society – continues to hold out the promise of a 'complete' development. It occurred, rather, on the basis of a normative profile of attributes for a citizenry. This profile was built up inside a specific investigative and administrative network which contained apparatuses like the popular school; that is, apparatuses capable of securing the systematic formation of these attributes. The fact that such an apparatus imposes norms for capacities and conduct; the fact that it is organised around techniques of moral supervision; and the fact that these techniques are embodied in unequal relations between differentially constructed social agents (the teacher-student couple) – none of these facts is grounds *per se* for an ethical or political critique of education in general or literary education in particular. They become so only if one considers that a true 'cultural politics' must be embodied in forms of social organisation in which social norms are not imposed until they have been organically realised in the breast of each individual.

In other words, they become so only if cultural politics is the imagined reconciliation of 'man's' divided ethical substance – of moral freedom and social necessity – in transparent communication and true community. But we have seen that this conception of cultural realisation plays a quite marginal and specialised role in the apparatus which made the actual formation of the cultural attributes of the 'community' an historical possibility. This conception is in fact the residual projection of the aesthetico-ethical practice of self-culture now deployed as a function of the technology of moral supervision itself. Hence, the social normativity which we find in the ethical discipline of literary education is not a disguised politics to be unmasked with the recovery of true community. It represents a *directly* ethical and aesthetic exercise of power. It indicates the form in which literary education functions as an irreducible and, for us, ineluctable ethical technology in the government of populations. Any critique of literary education seeking to engage with it must therefore be – in the specified sense – a local 'ethical' critique made, for example, in terms of alternative deployments of the disciplines of sensibility formation.

III

If the work of Baldick, Knights and Hohendahl represents the recent fortunes of the dialectic, then Stanley Fish's *Is There a Text in this Class?* is similarly representative of the pass which literary theory has come to as the travelling companion of the human sciences. In Fish's work the imperative to think 'the subject's' unthought being receives a distinctly phenomenological inflection. Fish is less concerned with specifying the precise structure of the literary unconscious than with describing the ambivalent moment of its surfacing in recognition and representation. The fact that his book represents one of the most sustained attempts in literary theory to reflect on the 'politics' of literary education – it is subtitled 'The Authority of Interpretive Communities' – makes it doubly significant from our point of view. Nonetheless, despite its concern with the process of 'becoming' a subject, and regardless of its institutional focus, Fish's version of theoretical clarification remains confined to the three theoretical figures whose migration from the human sciences brought literary theory into being in the first place. So, we can organise our discussion of Fish around the forms in which these figures surface in his work.

In the first place, Fish begins his discussion of the literary institution by rebutting charges that his conception of the indeterminacy of meaning leads him into relativism, nihilism and a model of literary education in which power replaces rationality. He argues that these charges will not stick because, although meaning is not objectively present in the poem or its writer's intentions, it is nonetheless radically constrained by the interpretive norms and procedures which bring it into being. According to Fish, such norms and procedures cannot be expressions of a wilful and open-ended subjectivity. In fact, they constrain interpretation not, however, through their presence in the object, but as subjectivity's unthought – in this case institutional – conditions of possibility.

> It is just that these norms are not embedded in the language (where they may be read out by anyone with sufficiently clear, that is, unbiased, eyes) but inhere in an institutional structure within which one hears utterances as already organised with reference to certain assumed purposes and goals . . . interpretive activities are not free, but what constrains them are the understood practices and assumptions of the institution and not

the rules and fixed meanings of a language system. (Fish, 1980, p. 306)

Interpretation is thus constrained by the radical 'finitude' of 'the subject'. It should come as no surprise to learn that this finitude has another side, however. If the interpretive norms set limits to subjectivity, confining it to the stipulative authority of the literary institution, they are nonetheless the means by which these limits can be evaded. They are, according to Fish, simultaneously the form in which determinant recognition is recalled to its conditions of possibility and is thereby freed to assume a new shape. The finitude imposed by institutional norms and procedures is thus also an 'analytic', recovering for subjectivity the conditions of its own realisation in interpretation and hence making it mobile across the whole field of interpretive positions. In short, the terrain on which Fish constructs his theory of literary education is that of the 'analytic of finitude'.

In the second place, on this terrain, as in the other versions of literary theory, 'the subject' (Fish's 'reader') takes on the now familiar ambivalence of the 'transcendental-empirical couple'. From one perspective, the reader is a product of training in a number of limited and empirical norms and procedures. The recognition of literariness, says Fish (ibid., p. 343), results not from the unconditional perception of literary properties but from 'running one of a number of well-defined interpretative routines' – a remark which at first seems to parallel our own earlier account of the artefactual character of the aesthetic. At the same time – and this marks the difference between the two accounts – the literary reading is also the place where these interpretative routines are themselves given to, and hence transcended by, consciousness. The ambivalence of the resulting transcendental-empirical couple is well enough represented in the remark from which the last quotation was taken.

A student of mine recently demonstrated this knowledge when, with an air of giving away a trade secret, she confided that she could go into any classroom, no matter what the subject of the course, and win approval for running one of a number of well-defined interpretive routines: she could view the assigned text as an instance of the tension between nature and culture; she could look in the text for evidence of large mythological oppositions; she could argue that the true subject of the text was its own composition, or that in the guise of fashioning a narrative the speaker was fragmenting and displacing his own anxieties and fears. (Loc. cit.)

Moving between a mechanism of perception of which she is the effect, and a transcendental reflection on this mechanism, Fish's student assumes the familiar double form of 'the subject' in the human sciences. Given these circumstances, it is hardly surprising that Fish's discussion of literary meaning is organised around the ritual opposition between 'description' (empirical recognition) and 'interpretation' (transcendental reflection). Fish attempts to defend the rights of interpretation by reconciling this difference. But he does so without the least awareness that the opposition between description and interpretation is a permanent and unresolvable feature of the figure of 'the subject', which he has inherited from the human sciences.

In the third and final place, it is inevitable given these theoretical circumstances that Fish will formulate the central problem of literary studies – and of the 'authority of interpretive communities' – in terms of the relation between the unconscious and the *cogito*. On one side, the interpretive norms make consciousness possible from a place which is not that of consciousness (the 'institution') and this drives them into the domain of the unthought, in Fish's view. In fact, it is the unthought characteristic of membership in interpretive communities that sets limits to doubt and the indeterminacy of meaning. These limits exist, says Fish (ibid., pp. 331–2), 'because the mental operations we can perform are limited by the institutions in which we are *already* embedded. These institutions precede us, and it is only by inhabiting them, or being inhabited by them, that we have access to the public and conventional senses they make.'

But on the other side, it is the very fact that such membership is characterised as unthought or 'taken for granted' that forms the imperative to think it: to drag back into consciousness that which eludes it while making it possible, and hence to free it from the fixity of its unconscious determination. Hence, hard on the heels of his celebration of 'tacit knowledge', Fish (ibid., p. 366) speaks with great assurance on the virtue and rewards of enlightenment: 'The greatest rewards of our profession are reserved for those who challenge the assumptions within which ordinary practices go on, not so much in order to eliminate the category of the ordinary but in order to redefine it and reshape its configurations.'

In fact, the relation between the unconscious and the *cogito* is a highly problematic and unstable one for Fish, because through it he organises his meditation on the role of authority in literary education. On the one hand, he is driven to affirm that interpretive régimes are inescapably tacit or unconscious as this, in his view, is the only thing that saves interpretation from relativism, and pedagogical authority from the cynical exercise of power. As long as we take a particular régime for granted we 'believe in it', says Fish (ibid., p. 364); and because we believe in it we teach it in good faith to our students. On the other hand, he is driven to affirm the necessity of recovering the unthought for consciousness; because unless this is achieved 'the subject' will remain a slave to objective meaning, which Fish regards as nothing more than the blind imposition of a specific interpretive régime. Needless to say, this 'dilemma' is as unresolvable as it is unproductive. It is simply a product of those circumstances which bring the figure of 'the subject' into being between the surfaces of the *cogito* and the unconscious. The best that Fish can manage is to stage an oscillation: the subject 'thinks the unthought' and changes régimes (thereby escaping the blind authority of the taken-for-granted); at the same time the subject finds itself in a new régime in which it was 'always already' tacitly in place (thereby escaping the cynical authority of deracinated consciousness).

> When his beliefs change, the norms and values to which he once gave unthinking assent will have been demoted to the status of opinions and become the objects of an analytical and critical attention; but that attention will itself be enabled by a new set of norms and values that are, for the time being, as unexamined and undoubted as those they displace. (Ibid., p. 319)

Interestingly enough, it is precisely in this movement between unthought commitment and theoretical reflection that Fish – obedient to the logic of the human sciences which dictates that even foundations must have foundations – attempts to comprehend his own position and authority as a teacher-critic. Not surprisingly, in doing so he simply reproduces the initial oscillation at a higher level. Fish is the exemplary subject who braves the unconscious depths of the literary institution, dragging it back to the full light of consciousness, and freeing us from the blind authority of objective meaning by thinking its unthought norms. But he is also exemplary in a second quite different way. He reminds us that it is only through our unthought 'habitation' of some particular régime – in which our subjectivity is 'always already' in place – that we can escape the nihilistic authority of unconstrained consciousness. Hence Fish remarks that his theory of interpretation as movement across different interpretive régimes is not one that can be 'lived by'. But the reader should not mistake this for intellectual modesty, because Fish's coda is that it is a theory that one cannot help but 'live out'.

If in the first model we found the project to supercede the 'present state' of literary studies, rooted in a certain conception of the relation between ethics and politics, then in the second model we find it deploying a certain conception of the relation between politics (authority) and knowledge. This relation is one in which the teacher-critic seeks to elude his aesthetico-ethical authority – generated through his exemplary position in the machinery of moral supervision – by staging a double feint. First, in the direction of theoretical knowledge. Here, by deploying a form of representation supposedly capable of equalising teacher and taught on the democratic platform of rational awareness, the teacher-critic seeks to *abolish* his authority, transforming its unthought practice into theoretical reflection. Second, in the direction of a rhetoric of commitment. Here, by appearing to purge it of all tendentiousness and deploying it as the universal form of 'the subject's' becoming or 'being in the world', he attempts to *domesticate* his authority, reconverting theoretical awareness into tacit practice.

Needless to say, I am more interested in 'being in the classroom'. In order to return to this less exalted, but also less fraught, space let us summarise the consequences of our genealogy for Fish's account of literary education.

First, we have argued that capacities for reading and interpreting literature do not have a single general location or logic, in the space between 'the subject's' empirical perceptions and a transcendental reflection on their conditions of possibility. Instead, we have seen that such capacities – for example, the Renaissance oratorical 'praise of authors'; the 'formulaic' percipience of the audience for the oral epic; the dialectical movement between form and meaning in Romantic self-culture – are built up piecemeal-fashion through the practical mastery of special ensembles of techniques, exercises and perceptual routines. These ensembles are not embodied in 'the subject' and are instead maintained in definite apparatuses (for example, the grammar school) and instituted relationships (between the aspiring epic singer-composer and the master he imitates). As such they need possess no common form: think of the difference between the gradual mastery of the oral formulary in the relation of imitation of the master, and the practice of ethical division and reconciliation through which the Romantic aesthete shapes the relation to his 'self'. It is, therefore, something of a fiction to unify these dispersed ensembles under the single heading of 'interpretive routines'. They possess no necessary relation to each other, nor do they share the same range of functions or participate in the same 'forms of living'.

In other words, it is misleading to conceive of these ensembles as 'conditions of knowledge' or as chains of 'subject positions'. They do not subtend a single general surface of 'empirical recognition', and hence they are not stitched together by the promise of 'the subject's' mobility across this surface. Rather, their mode of existence appears to be that of contingent activities, exercises and techniques, whose practical mastery is responsible for the formation of specific non-aggregative capacities: for example, Matthew Arnold's highly developed capacity to intensify the 'morally coded' and the 'spontaneously perceived' in the practice of reconciliation through which he shaped the attributes of the ethical exemplar. These procedures for the formation of psychological capacities and ethical attributes can be treated as quite analogous to the ones that Marcel Mauss (1973) describes for physical capacities, built up through piecemeal 'techniques of the body'.

By posing the problem of the acquisition of literary capacities in terms of the 'conditions of recognition' or 'subject positions', the problematic of literary theory – in this instance in Fish's rendition of it – collapses the historically contingent and differentiated activities that have been called 'reading literature' into the single general figure of 'the subject'. This collapse is signalled by a particular circularity in Fish's argument. On the one hand, Fish (ibid., p. 313) poses the problem of the literary reading in terms of its necessary dependence on enabling practices or 'circumstances': 'The answer to the question "How did he get from her words to the circumstances within which she intended him to hear them?" is that he must already be thinking within those circumstances in order to be able to hear her words as referring to them.' But on the other hand, says Fish (ibid., p. 316), the hearer or reader only comes to occupy these enabling practices or circumstances because they are 'informed by tacitly known purposes and goals'; and these purposes and goals are none other than the meaning or interpretation which they (the practices or circumstances) are supposed to make possible. In other words, the capacity for interpretation depends on a prior mastery of interpretive procedures; but the mastery of interpretive procedures depends on a prior capacity for interpretation.[3]

What this circularity shows is that by posing the problem of literary capacities in terms of subjectivity and its conditions of possibility – in fact in terms of the 'analytic of finitude' – Fish forfeits all possibility of describing their formation and maintenance. Despite his claims to ground interpretive capacities in institutional trainings, Fish (ibid., p. 316) cannot finally distinguish capacities *acquired* on the basis of the mastery of practical techniques from *pre-given* capacities; or, the acquisition of capacities from their exercise: 'The distinction, then, is between already having an ability and having to acquire it, but it is not finally an essential distinction, because the routes by which that ability could be exercised on the one hand, and learned on the other, are so similar.' Of course, they are similar only if one is committed to the idea that the dispersed cultural technologies, in which literary capacities have been built up, are all somehow whistled into existence by the interpretive 'purposes and goals' which they make possible. But as we have seen in the case of modern criticism itself, the acquisition of capacities inside cultural apparatuses is a protracted and contingent affair. In this case it is achieved on the basis of imperatives (to intervene in the sensibilities of whole populations) and forms of social organisation (the popular school as an apparatus of moral supervision) in relation to which the interpretive operation which Fish treats as foundational is nothing more than a mildly interestingly by-product. To describe such cultural technologies it is necessary to move off the terrain of 'the subject' altogether.

Second, we have seen that the imperative of theoretical clarification is not something arising from the nature of subjectivity or as a function of a single general relation – recognition, interpretation – linking reader and text. The imperative is given foundational standing in Fish's account, because he assumes that the indeterminacy of recognition or its (shifting) determination by unthought norms is constitutive of subjectivity or reading in general. Indeed, Fish purports to demonstrate this assumption in his record of an 'experiment', in which he directed a literature class to interpret what was in fact a bibliographical list for an assignment as a seventeenth-century religious poem. This the class proceeded to do, using an array of typological and exegetical procedures; and Fish treats this accomplishment as proof of the indeterminacy of recognition, or of the fact that its apparently determinate character is dependent on unthought norms always open to change: 'Skilled reading is usually thought to be a matter of discerning what is there, but if the example of my students can be generalised, it is a matter of knowing how to *produce* what can thereafter be said to be there. Interpretation is not the art of construing but the art of constructing' (ibid., p. 327).

Fish has no qualms about generalising. If recognition has its character by virtue of the nature of subjectivity, then all recognition must share the same interpretative form. Hence that which appears to be a description of presented features must itself be an interpretation or 'construction' of them. The idea that the original assignment list exists in a different modality to the interpretative one of poetry – the modality of description or unproblematic recognition – must therefore be false. According to Fish (ibid., p. 329), 'the assignment we all see is no less the product of interpretation than the poem into which it was turned. That is, it requires just as much work and work of the same kind, to see this as an assignment as it does to see it as a poem.'

However, Fish's *tour de force* does not demonstrate what it purports to; and it is not difficult to show that it is much closer to I. A. Richards' initial 'experiments' in practical criticism than Fish perhaps would wish. All that Fish's 'experiment' shows is that it is possible to come to doubt a particular recognition under certain prescribed circumstances; these circumstances being, for example, when someone is required to apply exegetical techniques to a bibliographical list. From this it does not follow that such a doubt is possible under all circumstances, or that Fish's problematising regimen stands in any important relation to those other circumstances in which bibliographical lists are treated as bibliographical lists. In other words, it does not follow that recognition or meaning is indeterminate *per se*, or that it was always on the cards that this particular recognition would enter the arena of doubt.

Doubt, Wittgenstein (1969) reminds us, has conditions too; and these conditions do not, as Fish assumes, have the single general form of a gap between empirical recognition and its unthought conditions. Recognition is not always potentially problematic. It must be *problematised* through circumstance, norm or decision. For example, a rhetorical description of the figures (metaphor, metonomy, synedoche), or a philological description of a particular compositional formulary (Lord's description of the oral epic), may indeed be a quite determinate description of presented features. (Of course, this is not to say that such descriptions will be invariably correct, only that here tropes, and there compositional formulas, are being described according to their presented features.)

This is not to make some claim for the transcendental objectivity of such features, however. Their description clearly depends on specific perceptual routines and descriptive techniques: in Lord's case, techniques of morphological classification (substitution in parallel verbal contexts) common to philology and structural linguistics. But it is to say that the deployment of these routines and techniques is not automatically governed by the relation between recognition and doubt. Such deployments do indeed determine what counts as knowledge under certain circumstances, but they are not themselves automatically in the circle of knowledge or doubt. This does not mean, says Wittgenstein, that we know them with certainty or (on the other hand) that they are always just beyond the reach of knowledge. Neither does it mean, *pace* Fish, that when we use them thus we are being uncritical, and that it is always possible that we might come to doubt them. What it means is that not all human activities fall within the sphere of knowing and doubting. It means that some of the activities that we call description – as, for example, when the rhetorician describes a metaphor to someone who is expected to learn how to use metaphors – do not fall within the sphere of knowing and doubting. It means that knowledge and doubt are the accomplishment of special techniques and activities not co-extensive with 'subjectivity'.

In this sense, then, the philological description is indeed determinate as is the recognition of Fish's bibliographical list. The fact that it is possible under certain circumstances to bring the latter within the circle of doubt is not a fact about the list itself, its recognition or its reader. It is a fact about these special circumstances. If, as Fish says, the determinacy of recognition is not a transcendental fact about the object, then its indeterminacy is not a transcendental fact concerning 'the subject'. In short, the recognition of the list must be *made* indeterminate; that is, its indeterminacy must be secured through a practice of problematisation deploying problematising norms and techniques. How does Fish achieve this? Well – and this is precisely what vanishes from his account through the double feint around authority – he *requires* his students to problematise this recognition.

In saying 'treat this list as a poem', Fish is not showing that lists exist in a sphere of recognition and doubt in which they might at any moment – in any sort of social relationship – come to be treated as poems. Nor, consequently, is he showing that recognition of the list is the result of the same sort of (interpretive) activity as recognition of the poem. He is simply enforcing circumstances in which the list will not be used or described as a list. In short, he is levying the imperative of theoretical clarification as a *norm*. The correct formulation of the problem is *not*: this list *cannot* be described only interpreted, *but*: under these circumstances we *do not* describe it. 'These circumstances' are precisely the relations of supervision and correction that characterise the literature lesson, and nothing about the list or its readers dictates that these circumstances must apply. (Of course, nothing dictates that they must not apply either.) We thus verify through a contemporary example the historical point made in Chapter 6: the imperative to recover for consciousness that which makes it possible while eluding it does not derive from 'the subject' but from the contingent intellectual action in which the positive sciences were redeployed in the space of representation. Fish demonstrates again that literary theory deploys the imperative as a pedagogical norm in the régime of moral supervision. (Not that this is necessarily a bad thing.)

Third, the insufficiency of Fish's meditation on 'the authority of interpretative communities' should now be readily apparent. Authority in this area resides neither in the unthought character of interpretive norms, nor in the threat of an unconstrained consciousness imposing itself at will on traditional ('embodied') wisdom. Power here is exercised neither through the failure of knowledge nor through its tyrannical success. In short, it does not derive from relations of recognition and reflection linking 'the subject' to the poem. Rather, it is a function of the relations of supervision and correction linking two differently specified individuals – the student and the teacher-critic – in a highly specialised relationship. In the example we have just discussed, the fact that the students come to interpret the list as a poem signifies neither their escaping the blind authority of the unthought, nor their acceptance of the true authority of their 'being in the world'. Instead, it indicates that they are acting in accord with the imperative to problematise and clarify recognition, an imperative deployed as a pedagogical norm or 'task of behaviour'.

It is not in the students' subjectivities that their uncertainty regarding the status of the list arises (if it arises). It is in their relation to their teacher. This relation, which we have described as the form in which the technology of moral supervision was deployed in the popular school, provided the imperative of the human sciences with its object: a category of individuals whose openness to the corrective force of 'moral observation' means that their perceptions are open to problematisation. 'Recognition' in modern criticism is thus a function not of the relation between the two sides of subjectivity, but of the instituted relation of supervision and correction linking two differently constituted social agents. It is the surface on which the exemplary attributes of the teacher-critic are moulded, and then unceasingly exercised and maintained. It is simply not the case that the institution of recognition can be founded in a theoretical recovery of its 'unthought' conditions, and that through this foundation 'the subject' will escape the authority of recognition by acquiring mobility across all its possible forms. This utopian project is simply the result of taking the imperative of clarification at its word, instead of as an ethico-intellectual exercise deployed as a pedagogical norm.

Finally, we are now in a position to call into question the conception of the relation between politics and knowledge lying at the heart of the renovatory project of literary theory. We have seen that authority in modern criticism is not a function of the relation between 'the subject' and the text. It does not have a 'bad' form, deriving from 'the subject's' failure to think its unthought formation and hence claim the radical equality of enlightenment. But neither does it have a 'good' form, deriving from the fact that 'the subject' is always already 'at home' in the norms and categories which relate it to the world. Hence authority cannot be abolished through a reflexive action in which subjectivity theorises its own possibility and thereby subordinates authority to knowledge. But neither can it be domesticated through a gesture of belief or commitment in which 'the subject' finds itself 'always already in place', thereby purifying authority in the comforting ontology of 'being' and 'becoming'. Instead, authority in modern criticism is the inescapable product of the pedagogical imperatives and techniques, and the purpose-built relations of supervision and correction deployed in the teacher-student couple.

We have seen that if knowledge of the poem in modern criticism is inseparable from a certain 'clarifying' knowledge of its reader – if the poem is in fact a surface always revealing ethical incompleteness and intellectual failure – this is because literature's predominant contemporary deployment or mode of existence is as a focus and support for these relations of supervision and correction. In short, knowledge in modern criticism is inseparable from the instituted relations and activities through which a special form of aesthetico-ethical power is generated and exercised. We have already seen that this form of power does not operate on individuals indirectly, through their unconscious, by blocking knowledge. Instead, it takes hold of individuals directly (by requiring the exercise of certain skills and techniques; by instituting certain relations of emulation and correction between them) where it in fact *produces* knowledge (of the state of the sensibility; of the level of theoretical awareness). And this means that strategies to modify current critical practices cannot assume the global form of a reduction of authority to knowledge: one that would reconstruct the supervisory relations of criticism on the basis of a single fundamental knowledge of its object and subject. Rather, such strategies must make their calculations *within* the inescapable relations of authority in which aesthetico-ethical power *and* knowledge are formed in modern literary education.

IV

It is possible to suggest, then, that the 'present state' of literary education does not confront us as a unity organised around the imperative to reconcile culture and society, or the imperative to clarify the literary unconscious. It seems inescapable that these twin imperatives, and the figures of 'man' and 'the subject' that they support, are themselves functions of the form in which the Romantic aesthetic and the human sciences were deployed within the supervisory mechanism of literary pedagogy. As such they are in no position to effect an 'unmasking' of literary education: to reveal its ethics and authority as a diguised politics and to reconstruct it on the basis of a universal ethics and a rational knowledge. Quite the reverse. We have seen that they are in fact the twin forms through which the supervisory relations at the heart of literary education take hold of individuals: doing so in accordance with a specific machinery of cultural formation, and with the exemplary role of the teacher-critic in this machinery.

The attempt by critics like Baldick, Knights, Hohendahl and Fish, to make one or both of these imperatives serve as an absolute historical or theoretical horizon for the present, leads them to both *under* and *over*-estimate the importance and potential of literary education. It leads them to an under-estimation because, as a result, the apparatus of literary education is reduced to the function of a cipher for a process of historico-ethical development or theoretical clarification, taking place on the universal terrains of culture and knowledge. From here arises the complacent tendency to dismiss literary pedagogy as an ideology or as a pre-theoretical knowledge. This is done in the name of the 'complete' development of human capacities to be achieved, it is said, through the aesthetic totalisation of social relations or their reduction to a theoretical knowledge. But we have seen that literary education does not have the form of an ideology or a pre-theoretical knowledge. It is an irreducible ethical technology: a specialised form of that larger governmental apparatus whose historic achievement was to raise the cultural levels of whole populations through the forms in which it supervised their individual members.

At the same time, this same tendency to generalise from the twin pedagogical imperatives leads to a misplaced over-estimation of literary education's scope and significance. If English and modern criticism are not currently realising their vocation to complete 'man', it is argued, then this is only because they are blocked by some contingent impediment: by the confinement of criticism to ethics and aesthetics, which signals its isolation from the 'actual and growing social force' in which the promise of culture might be fulfilled; or by its restriction to a pre-theoretical form of empirical experience, whose theoretical reconstruction will liberate the 'grammar' of all possible experiences. Hence, as we have noted – particularly in the case of Marxist criticism – the denunciation of literary education as ideology is inseparable from the project to restore it to its former glory and true vocation: either by ending its isolation from 'the way of life as a whole'; or by transforming it into a fundamental knowledge of 'the subject's possible formations; or – as with Jameson – by both strategies at once.

But the same remarks apply here as in the case of under-estimation. English and modern criticism are not and never were, in practice or in principle, vehicles for a 'complete' development of human capacities. Their current standing is entirely due to their role in the training of sensibilities – particularly the exemplary sensibility of the teacher-critic – inside the apparatus of public education. This apparatus, we have seen, forms cultural attributes on the basis of a (shifting) profile, arising from a larger network of governmental institutions. These include the institutions of public health, penality, family management, sexuality and social assistance, which are individually and collectively capable of specifying and shaping a definite range of 'social' attributes without the help of 'culture and criticism'.

To suggest – as Frederick Jameson (1981, pp. 96, 74) does – that literary culture might be responsible for this entire complex; that it might complete 'man' through 'the reconstruction of the materials of cultural and literary history in the form of this new "text" . . . which is cultural revolution'; and that it must therefore 'restore a perspective in which the imagery of libidinal revolution and of bodily transfiguration once again becomes a figure for the perfected community' – all this can only be taken as a sign that the forms in which modern criticism is able to reflect on itself are radically disconnected from the actual forms of social organisation responsible for governing the present. Literary education is simply not that important. But then, by the same argument, neither is it that unimportant.

The contours of literary education – the forms in which it confronts us in the present – are, I have argued, the results of a specific set of historical circumstances. These were the circumstances in which literary pedagogy, having emerged as a privileged embodiment of the technology of moral supervision, permitted the exemplary discipline of the Romantic aesthetic and the clarificatory practice of the human sciences to meet, in a being characterised by a certain ethical and intellectual incompleteness.

To some extent this being represents the entire population of the school system, because these attributes – particularly ethical incompleteness – are a function of the techniques of supervision and correction on which popular education is based. The most intense development of these characteristics is reserved, however, for the special stratum of literary intellectuals and English teachers. As the privileged personification of the machinery of 'moral observation' in which 'the true character and disposition is revealed', the teacher-critic himself cannot exist outside the forms of ethical self-shaping and theoretical clarification on which his exemplary formation depends.

Nevertheless, if the meeting of the Romantic aesthetic and the human sciences in the supervisory organisation of the school indicates the contours in which modern literary education came into being, it also signals the lines along which it is open to change. I have argued that these lines do not meet in a single revolutionary nexus, in which the ethical technology of literary education will be overthrown and reconstructed as a rational politics or a true knowledge. Instead, it seems to me that they assume the form of four co-ordinates, each moving at a tangent to the others and defining not a single programme for change but a field of possible initiatives, each with its own limits and logic. In summarily describing these four co-ordinates I will bring this study to a close.

The *first* co-ordinate, and no doubt the most important, is that formed when the literary text began to absorb the techniques of moral supervision, whose first home had been the playground and the classroom. These were the circumstances in which English came into being: bringing the life of the child into the formative space of the school; acquiring in the process the latter's 'closeness to life'; and giving birth to the demand for a teacher whose knowledge of literature would also support a supervisory knowledge of the child who read it. However, if the functions of moral supervision thus acquired by English have been responsible for its remarkable importance in the system of public education – in the training of teachers in particular – they also mark the site of a crucial instability. And this is not because they are about to be unmasked as ideology. It is, rather, that *other* instrumentalities have also supported these functions and continue to do so.

The emergence of English was, we have observed, inseparable from the deployment of 'experimental pedagogy': that mix of progressive education and educational psychology which was able to capitalise in its own way on the powers of observation and correction generated in the playground and the classroom. These disciplines have also laid claim to a supervisory knowledge of the 'true character and disposition' of the child. They represent powerful alternative investments of the tactics of 'supervised freedom' and 'correction through self-expression', which advocates of English wrongly assume to derive from the expressive powers of literature. For this reason English has never been without its psycho-therapeutic wing, whose early forms we noted in the work of Margaret McMillan and J. A. Green, and whose later versions are clearly visible in the writings of Marjourie Hourd, David Holbrook and Dorothy Heathcote.

But for the same reason it has been possible from the outset that the psychological use of the pedagogical disciplines could simply displace their literary use as English, shifting the functions of sensibility formation completely into the socio and psycho-therapeutic register. There are two reasons for taking this possibility seriously. First, if Donzelot's (1979, pp. 169–217) account of the role of psychological techniques in French education is correct, then it seems that in some national systems literary pedagogy has never assumed the importance in cultural regulation that it has in the Anglo-American context. Second, the recent expansion of sex education and 'human relations' education in the English, American and Australian school systems indicates that the extent to which 'moral training' occurs in an aesthetico-ethical, as opposed to a psycho-therapeutic, register is contingent and changeable, and is indeed in the process of changing.

The *second* co-ordinate is that formed when the dialectical practice of Romantic self-culture was redeployed as a discipline in the school system. With the migration of the techniques of moral supervision to art and literature, there arose the demand for a specialist teacher who could exercise the non-coercive functions of 'moral observation' on the surface of the literary text. These were the circumstances in which the dialectic of intellect and feeling, form and meaning, lost its caste deployment as a means of shaping a particular relation to the self, and reappeared as a 'task of behaviour' in the formation of the English teacher. In this new deployment the relation to the self is only achieved through a relation to another for whom the dialectic provides a window for ethical invigilation and correction. In short, ethical criticism was generalised, to a degree, when its exemplary functions were harnessed to the normalising functions of the apparatus of moral supervision.

If this has meant the almost complete eclipse of the man of letters – he now appears only as a 'personality' in the system of mass communication – it has also witnessed the remarkable multiplication of his exemplary attributes in the corps of popular teachers. Far from being a sign of the deracination of an erstwhile organic or popular culture, the shift of criticism into the educational apparatus has witnessed an unprecedented dissemination of its special culture of the self. But, this shift also marks the site of an important instability in literary education, formed at that point where Romantic criticism meets the other disciplines of the humanities in the modern university.

Romantic criticism, we have seen, did not emerge as a knowledge but as an ethical practice: an exercise of self-culture based not in some deeper knowledge of literature or psychology, but in the special ritual of ethical division and the 'practice of the self' that accompanied it. It is surely one of the more remarkable facts about the modern humanities that, at the centre of their conception of 'man's' cultural completion, we should find a formerly esoteric ethical practice generalised through its re-deployment as an instrument of moral supervision in a governmental pedagogy. The practice of the ethical dialectic is thus both a mainstay of, and an embarrassment to, literary education: a mainstay because it marks the place of English in the pedagogical 'government of populations', which is responsible for its enrolments and importance; an embarrassment because this practice defies all protocols for rational knowledge and proceeds as a species of sensibility training with an inescapable disciplinary function. Thus, while the future of ethical criticism remains secure as long as literary pedagogy retains its governmental function, it has no future apart from this function and represents an immoveable obstacle to all attempts to subject literary education to a rational reconstruction.

This is not the case with literary theory, however, whose formation marks the *third* co-ordinate on which literary education came into being and along which it is open to change. Although it was formed in that moment when 'the subject' of the human sciences overlapped the 'man' of Romantic criticism in the educable individual provided by the school, it is possible for literary theory to outlive this moment, in some form. Unlike the Romantic ethical dialectic, the imperative of theoretical clarification has a future beyond its pedagogical deployment, because of its attachment to the field of the human sciences. This is not to say, however, that this pedagogical use is a merely contingent 'application' of the 'pure' knowledges of linguistics, sociology and psychology. The sciences of man are, we have seen, irreducibly pedagogical in that they are grounded not in the nature of 'the subject', but in a specific intellectual action – to think subjectivity's unthought conditions – arising as a contingent strategy in response to the emergence of the positive sciences. It is the dependence of the human sciences on their positive parent sciences (philology, economics, biology) that guarantees their place in the university; and it is literary theory's dependence on the human sciences that promises it a future outside its supervisory deployment in literary pedagogy. But it is this very promise that marks a third area of instability in English and modern criticism; because outside of its pedagogical deployment literary theory is unable to function as a species of criticism – it parts company with the aesthetic – and is in fact nothing more than a minor branch of one or another human science.

Such a divorce would mean that literary theory would lose its current importance which, as we saw in the case of Fish, is wholly dependent on its continuing to support the supervisory functions of criticism. In the area of semiotics, for example, literary theory would not assume the form of a 'literary semiotics', but would be displaced by a semiotics applied to literary (amongst other) texts. This is the case with Greimas' *Structural Semantics*, for example. Here, courtesy of the three theoretical figures of the human sciences, philology is redeployed under the sign of 'conditions of representation', but quite independently of the Romantic aesthetic. Greimas thereby produces a semantics of narrative which will not support the techniques of aesthetico-ethical supervision and which, as a direct consequence, is quite marginal to the teaching of literature and criticism. (Greimas' work can be contrasted with Todorov's in this regard, the latter retaining the dialectic of form and meaning at the centre of his conception of 'self-regulating form'.) The price of a future beyond its pedagogical deployment is that literary theory becomes a marginal branch of the social sciences.

All the same, no matter how far literary theory moves in the direction of the human sciences, it is always possible for it to be recuperated for criticism and pedagogy. This possibility is contained in the figure of 'the subject' and the pedagogical imperative (to 'think the unthought') which literary theory inherits from the human sciences. Hence, even Greimas treats the various levels of his narrative grammar – one, the 'actantial', being nothing more than a codification of Propp's philological morphology of folk tales – as the unconscious stages through which narrative must pass in its passage to 'manifestation' in consciousness. And this allows Jameson to redeploy the grammar as the calculus of a failed consciousness ('ideological closure'). Once redeployed in this manner the fragile purity of the semiotics of literature is plunged once more into the chaotic proliferation of foundations – Greimas' narrative grammar is forced to cohabit with sociological and psychoanalytic structures – which threatens to undo the entire enterprise of literary theory.

Moreover, the failure of the intellect, which Jameson marks through the 'ideological closure' of narrative, is inseparable from a certain ethical incompleteness: the familiar failure to reconcile culture and society and thereby release the 'political unconscious' in an aesthetic totalisation of social relations. Jameson's work – ironic as this may seem given his project for 'cultural revolution' – thus exemplifies the forces pulling literary theory back into the orbit of the technology of moral supervision, where it functions as one of the two poles of modern criticism. In short, we can say that through its attachment to the human sciences, literary theory exposes modern criticism to two sorts of mutation: to marginalisation and fragmentation through absorption into the human sciences proper; and to the chaos of foundations and disciplinary 'contamination' resulting from its recuperation for the supervisory tasks of literary education.

However, more important than either of the preceding two co-ordinates – second only to the initial pedagogical emergence of English – is the *fourth* co-ordinate: that formed by criticism's own 'positive sciences' rhetoric and philology. We have seen that both the Romantic aesthetic and the human sciences – the twin forms whose imperatives of ethical reconciliation and theoretical clarification give shape to modern criticism – can be understood as optional strategies formed in response to the emergence of the positive sciences. In these two strategies rhetoric and philology undergo a double marginalisation: appearing in the one as a source of purely formal insights that will become clichés unless reconciled with 'experienced meaning'; and in the other as the locus of a pre-theoretical empiricism in need of theoretical clarification. (We can see both proscriptions, fused in the heat of pedagogy, in Richards' (1929, pp. 292–310) stigmatisation of 'technical presuppositions' as both formalist and empiricist.)

But we have noted that this double marginalisation of the positive sciences is also a double re-deployment. Subject to an ethical redeployment in the romantic aesthetic, a rhetorical schema like the division between ornament and thought assumes a new form in the dialectical division between form and meaning, and a new function as the schema for a practice of ethical reconciliation or self-culture. Whereas, redeployed in the human sciences, a philological technique like morphological description (through substitution in parallel verbal contexts) reappears as the unthought conditions of representation that 'the subject' must recover. Thus, no matter how strenuously modern criticism attempts to marginalise rhetoric and historical philology as 'mechanical' (Richards) or 'antiquarian' (Jameson), it remains indissolubly wedded to them at the level of its conditions of possibility.

It is for this reason, as we observed in the conclusion to Chapter 7, that the twin projects to realise 'man' – through a reconciliation of his ethical division or a theoretical recovery of his unconscious being – remain under permanent threat of dissolution from the Trojan Horse of historical philology. Philological time owes nothing to 'man'. As such it is capable of scattering literary capacities across the dispersed cultural technologies in which they are formed, threatening in the process to reveal the twin projects of modern criticism as the local imperatives of one such technology. I have already indicated that the present study is, in part, an attempt to capitalise on these effects and as such itself can be taken as an articulation of the fourth region in which literary education is open to change.

Historical philology is, in principle at least, capable of dissolving the Romantic aesthetic and the (cultural) human sciences. It can do so by deploying a description of texts – of their compositional technologies and historical deployments – which is not contingent on the ethical or theoretical transformation of the bearer of the description. In other words, it deploys a description which does not generate a 'pedagogical imperative', and is not therefore part of the system of sensibility training or self-problematisation. We saw that it was for this reason that Wimsatt and Brooks constructed their *Short History*, in part as a defence against the historical philology of the American graduate schools. Their complaint that these schools removed criticism from its humanising vocation is the complaint that philology removes knowledge of texts from the supervisory knowledge of their readers. Somewhat ironically, but for precisely the same reason, we find critics like Frye, Hartman and Jameson seeking to contain historical philology by invoking the 'dialectic' between 'historical' and 'ethical criticism'. Without such strategic recuperations the description of literature forfeits its pedagogico-ethical function altogether, and assumes the form of a specialist historical knowledge quite marginal to the 'governmental' training of sensibilities.

However, for this very reason pragmatic limits are set to the extent to which historical philology can escape its redeployment as criticism and pedagogy. The themes of the Romantic aesthetic (the historico-ethical completion of 'man') and the human sciences (the theoretical rehabilitation of 'the subject') resurface in the heartlands of historical description – so powerful is the pull of the technology of moral supervision which forms the base of the educational pyramid.

Such are the four co-ordinates which organise the historical surfaces on which modern literary education first appeared, and which delineate the contours on which it is open to modification. It will be observed that these possible changes do not have a single general form, as is presupposed by the twin projects to reconstruct the ethical functions of literary pedagogy on the basis of a rational politics or a true knowledge. Literary education is not open to a general critique or a total supercession. The strategies available to those working within its four co-ordinates are both less global and more various. They must be formed on the basis of calculations made in one or more of the four regions whose topographies we have just sketched.

● *First*, in the crucial region formed by the deployment of techniques of moral supervision in the machinery of cultural regulation. Here the problem of literary education must be posed in terms of the relation between the aesthetico-ethical embodiment of these techniques in English, and their increasingly powerful and no less fundamental psycho-therapeutic deployment in the psychological *savoirs*.

● *Second*, in the domain of Romantic critical practice. Calculation must take into account the continuing importance of the teacher-critic in the machinery of moral supervision, in relation to the instability in the field of knowledge caused by the 'archaic' presence of his 'practice of the self'.

● *Third*, in the field of literary theory, strategies must be calculated in terms of its problematic adjacency to the field of the human sciences. This is an adjacency which promises to free literary theory from its supervisory deployment (but only at the cost of disconnecting it from aesthetics and criticism), while never completely insuring it against the possibility of further pedagogical recuperations.

● *Finally*, in the region of the positive sciences the problem of literary education confronts us in the form of a specific mode of historical description: one able to dissolve criticism's twin projects for 'man's' cultural completion (and hence open up the whole terrain of the historical technologies in which literary capacities are actually formed) but which in doing so removes knowledge of literature from the domain of sensibility formation altogether.

These, then, are the four strategic areas of literary education which it becomes possible to occupy on the basis of the genealogy I have undertaken. Perhaps they seem fiddling and inglorious to those who continue to raise their eyes to 'criticism and culture' in the hope of glimpsing the forms of 'man's' cultural apotheosis. They exemplify, however, the lowering of the temperature of the debate surrounding English and modern criticism, which has been the objective of these concluding remarks. Such a lowering is, it seems to me, a small price to pay in order to re-engage with the forms in which literary education is actually deployed.

Notes and References

1 Introduction

1. The following citational conventions are used in this work: all emphases are those of the quoted authors, as are round brackets; square brackets indicate my interpolations.
2. Other works treating English as the promised reconciliation of the ethical division are Bantock (1967), Gribble (1983), Shayer (1972), Knights (1978), Thompson (1969), Dixon (1967) and Whitehead (1966).
3. Further examples of the analysis of English as a 'disguised politics' or moralising ideology can be found in Anderson (1969), Baldick (1983), Eagleton (1983), Widdowson (1982), Doyle (1981), Jameson (1981) and Hohendahl (1982).
4. For other instances of the model of theoretical clarification *see*: Belsey (1980), Fish (1980), de Man (1971), Jameson (1981), Pecheux and Fuchs (1982), McCallum (1983), Frye (1951; 1957), Barthes (1974) and Macherey and Balibar (1978).

2 Government

1. Given that monitorial schools did not exist in any numbers until the second decade of the century, it is clear that monitorialism and the 'progressive' critique of 'rote learning' in favour of play and self discovery are in fact contemporaneous. In other words, the tactics of supervised freedom and the 'personal' relation between teacher and student do not represent a fundamental critique of monitorialism arising from its 'failure', but an alternative implementation of the pedagogical disciplines. The specially-trained sympathetic teacher does not replace the machinery of normalising observation but, as it were, refocuses it and makes it operative in the personal register.
2. This combination of social and spiritual grooming is well enough illustrated in Blake's description of the annual procession of Sunday school children to St Paul's, in his *Holy Thursday*.

   Twas on a Holy Thursday their innocent faces clean
   The children walking two and two in red and blue and green
   Grey headed beadles walked before with wands as white as snow
   Till into the high dome of Pauls they like Thames waters flow.

3. See also Spufford (1979).
4. In other words, contra Thompson and Simon, there is no need to assume that social progress is dependent on secularisation or the conversion of ethical practices into social and political forms based on

292

universal reason. If in the Sunday school popular religious practices were 'ethicised' through their incorporation in new forms of social discipline, they nonetheless continued to inform the techniques of personal and social discipline required by a wide variety of reform movements.

5. In addition to Kay-Shuttleworth's own pioneering *Moral and Physical Condition* – which, it can be noted in passing, was praised by Engels – we can mention the following as further manifestations of the statistico-moral 'surface' on which the need for a governmental popular education first appeared: Jelinger Symons' *Tactics for the Times*; Mary Carpenter's *Reformatory Schools*; Joseph Fletcher's *Education: National, Voluntary, and Free* (supplemented by an elaborate statistical cartography linking the provision of education county by county to everything from improvident marriages to crimes against property and murder); the educational reports of the London and Manchester Statistical Societies; the publications of the Central Society of Education; and, of course, the Blue Books and statistical appendices of the various parliamentary select committees and commissions of inquiry. For further discussions of the way in which the deployment of moral statistics brought the life of the population within the sphere of government, see Hacking (1982).

6. This sort of calculation, in which the cost of labour is factorised along with that of the physical and mental capacities of the population needed to sustain a certain standard of life and consumption, is formative of the 'social' sphere. For further discussion see Hirst (1981).

7. For a parallel account of the governmental techniques and strategies that defined popular education as an apparatus for managing the 'moral topographies' of the nineteenth-century city, see Jones and Williamson (1979).

8. For an authoritative description of this transformation in the 'moral architecture' of the popular school, see Seaborne (1971, pp. 131–62). Seaborne emphasises Stow's indebtedness to Samuel Wilderspin, whose model infant school in Glasgow was one of the first to incorporate a gallery.

9. The effect of Kay-Shuttleworth's pupil-teacher scheme can be gathered by looking at the apprenticeship figures for 1850, four years subsequent to its introduction. In this year the Committee's Minutes record that whilst there were only 53 students in the fourth year of their apprenticeships, 1658 were setting out on their new careers, attracted by the new conditions (cited in Sturt, 1967, p. 193). Given that these students were overwhelmingly from the working and lower-middle classes, it is clear that the new measures provided the conditions for the formation of a new socio-moral stratum.

10. For further discussion see Rich (1933).

3 Culture

1. In fact, popular pedagogy remained overwhelmingly oral throughout

the nineteenth century. In his attack on the 'rote learning' of the monitorial system, Stow inveighed against 'the prejudice that books and the mere power of reading do form knowledge'. It was not the book that lay at the centre of the new education, but something quite different:

> The human voice and action, and *the mental sympathy of the gallery*, simplify education, impress knowledge more lastingly on the mind, and save much of the drudgery to the pupil, although the labour of the master, as a trainer, may be increased, . . .
>
> for, as we have already stated, the master himself is the best book, the most natural and efficient means of communication, and the result in all cases proves the truth of this position by its efficiency and power. (Stow, 1850, p. 177)

It is hardly surprising, then, that when literature first surfaced in this oral environment it was in the form of recitation and paraphase; or, that right until the end of the century, the scholars supplied to the training colleges were poor readers by modern standards.

2. This is not to say that the practice of self-culture did not have a pedagogical form. It did: not, however, as a normalising technique in the space of the popular classroom, but as the form of the relation between the *private tutor* and the 'young gentleman' he was contracted to cultivate. Here, as outlined in Herbart's *The Science of Education*, the problem was not to secure a whole classroom's internalisation of social norms embodied in the teacher's 'moral observation'. Rather, it was to determine the precise moment at which the tutor should *withdraw* from the tutelary relationship, leaving the young master free to pursue his own 'practice of the self'. Even as late as the first decades of this century, we find the progressive educationist Edmund Holmes (1914) criticising the 'neo-Herbartians' for their attempt to apply the high-bourgeois model of individual tutelary cultivation to the supervisory form of the popular classroom.

3. Since the writing of these remarks two works have appeared which provide them with supplementary confirmation. Philip Kain's (1982) *Schiller, Hegel, and Marx: State, Society, and the Aesthetic Ideal of Ancient Greece*, a detailed textual commentary showing the dependence of Marx's analysis of the commodity form and alienated labour on Schiller's account of aesthetic activity and the aesthetic state. And Stephen Gaukroger's (1986) 'Romanticism and Decommodification: Marx's Conception of Socialism', which shows the utopian consequences of this dependence for Marx's project for a society based on unalienated labour.

4. It is for this reason that the Romantic conception of the dialectically reconciled or 'organic' work of art has continued to function as a privileged model for Marxian ideas of socialist society. Consider Trotsky's (1971, p. 230) visionary claim that in such a society 'Art then will become more general, will mature, will become tempered, and will become the most perfect method of the progressive building of life in every field.'

5. See Radzinowicz, L. (1956), vol. 4.
6. These and a number of other important facts concerning the cultural profile of the early inspectorate are derived from Ball (1963) and Roberts (1960).
7. Of course, this is not to say that the inspectors did not understand what they were doing, only that this understanding derived not from their ethical culture but from the emerging bureaucracy whose agents they were. Joseph Fletcher is a case in point. The exercise of self-culture provided him with the 'beautifully balanced mind' through which he exercised his function of ethical invigilation. But this function was itself a strategy deployed within the vast statistico-governmental specification of popular education which Fletcher could do no more than summarise in his *Education: National, Voluntary and Free*. This is not at all to belittle Fletcher and his cohort. Quite the reverse: it was precisely their capacity to master the new forms of investigation and administration that gave the inspectors a far more important role in the 'culture' of the population than the literary intelligentsia.

4 English

1. For further discussion see Bacon (1980).
2. For a detailed textual commentary on the dependency of Arnold's educational writing on Kay-Shuttleworth's, see Mason (1983).
3. Phillips (1937), Viola (1942) and Richardson (1949) provide further instances.
4. See also McNary (1908).
5. H. Caldwell Cook's (1917) *The Play Way* provides an early exemplification of the 'drama-in-education' programme.
6. Richard Rainolde's *The Foundation of Rhetoric* provides the Renaissance schoolboy with the following headings for praising an author. Rainolde advises:

> First make a proemium or beginning
> to your comparison.
> Then compare them of their countrees.
> Of their parentes.
> Of their auncestours.
> Of their education.
> Of their actes.
> Of their death.
> Then adde the conclusion. (Rainolde, 1563, p. xlvii)

7. In this regard Henry Sidgwick's response to the question 'Can culture be taught?' typifies the late nineteenth-century 'liberal' opinion of the universities:

> We can doubtless acquire knowledge through teaching, but can we acquire the love of knowledge, the ardour for seeing things as they

are, which I have assumed to be an essential element of culture? . . .
Experience shows that the love of knowledge and beauty can be
communicated through intellectual sympathy: there is a beneficent
contagion in the possession of it; but it must be admitted that its
acquisition cannot be secured by any system of formal lessons.
(Sidgwick, 1904, p. 355)

8. That the unstable relation between the invigilatory and 'academic'
forms of examination continues to define the space in which the
problem is posed is indicated by the following remarks. They are taken
from a book entitled, significantly, *English Versus Examinations*.

But between English and the characteristic school examinations
there must be a tension. At every point, from primary school to
university, examinations through their side-effects threaten the
most precious and vulnerable parts of English teaching. In this, I
think most of the contributors to this handbook would agree with my
sense of what English teaching is, though I define it crudely. Plainly
enough I mean an activity which draws in as much of the pupils'
genuine joys, interests, fears and energies as possible . . . I mean too
a discipline which allows the pupil to discover or confirm something
of himself and of others through the compelling indirectness of the
imagination exercised through writing, or through the utter
simplicity of the fancy in pure play . . .
The question of English *versus* Exams is natural not wilful. For
examinations necessarily are the terrain of the measurable, and our
prime concern is with the play of the sensibility. (Jackson, 1983, p. 10)

Little did Stow realise – when he first enclosed the slum children in a
supervisory simulacrum of their 'real life at play' – the problems he
would pose for those charged with integrating the literary version of
this simulacrum into a national education system.
9. For a discussion of the American developments see Warner (1985).
10. Of course, in expressing social aptitudes in terms of averages the
psychologists took themselves to be describing the ontological laws
and forms of human nature. Georges Canguilhem provides a brilliant
analysis of a parallel manoeuvre in Quetelet's anthropometrics, where
the formulation of an average height for man is treated as the
expression of a natural law. Canguilhem comments:

The interest of Quetelet's conception lies in the fact that in his notion
of true average he identifies the ideas of *statistical frequency* and
norm, for an average which determines that the greatest divergences
are the most rare is really a norm . . .
If it is true that the human body is in one sense a product of social
activity, it is not absurd to assume that the constancy of certain traits,
revealed by an average, depends on the conscious or unconscious
fidelity to certain norms of life. Consequently, in the human species,
statistical frequency expresses not only vital but also social

normativity. A human trait would not be normal because frequent but frequent because normal, that is, normative in one given kind of life . . . (Canguilhem, 1966, pp. 90–1)

What goes for bodily traits is even more obviously the case for mental ones.
11. For an interesting discussion of the social uses of child psychology, including the work of Isaacs, see Riley (1983).

5 Two Models

1. See, for example, Cain (1984).
2. In other words, I am not suggesting that we dismiss the 'Romantic revolt' against the rhetorical formulas as a fiction: only that we see it as a by-product of a much larger series of transformations in cultural technologies, rather than as an exemplary 'return to experience'. Elizabeth Eisenstein (1979, I, pp. 70–88; 119–132, 232–43) provides a detailed account of some of these changes. For example, once the task of preserving and reproducing knowledge passed from the copyist and rhetorician to the printed book, the repetitional eloquence of rhetoric began to lose its importance and value. Print gave greater 'epistemological security' and was a central determinant of the transformation of the rhetorical formula into the cliché. (I am indebted to Jeffrey Minson for this reference.)
3. For example, in his often repeated anecdote concerning a visit to a 'sublime' cataract, Coleridge (1817, II, pp. 224–5) castigates a fellow literary tourist for failing to achieve the appropriate reconciliation of beauty and terror. It is this reconciliation, Coleridge says, which transforms natural into ideal beauty and overcomes the division between subject and object. The hapless tourist had described the waterfall as merely 'pretty'.
4. Hardison's description of the Medieval and Renaissance use of the 'theory of praise' provides us with one example of what it means to call the acceptable paraphrase an 'institution'. Beginning with (Tiberius Claudius) Donatus' *Interpretationes Virgilianae*, the idea that the *Aeneid* was in effect a piece of epideictic oratory in praise of Aeneas provided the framework for a centuries-long canonical paraphrase of the poem. This paraphrase was particularly durable because it also functioned as a recipe for composing similar pieces of oratory. Hardison (1962, p. 34) comments in relation to Fulgentius, a later expositor, that: 'he regards the theory of praise both as a critical device for discovering the moral content of poetry and as a set of prescriptions guiding the composition of didactic poems.' It is interesting to note that the moral effect of such a reading is a function of this technique of paraphrase, because the *Aeneid* is treated as a repository of ethical patterns which are to be committed to heart and emulated. The moral effect of Romantic criticism, on the other hand, is the product of a ritual aesthetic exercise in which every paraphrase must be subjected to a formal observation that robs it of its didactic purpose.

6 The Pedagogical Imperative

1. For this reason Ian Hacking (1975) argues that there was no 'problem of meaning' as long as the problematic of representation held sway. Hobbes, for example, spoke of meaning in terms of a 'discourse' or chain of ideas (representations) underlying the 'discourse of words'. But this chain of ideas was itself quite 'visible' – one only had to inspect it in order to form 'clear and distinct ideas' – because it consisted of the mind's own operations (analysis and synthesis) which were duplicated (represented) in the chain of words. For further discussion see Foucault (1966, 46–125).

2. One can see this clearly enough in Arnold's *Culture and Anarchy*. Neither 'Hebraism' (strict adherence to the moral code issuing in conscientious action) nor 'Hellenism' (pursuit of knowledge and beauty for their own sakes) can function as a point of rest for the goal of culture. This is too often overlooked by those who criticise Arnold for his alleged specification of culture simply in terms of distinterested judgement. 'It is all very well', says Arnold (1869, p. 135), 'to talk of getting rid of one's ignorance, of seeing things in their reality, seeing them in their beauty; but how is this to be done when there is something [i.e. sin] which thwarts and spoils all our efforts?' In other words, it is not disinterestedness as such, but the continuous movement of mutual modification between the two ethical poles that constitutes culture as a permanently incomplete shaping of the self.

3. In this regard the 'social' mobilisation of aesthetics in the school system parallels the development of other more overtly regulative knowledges (for example, criminal anthropology in the prison system). The tactic of achieving regulation through a corrective knowledge aimed at specifying individual attributes in relation to social norms is common. Indeed, Maria Montessori's project for a pedagogical anthropology, with its classification of more and less educable types, might be thought of as linking the two forms. For further discussion see Pasquino (1980).

7 Exemplary Knowledge

1. I hope that it is clear by now that this and similar remarks are in no sense intended as criticisms of Romantic and post-Romantic critical practice. We have seen that when Friedrich Schlegel looks at Goethe's *Wilhelm Meister* he finds there the signs of his own ethical incompleteness. On the other hand, when a literary philologist like August Boeckh (1877) examines one of the classical texts, he finds a tissue of interlinked lexical, historical and generic phenomena. But the fact that in the former case 'looking at the text' means activating a special ethical practice of the self, while in the latter it is the product of the apparatus of philological description, makes neither activity intrinsically more important than the other. It is only their *difference* that I wish to insist on.

2. See, for example, Culler's (1983, pp. 89–134) remarks on 'supplementation' and the 'openness of contexts'. Or, for an even more euphoric hymn to openness, see Cixous (1974), which should be read in conjunction with John Frow's (1986) commentary on it.
3. For a summary exemplification of the tendency to link up all three forms of the unconscious see Coward and Ellis (1977).
4. It is possible to get some sense of this outcome by looking at August Boeckh's account of philology. Significantly, he begins by distinguishing philology from (universal) history and by denying the latter's claims to represent the past.

> History and philology are, in the general view, closely related. In isolating the philological from the historical activity, one must refer to the known history as philological material. History is the restoration of the tradition concerning the past as a body of knowledge; it is not the representation of the past. The aim of philology is not the writing of history; it is the recognition of the knowledge set down in the writing of history. (Boeckh, 1877, p. 9)

Philology's task is thus to 're-cognise' the special bodies of knowledge preserved in the archive, but to do so without emending them as criticism does.

> Philology thinks *about* this knowledge. Criticism that emends the text is not philological knowledge; it [philological knowledge] aims simply to present the alien knowledge as it truly is . . . Its claim is this: to reproduce the alien idea as assimilated to itself, omitting nothing through which the total of philology is taken away. Philology stands over against this knowledge so as to view it objectively. This reproduced knowledge is then formed into a larger whole so as to point out its place in thought with what knowledge has already been relearned. (Ibid., p. 18)

Boeckh's conception of philology as the discipline that relearns 'what has been known', but preserves what is alien or discontinuous in the special knowledges of the archive, has an unexpectedly modern ring to it. (Although Boeckh himself thought that these knowledges would eventually form a totality if philology advanced far enough.)

8 Conclusion

1. This characterisation might seem to be belied by some recent incarnations of literary theory, which in fact stress the disunity or 'splitting' of 'the subject'. Whether through a discussion of (linguistic) enunciation or the (psychoanalytic) 'mirror phase', these versions treat recognition or signification as only temporary 'fixings' of the process of 'subject formation' which promises to disperse subjectivity across all its possible forms. (See, for example, Cixous (1974) and Belsey (1980).) It

should be clear from our discussion of the human sciences, however, that this valorisation of the disunity of subjectivity is simply an optional variant of (someone like) Frye's stress on its unity. The analytic of finitude supports *both* the idea of a determinate subjectivity fixed by the operation of inexorable laws *and* that of an indeterminate one in which subjectivity is opened to all its possible forms by bringing these laws within the sphere of representation. We have argued that human capacities and attributes are neither determinate nor indeterminate in this manner, being the local achievements of definite and untranscendable cultural technologies. As a consequence it makes no sense to talk of 'all possible' forms of subjectivity, only of 'some actual' ones. For further discussion see Adams and Minson (1978); Hirst and Woolley (1982, pp. 118–39); and also the remarks on Stanley Fish later in this chapter.

2. Compare our account of the transition from eighteenth-century 'universal rhetoric' to Romantic criticism (given in Chapter 6) with that provided by Hohendahl. Hohendahl takes the universalism of eighteenth-century criticism at its word, treating it as a function of the temporary identity of bourgeois cultural ideals and political interests. The Romantic stress on the recondite and exemplary character of culture is then seen as a retreat from this universalism, as the result of the divergence between culture and society. If our genealogy is correct, however, then something like the opposite is the case. We saw that Kames' claims for the universality of taste are in fact accompanied by his pronouncement that only the few ('nature's favourites') possess it. Defined by the problematic of representation, eighteenth-century philosophical rhetoric did not generate a pedagogical imperative. The stress on the élite and exemplary nature of culture in the Romantic aesthetic, on the other hand, is a function of its intensely pedagogical character. In this aesthetic, human nature is not given, it must be produced by a work on the self; and this is what eventually permitted its deployment in the 'social' sphere as an instrument of sensibility formation.

3. In fact this circularity is inescapable for all accounts which attempt to discuss the 'formation of the subject' in terms of a general relation of recognition or representation. Hirst (1976), for example, has shown its disabling presence in Althusser's conception of subject formation via 'interpellation'. But it is a general feature of all accounts which treat the 'becoming' of the subject in terms of a mutually constitutive relation between the conditions of seeing and that which is seen. At some point all such accounts are forced to assume that a capacity for recognition, whose *formation* they purport to describe, *already exists*. Its prior existence turns out to be a condition for the process of interpellation – or the 'exchange of looks', or the relation between 'enunciation and enounced' – which supposedly explains how the capacity is formed. For an exhaustive analysis of this problem as it afflicts recent theory of the cinema see Williamson (1983).

Bibliography

ABRAMS, M. H. (1953) *The Mirror and the Lamp: Romantic Theory and the Critical Tradition* (London, Oxford University Press).

ADAMS, P. and MINSON, J. (1978) 'The "Subject" of Feminism', *m/f*, 2, pp. 43–62.

ADORNO, T. *et al.* (1969) *The Positivist Dispute in German Sociology* (London, Heinemann).

ALTICK, R. D. (1957) *The English Common Reader: A Social History of the Mass Reading Public 1800–1900* (Chicago, University of Chicago Press).

ANDERSON, P. (1969) 'Components of the National Culture', in A. Cockburn and R. Blackburn (eds) *Student Power* (Harmondsworth, Penguin Books).

ARCHER, M. (1984) *Social Origins of Educational Systems* (London, Sage Publications).

ARCHER, M. and VAUGHAN, M. (1971) *Social Conflict and Educational Change in England and France, 1789–1848* (Cambridge, Cambridge University Press).

ARNAULD, A. (1662) *The Art of Thinking: Port-Royal Logic* (reprinted New York, Bobbs-Merrill, 1964).

ARNAULD, A. and LANCELOT, C. (1660) *General and Rational Grammar: The Port-Royal Grammar* (reprinted The Hague, Mouton, 1975).

ARNOLD, M. (1869) *Culture and Anarchy* (reprinted Cambridge, Cambridge University Press, 1932).

ARNOLD, M. (1873) *Literature and Dogma* (London, Thomas Nelson).

ARNOLD, M. (1888) *Essays in Criticism* (Second Series) (London, Macmillan).

ARNOLD, M. (1889) *Reports on Elementary Schools, 1852–1882*, F. R. Sandford (ed.) (London, Macmillan).

ARNOLD, M. (1966) *Culture and the State: Matthew Arnold and Continental Education* (New York, Teachers College Press).

ARNOLD, M. (1973) *Matthew Arnold on Education* (Edited with an Introduction by G. Sutherland), (London, Penguin).

BACON, A. (1980) 'Attempts to Introduce a School of English Literature at Oxford: the National Debate of 1886 and 1887', *History of Education*, 9, pp. 303–13.

BALDICK, C. (1983) *The Social Mission of English Criticism 1848–1932* (Oxford, Clarendon Press).

BALDWIN, T. W. (1944) *William Shakespeare's small Latine and lesse Greeke* (Urbana, University of Illinois Press).

BALL, N. (1963) *Her Majesty's Inspectorate 1839–1849* (London, Oliver and Boyd).

BANTOCK, G. H. (1967) *Education, Culture and the Emotions: Further Essays in the Theory of Education* (London, Faber and Faber).

BARTHES, R. (1974) *S/Z* (New York, Hill and Wang).

301

BATE, W. J. (1952) *Criticism: The Major Texts* (New York, Harcourt, Brace, Jovanovich).

BELSEY, C. (1980) *Critical Practice* (London, Methuen).

BENNETT, T. (1979) *Formalism and Marxism* (London, Methuen).

BOARD OF EDUCATION (1921) *The Teaching of English in England* (The Newbolt Report) (London, HMSO).

BOARD OF EDUCATION (1925) *Report of the Departmental Committee on the Training of Teachers for Public Elementary Schools* (London, HMSO).

BODKIN, M. (1934) *Archetypal Patterns in Poetry* (London, Oxford University Press).

BOECKH, A. (1877) *On Interpretation and Criticism* (reprinted Norman, University of Oklahoma Press) (Lectures given between 1820–1850).

BROOKS, C. (1947) *The Well Wrought Urn: Studies in the Structure of Poetry* (London, Methuen).

BROWER, R., VENDLER, H. and HOLLANDER, J. (1973) *I. A. Richards: Essays in his Honour* (New York, Oxford University Press).

CAIN, W. E. (1984) *The Crisis in Criticism: Theory, Literature, and Reform in English Studies* (Baltimore, The Johns Hopkins University Press).

CANGUILHEM, G. (1966) *On the Normal and the Pathological* (Dordrecht, D. Reidel).

CARLYLE, T. (1839) *Chartism*, in A. Shelston (ed.) *Selected Writings*, (Harmondsworth, Penguin Books, 1971).

CARPENTER, M. (1851) *Reformatory Schools (For the Children of the Perishing and Dangerous Classes and for Juvenile Offenders)* (London, C. Gilpin) Reprinted Woburn Press, 1968).

CENTRAL SOCIETY OF EDUCATION (1838) *Second Publication of 1838* (reprinted London, Woburn Press, 1968).

CIXOUS, H. (1974) 'The Character of "Character" ', *New Literary History*, v, pp. 373–402.

COLERIDGE, S. T. (1817) *Biographia Literaria*, edited by J. Shawcross in 2 vols (Oxford, Oxford University Press, 1907).

COLERIDGE, S. T. (1972) *On the Constitution of the Church and State* (London, J. M. Dent).

COLLINS, J. C. (1887) 'Can English Literature Be Taught?', *The Nineteenth Century*, xxii, pp. 642–58.

COLLINS, J. C. (1891) *The Study of English Literature* (London, Macmillan).

COLQUHOUN, P. (1806a) *A Treatise on the Police of the Metropolis*, London (Seventh edition).

COLQUHOUN, P. (1806b) *A New and Appropriate System of Education for the Labouring People*, London. (Reprinted Shannon, Irish University Press, 1971).

COMMISSION ON ENGLISH (1968) *12,000 Students and Their English Teachers* (Massachusetts, College Entrance Board).

COOK, H. C. (1917) *The Play Way* (London, William Heinmann).

COUSINS, M. and HUSSAIN, A. (1984) *Michel Foucault* (London, Macmillan).

COWARD, R. and ELLIS, J. (1977) *Language and Materialism* (London, Routledge and Kegan Paul).

CRAIG, A. R. (1847) *The Philosophy of Training* (London).

CRANE, R. S. (1967) *Critical and Historical Principles of Literary History* (Chicago, University of Chicago Press).

CULLER, J. (1983) *On Deconstruction: Theory and Criticism after Structuralism* (London, Routledge and Kegan Paul).

CURTIUS, E. R. (1948) *European Literature and the Latin Middle Ages* (London, Routledge and Kegan Paul).

DALE, R., ESLAND, G. and MACDONALD, M. (eds) (1976) *Schooling and Capitalism*, (London, Routledge and Kegan Paul).

DAWSON, E. (1908) 'A Model Literature Lesson', *Journal of Education* August, pp. 528–9.

DEWHURST, K. and REEVES, N. (1978) *Friedrich Schiller: Medicine, Psychology and Literature* (Oxford, Sandford Publications).

DICK, Malcolm (1980) 'The Myth of the Working-Class Sunday School', *History of Education*, 9, pp. 27–41.

DIXON, J. (1967) *Growth Through English* (Oxford, Oxford University Press).

DONZELOT, J. (1979) *The Policing of Families* (New York, Pantheon Books).

DOYLE, B. (1982) 'The Hidden History of English Studies', in Widdowson, P. (ed.) (1982).

DUNN, Henry (1837) *Principles of Teaching* (London).

EAGLETON, T. (1976) *Criticism and Ideology* (London, New Left Books).

EAGLETON, T. (1983) *Literary Theory: An Introduction* (Oxford, Basil Blackwell).

EAGLETON, T. (1984) *The Function of Criticism* (London, Verso Books).

EISENSTEIN, E. L. (1979) *The Printing Press as an Agent of Change: Communications and Cultural Formations in Early-Modern Europe* (Cambridge, Cambridge University Press).

ELLEDGE, S. (ed.) (1961) *Eighteenth-Century Critical Essays* (In two vols.) (Ithaca, Cornell University Press).

ENGLISH ASSOCIATION, THE (1917) *English Papers in Examinations for Pupils of School Age in England and Wales* (London, Pamphlet No. 37).

FARRAR, F. W. (1867) *Essays on a Liberal Education* (London, Macmillan).

FICHTE, J. G. (1794) 'The Vocation of the Scholar', in *The Popular Works of Johann Gottlieb Fichte*, translated by W. Smith (London, Trubner, 1889).

FISH, S. (1980) *Is There a Text in this Class?: The Authority of Interpretive Communities* (Cambridge, Mass., Harvard University Press).

FLETCHER, J. (1851) *Education: National, Voluntary, and Free* (London, James Ridgeway).

FOUCAULT, M. (1966) *The Order of Things* (London, Tavistock).

FOUCAULT, M. (1977) *Discipline and Punish* (London, Allen Lane).

FOUCAULT, M. (1978) *The History of Sexuality*, vol. 1 (London, Allen Lane).

FOUCAULT, M. (1984a) *Histoire de la Sexualite, 2: L'Usage des Plaisirs* (Paris, Editions Gallimard).

FOUCAULT, M. (1984b) *Histoire de la Sexualite, 3: Le Souci de Soi* (Paris, Editions Gallimard).

FROEBEL, F. (1977a) *The Education of Man*, in Robinson, D. N. (ed.) (1977a).

FROW, J. (1986) 'Spectacle, Binding: On Character', *Poetics Today*, in press.

FRYE, N. (1951) 'The Archetypes of Literature', *The Kenyon Review*, 13. (Reprinted in Bate, 1952).

FRYE, N. (1957) *Anatomy of Criticism* (New York, Princeton University Press).

FRYE, N. (1964) *The Educated Imagination* (Bloomington, Indiana University Press).

GAUKROGER, S. (1986) 'Romanticism and Decommodification: Marx's Conception of Socialism', *Economy and Society*, 15, pp. 287–333.

GOLDSMITH, J. M. (1972) *The Social Context of Education, 1808–1870* (Shannon, Irish Universities Press).

GOSSMAN, L. (1982) 'Literature and Education', *New Literary History*, 13, 2.

GREEN, J. A. (1912) 'Teachers, Doctors, and Mdme. Montessori', *The Journal of Experimental Pedagogy and Training College Record*, I, pp. 42–51.

GREEN, J. A. (1913) 'The Teaching of English', in three parts in *The Journal of Experimental Pedagogy and Training College Record*, I, 1912, pp. 226–32; II, 1913, 14–25, 201–209.

GREIMAS, A. J. (1966) *Structural Semantics: An Attempt at a Method*, reprinted in English (Lincoln, University of Nebraska Press, 1983).

GREIMAS, A. J. (1971) 'Narrative Grammar: Units and Levels', *Modern Language Notes*, 86, pp. 793–806.

GRIBBLE, J. (1983) *Literary Education: A Revaluation* (Cambridge, Cambridge University Press).

GROSS, J. (1969) *The Rise and Fall of the Man of Letters* (London, Weidenfeld and Nicolson).

HACKING, I. (1975) *Why Does Language Matter to Philosophy?* (Cambridge, Cambridge University Press).

HACKING, I. (1982) 'Biopower and the Avalanche of Printed Numbers', *Humanities in Society*, 3–4, pp. 279–95.

HALSEY, A. H., FLOUD, J. and ANDERSON, C. A. (eds) (1961) *Education, Economy, and Society* (New York, The Free Press of Glencoe).

HARDISON, O. B. (1962) *The Enduring Monument: A Study of the Idea of Praise of Renaissance Literary Theory and Practice* (Westport, Conn., Greenwood Press).

HARTMAN, G. H. (1973) 'Toward Literary History', in Polletta, G. T. (ed.) (1973).

HARTMAN, G. H. (1980) *Criticism in the Wilderness: The Study of Literature Today* (New Haven, Yale University Press).

HARTOG, P. J. (1918) *Examinations and their Relation to Culture and Efficiency* (London, Constable and Co.).

HAYDEN, J. (1969) *The Romantic Reviewers 1802–1824* (London, Routledge and Kegan Paul).

HEATHCOTE, D. (1968) *Drama in Education* (University of Newcastle-Upon-Tyne Institute of Education).

HERBART, J. F. (1804) *The Science of Education*, in Robinson, D. N. (ed.) (1977a).

HERNADI, P. (ed.) (1981) *What is Criticism?* (Bloomington, Indiana University Press).

HINDESS, B. (1983) *Parliamentary Democracy and Socialist Politics* (London, Routledge and Kegan Paul).

HIRST, P. Q. (1976) 'Althusser and the Theory of Ideology', *Economy and Society*, 5, 4.

HIRST, P. Q. (1981) 'The Genesis of the Social', *Politics and Power*, 3, pp. 67–83.

HIRST, P. and WOOLLEY, P. (1982) *Social Relations and Human Attributes* (London, Tavistock).

HOHENDAHL, P. U. (1982) *The Institution of Criticism* (London, Cornell University Press).

HOLBROOK, D. (1961) *English for Maturity: English in the Secondary School* (Cambridge, Cambridge University Press).

HOLBROOK, D. (1964) *English for the Rejected: Training Literacy in the Lower Streams of Secondary School* (Cambridge, Cambridge University Press).

HOLLINGWORTH, B. (1972) 'Developments in English Teaching in Elementary Schools Under the Revised Code 1862–1888', *Journal of Educational Administration and History*, 4, pp. 22–7.

HOLE, J. (1860) *'Light, More Light!' On the Present State of Education Amongst the Working Classes of Leeds* (reprinted London, Woburn Books, 1969).

HOLMES, E. (1914) *In Defence of What Might Be* (London, Constable).

HOURD, M. (1949) *The Education of the Poetic Spirit* (London, Heinemann).

HUMBOLDT, W. von (1836) *Linguistic Variability and Intellectual Development* (reprinted Coral Gables, University of Miami Press, 1971).

HUME, D. (1757) 'Of the Standard of Taste', in Elledge, S. (ed.) (1961).

HUNTER, I. (1984) 'After Representation: Recent Discussions of the Relation Between Language and Literature', *Economy and Society*, 13, pp. 397–430.

HUNTER, I. (1985) 'On Reflection Theory: Including Remarks on John Docker's *In A Critical Condition', Australian Journal of Cultural Studies*, 3, pp. 3–28.

INGESTRE, Viscount (1853) *Meliora or Better Times to Come*, Series I and II (London, John W. Parker). (Reprinted in two vols, London, Frank Cass, 1971).

ISAACS, S. (1930) *Intellectual Growth in Young Children* (London).

JACKSON, B. (ed.) (1965) *English Versus Examinations: A Handbook for English Teachers* (London, Chatto and Windus, 1960).

JAKOBSON, R. (1960) 'Linguistics and Poetics', in Sebeok, T. A. (ed.) (1960).

JAMESON, F. (1981) *The Political Unconscious: Narrative as a Socially Symbolic Act* (London, Methuen).

JOHNSON, L. (1979) *The Cultural Critics: from Matthew Arnold to Raymond Williams* (London, Routledge and Kegan Paul).

JOHNSON, R. (1976) 'Notes on the Schooling of the English Working Class 1780–1850', in Dale, Esland and MacDonald (1976).

JONES, K. and WILLIAMSON, K. (1979) 'The Birth of the Schoolroom', *I and C*, 6, pp. 58–110.

KAIN, P. J. (1982) *Schiller, Hegel, and Marx: State, Society, and the Aesthetic Ideal of Ancient Greece* (Kingston and Montreal, McGill-Queens University Press).

KAMES, Lord (Henry Home) (1762) *Elements of Criticism* (in two volumes), Edinburgh. (Reprinted New York, Garland Publishing, 1972).

KAY-SHUTTLEWORTH, J. (1862) *Four Periods of Public Education* (reprinted London, The Harvester Press, 1973).

KAY-SHUTTLEWORTH, J. (1868) *Memorandum on Popular Education* (reprinted London, Woburn Books, 1969).

KNIGHTS, B. (1978) *The Idea of the Clerisy in the Nineteenth Century*, (Cambridge, Cambridge University Press).

KRIEGER, M. (1969) 'Mediation, Language, and Vision, in the Reading of Literature', in Singleton, C. S. (ed.) *Interpretation: Theory and Practice* (Baltimore, The Johns Hopkins Press) (Reprinted in Polletta, G. T. (ed.) (1973).

LANCASTER, J. (1838) *Improvements in Education as it Respects the Industrious Classes of the Community* (London).

LAQUEUR, T. W. (1976) *Religion and Respectability: Sunday Schools and Working Class Culture, 1780–1850* (New Haven, Yale University Press).

LAQUEUR, T. W. (1976a) 'The Cultural Origins of Popular Literacy in England 1500–1850', *Oxford Review of Education*, 2, pp. 255–75.

LEAVIS, F. R. (1930) *Mass Civilisation and Minority Culture* (Cambridge, The Minority Press).

LEAVIS, F. R. (1933) 'The Literary Mind', in *For Continuity* (Cambridge, Cambridge University Press).

LEAVIS, F. R. (1943) *Education and the University: A Sketch for an 'English School'* (London, Chatto and Windus).

LEAVIS, F. R. (1952) *The Common Pursuit* (London, Chatto and Windus).

LEAVIS, F. R. (1952a) 'Literature and Society', in Leavis (1952).

LEAVIS, F. R. (1952b) 'Sociology and Literature', in Leavis (1952).

LEAVIS, F. R. (1952c) 'Bunyan Through Modern Eyes', in Leavis (1952).

LEAVIS, F. R. and THOMPSON, D. (1933) *Culture and Environment* (London, Chatto and Windus).

LEE, S. (1913) *The Place of English Literature in the Modern University* (London, Smith, Elder and Co.)

LOVETT, W. and COLLINS, J. (1840) *Chartism: A New Organisation of the People* (reprinted Leicester, Leicester University Press, 1969).

LORD, A. (1960) *The Singer of Tales* (Cambridge, Mass., Harvard University Press).

LOWE, R. A. (1979) 'Eugenicists, Doctors and the Quest for National Efficiency: an Educational Crusade, 1900–1939', *History of Education*, 8, pp. 293–306.

MCCALLUM, P. (1983) *Literature and Method: Towards a Critique of I. A. Richards, T. S. Eliot and F. R. Leavis* (Dublin, Gill and Macmillan).

MCMILLAN, M. (1904) *Education Through the Imagination* (London, George Allen and Unwin).

MCNARY, S. J. (1908) 'The Preparation of a Class for a Lesson in Literature', *The Pedagogical Seminary*, 15, pp. 484–91.

MACHEREY, P. and BALIBAR, E. (1978) 'Literature as an Ideological Form', *Oxford Literary Review*, 3, pp. 4–12.

MALLICK, D., MOSS, P. and HANSEN, I. (eds) (1982) *New Essays in the Teaching of Literature* (Proceedings of the Literature Commission Third International Conference on the Teaching of English), A.A.T.E., Adelaide.

DE MAN, P. (1971) *Blindness and Insight* (New York, Oxford University Press).

MARCHAM, A. J. (1979) 'Recent Interpretations of the Revised Code of Education, 1862', *History of Education*, 8, pp. 121–33.

MARCUSE, H. (1955) *Eros and Civilisation* (New York, The Beacon Press).

MASON, D. M. (1983) 'Matthew Arnold and Elementary Education: A Reconsideration', *History of Education*, 12, pp. 177–89.

MATHIESON, M. (1975) *The Preachers of Culture: A Study of English and its Teachers* (London, George Allen and Unwin).

MARX, K. (1975) *Early Writings*. Introduced by Lucio Colletti, translated by Rodney Livingstone and Gregor Benton, (Harmondsworth, Penguin Books).

MAUSS, M. (1973) 'Techniques of the Body', *Economy and Society*, 2, pp. 70–88.

MENET, J. (1867) *Practical Hints on Teaching* (London, Bell and Daldy).

MINSON, J. (1985) *Genealogies of Morals: Nietzsche, Foucault, Donzelot and the Eccentricity of Ethics* (London, Macmillan).

MULHERN, F. (1979) *The Moment of 'Scrutiny'* (London, New Left Books).

NEWBOLT, H. (1928) *The Idea of an English Association*, English Association Pamphlet, no. 70.

ORGEL, S. (1971) 'The Poetics of Spectacle', *New Literary History*, 2, pp. 367–89.

ORGEL, S. (1975) *The Illusion of Power: Political Theatre in the English Renaissance* (Berkeley, University of California Press).

ORGEL, S. (1978) 'The Renaissance Artist as Plagiarist', *English Literary History*, 48, pp. 476–95.

PALMER, D. J. (1965) *The Rise of English Studies* (London, Oxford University Press).

PARLIAMENTARY PAPERS A (1834–38) *Reports From Select Committees on the Education of the Poorer Classes 1834–38* (Shannon, Irish University Press, 1970).

PARLIAMENTARY PAPERS B (1886–88) *The Report of the Royal Commission on the Working of the Elementary Education Acts England and Wales 1886–1888* (The Cross Commission). In 6 vols (vols. 34–39) (Shannon, Irish University Press, 1970).

PASQUINO, P. (1980) 'Criminology: Birth of a Special Science', *I & C*, 7, pp. 17–33.

PECHEUX, M. and FUCHS, C. (1982) 'Language, Ideology and Discourse', *Praxis*, 6, pp. 3–20.

PEERS, E. A. (1914) 'Imagery in Imaginative Literature', in two parts in *The Journal of Experimental Pedagogy and Training College Record*, vol. ii, pp. 174–87, 261–81.

PESTALOZZI, J. H. (1781) *How Gertrude Teaches Her Children*, in Robinson, D. N. (ed.) (1977b).

PHILLIPS, M. (1937) *The Education of the Emotions through Sentiment Development* (London, Allen and Unwin).

POLLARD, H. M. (1956) *Pioneers of Popular Education 1760–1850* (London, John Murray).

POLLETTA, G. T. (ed.) (1973) *Issues in Contemporary Literary Criticism* (Boston, Little, Brown and Co.)

POLLETTA, G. T. (1973a) 'The Place and Performance of Criticism', in Polletta (1973).

QUILLER-COUCH, A. (1920) *On the Art of Reading* (Cambridge, Cambridge University Press).

RADZINOWICZ, L. (1956) *A History of English Criminal Law and its Administration from 1750*, in 4 vols. (London, Stevens and Sons).

RAINOLDE, R. (1563) *The Foundation of Rhetoric* (reprinted Menston, Scholar Press, 1972).

RANSOM, J. C. (1941) *The New Criticism* (Norfolk, New Directions).

RASK, R. K. (1811) *A Grammar of the Icelandic or Old Norse Tongue* (reprinted Amsterdam, John Benjamins, 1976).

RICH, R. W. (1933) *The Training of Teachers in England and Wales During the Nineteenth Century* (Cambridge, Cambridge University Press).

RICHARDS, I. A. (1924) *Principles of Literary Criticism* (London, Routledge and Kegan Paul).

RICHARDS, I. A. (1929) *Practical Criticism* (London, Routledge and Kegan Paul).

RICHARDS, I. A. (1955) *Speculative Instruments* (New York, Harcourt, Brace and World).

RICHARDSON, H. (1913) 'Character: Its Analysis and Measurement in C.G.S. Units', *The Journal of Experimental Pedagogy and Training College Record*, II, pp. 189–98.

RICHARDSON, M. (1949) *Art and the Child* (London, University of London Press).

RILEY, D. (1983) *War in the Nursery: Theories of the Child and Mother* (London, Virago Press).

ROACH, J. (1971) *Public Examinations in England 1850–1900* (Cambridge, Cambridge University Press).

ROBERTS, D. (1960) *Victorian Origins of the British Welfare State* (New Haven, Yale University Press).

ROBERTSON, G. C. (1889) *Elementary Lessons on Psychology* (London).

ROBINSON, D. N. (ed.) (1977) *Works on Psychometrics* (Binet, Simon, Galton, Stern) (Washington, University Publications of America).

ROBINSON, D. N. (ed.) (1977a) *Psychometrics and Educational Psychology* (vol. I, J. F. Herbart, F. Froebel) (Washington, University Publications of America).

ROBINSON, D. N. (ed.) (1977b) *Psychometrics and Educational Psychology* (vol. II, J. H. Pestalozzi) (Washington, University Publications of America).

ROSE, N. (1979) 'The Psychological Complex: Mental Measurement and Social Administration', *Ideology and Consciousness*, 5, pp. 5–71.

RUSK, R. (1929) *Experimental Education*, (London, Longmans, Green & Co).

RUTHVEN, K. K. (1979) *Critical Assumptions* (Cambridge, Cambridge University Press).

SALMON, D. (1932) *The Practical Parts of Lancaster's 'Improvements' and Bell's 'Experiments'* (Cambridge, Cambridge University Press).

SAMPSON, G. (1921) *English for the English* (Cambridge, Cambridge University Press).

SAMPSON, G. (1935) 'Literature in the Classroom', *Essays and Studies*, XX, pp. 123–34.

SAUSSURE, F. de (1916) *Course in General Linguistics* (translated and introduced by R. Harris, London, Duckworth, 1983).

SCHILLER, F. (1780) *Essay on the Connection between the Animal and the Spiritual Nature of Man*, in Dewhurst, K. and Reeves, N. (1978).

SCHILLER, F. (1795) *On the Aesthetic Education of Man*. Edited, translated and introduced by E. Wilkinson and L. A. Willoughby (Oxford, The Clarendon Press).

SCHILLER, F. (1801) 'On the Sublime', in Schiller (1879).

SCHILLER, F. (1879) *Essays Aesthetical and Philosophical* (London, Bohn).

SCHILLER, F. (1966) *Naive and Sentimental Poetry* and *On the Sublime*, translated by J. A. Elias, (New York, Frederick Ungar).

SCHLEGEL, A. W. (1808) *Lectures on Dramatic Art and Literature*, in Wheeler, K. M. (ed.) (1984).

SCHLEGEL, F. (1800) 'On Goethe's *Meister*', in Wheeler, K. M. (ed.) (1984).

SEABORNE, M. (1971) *The English School: its Architecture and Organisation 1370–1870* (London, Routledge and Kegan Paul).

SEBEOK, T. A. (ed.) (1960) *Style in Language* (Cambridge, Mass., The M.I.T. Press).

SHAFTESBURY, Lord (Anthony Ashley Cooper) (1711) *Characteristicks (Of Men, Manners, Opinions, Times)*; Standard Edition in two volumes, edited and translated by G. Hemmerich and W. Benda, (Berlin, N. D. Fromann-Holzboog).

SHAYER, D. (1972) *The Teaching of English in Schools 1900–1970* (London, Routledge and Kegan Paul).

SIDGWICK, H. (1904) *Miscellaneous Essays and Addresses* (London, Macmillan).

SIMON, B. (1960) *Studies in the History of Education 1780–1870* (London, Lawrence and Wishart).

SIMPSON, D. (ed.) (1984) *German Aesthetic and Literary Criticism: Kant, Fichte, Schelling, Schopenhauer, Hegel* (Cambridge, Cambridge University Press).

SIMPSON, J. (1836) *The Philosophy of Education* (With its Practical Application to a System and Plan of Popular Education as a National Object) (Edinburgh, Adam & Charles Black).

SPUFFORD, M. (1979) 'First Steps in Literacy: the Reading and Writing Experiences of the Humblest, Seventeenth-Century Spiritual Autobiographies, *Social History*, 4, pp. 407–35.

STATISTICAL SOCIETY OF LONDON (1839) *Journal of the Statistical Society of London*, 1, (London, Charles Knight).

STOW, D. (1850) *The Training System, the Moral Training School, and the Normal Seminary* (London, Longman, Brown, Green).

STURT, M. (1967) *The Education of the People* (London, Routledge and Kegan Paul).

SULLY, J. (1890) *The Teacher's Handbook of Psychology* (London, Longmans, Green & Co.).

SUTHERLAND, G. (ed.) (1972) *Studies in the Growth of Nineteenth Century Government* (London, Routledge and Kegan Paul).

SYMONDS, J. A. (1907) *Essays Speculative and Suggestive* (London, Smith, Elder & Co.).

SYMONS, J. (1849) *Tactics for the Times: As Regards the Conditions and*

Treatment of the Dangerous Classes (London, John Ollivier) (Reprint, Garland, 1984).

TAINE, H.-A. (1863) *The History of English Literature* (in 4 vols.) (reprinted New York, Frederick Ungar, 1965).

THOMPSON, D. (ed.) (1969) *Directions in the Teaching of English* (Cambridge, Cambridge University Press).

THOMPSON, E. P. (1963) *The Making of the English Working Class* (London, Pelican Books).

TODOROV, T. (1973) *Introduction to Poetics*, published in French as *Poetique* (Paris, Editions du Seuil) (reprinted in English in an expanded form by the University of Minnesota Press, 1981).

TODOROV, T. (1977) *Theories of the Symbol* (Ithaca, Cornell University Press).

TODOROV, T. (1981) 'Poetics, Past and Future', (Preface to the English edition of Todorov (1973)).

TOLSTOY, L. (1930) *What is Art? and Essays on Art* (London, Oxford University Press).

TROTSKY, L. (1971) *Literature and Revolution* (Ann Arbor, University of Michigan Press).

VAN DER EYKEN, W. (1973) *Education, the Child and Society: A Documentary History 1900–1973* (Harmondsworth, Penguin Books).

VIOLA, W. (1942) *Child Art* (London, University of London Press).

LA VOLPA, A. J. (1980) *Prussian Schoolteachers: Profession and Office, 1763–1848* (Chapel Hill, University of North Carolina Press).

WARNER, M. (1985) 'Professionalisation and the Rewards of Literature: 1875–1900', *Criticism*, xxvii, pp. 1–28.

WARREN, A. H. (1950) *English Poetic Theory 1825–1865* (Princeton, Princeton University Press).

WATSON, F. (ed.) (1921) *The Encyclopaedia and Dictionary of Education* (in four volumes) (London, Pitman).

WELLEK, R. (1955) *A History of Modern Criticism: 1750–1950* (in four volumes) (London, Jonathan Cape).

WELLEK, R. (1981) 'Literary Criticism', in Hernadi, P. (ed.) (1981).

WELLEK, R. and WARREN, A. (1949) *Theory of Literature* (London, Jonathan Cape).

WHEELER, K. M. (ed.) (1984) *German Aesthetic and Literary Criticism: The Romantic Ironists and Goethe* (Cambridge, Cambridge University Press).

WHITE, H. O. (1935) *Plagiarism and Imitation During the English Renaissance* (Cambridge, Mass., Harvard University Press).

WHITEHEAD, F. (1966) *The Disappearing Dais* (London, Chatto and Windus).

WHITEHEAD, F. (1969) 'Why Teach English', in Thompson, D. (ed.) (1969).

WIDDOWSON, P. (ed.) (1982) *Re-Reading English*, (London, Methuen).

WILDERSPIN, S. (1823) *The Importance of Educating the Infant Children of the Poor* (London).

WILLIAMS, R. (1958) *Culture and Society 1780–1950* (London, Chatto and Windus).

WILLIAMS, R. (1961) *The Long Revolution* (London, Chatto and Windus).

WILLIAMS, R. (1971) 'Literature and Sociology', *New Left Review*, 67, reprinted in Williams (1980).

WILLIAMS, R. (1973) 'Base and Superstructure in Marxist Cultural Theory', *New Left Review*, 82, pp. 1–16.

WILLIAMS, R. (1980) *Problems in Materialism and Culture* (London, Verso and New Left Books).

WILLIAMSON, D. G. (1983) *Reconsidering Film Theory*, Ph.D. thesis, Griffith University, Australia.

WIMSATT, W. K. and BROOKS, C. (1957) *Literary Criticism: A Short History* (New York, Alfred A. Knopf).

WINTERS, Y. (1947) *In Defence of Reason* (Chicago, Swallow Press).

WITTGENSTEIN, L. (1953) *Philosophical Investigations* (Oxford, Basil Blackwell).

WITTGENSTEIN, L. (1969) *On Certainty* (Oxford, Basil Blackwell).

ZIMMERN, A. (1900) 'Literature as a Central Subject', *Journal of Education*, September, pp. 557–9.

Index